SCIENCE FOR SOC

GW00975946

SCIENCE FOR SOCIAL SCIENTISTS

JOHN LAW and PETER LODGE

MACMILLAN PRESS
LONDON

First published 1984 by
THE MACMILLAN PRESS LTD
London and Basingstoke
Companies and representatives
throughout the world

ISBN 0 333 35100 2 (hardcover)
ISBN 0 333 35101 0 (paperback)

Printed in Hong Kong

Contents

PART II THE ACQUISITION OF KNOWLEDGE

PART III INTERESTS AND THE DEVELOPMENT OF SCIENTIFIC KNOWLEDGE

Acknowledgements

Amongst those who read earlier versions of this text, we would particularly like to thank Michel Callon, Jean-Pierre Courtial and Serge Bauin. We would also like to thank the following for kind permission to reproduce redrawn versions of illustrations and maps: D. H. Hubel, T. N. Wiesel and the Physiological Society for figure 2.1; R. L. Gregory and Weidenfeld & Nicolson for figures 2.2, 2.3 and 2.4, which are taken from *The Intelligent Eye*; London Transport for figure 7.1 (London Transport Underground Map, Registered User Number, 83/E/214); The Ordnance Survey for figure 7.2 (Crown Copyright Reserved); Charles H. Hayward and Evans Brothers Ltd for figures 10.1 and 10.2 from *The Complete Book of Woodwork*; the Ford Motor Car Company for figures 7.3 and 7.4.

J. L.
P. L.

List of Illustrations

Endnotes

1 Introduction

Science and technology are everywhere around us. From penicillin to the micro-chip, from the atom bomb to genetic engineering, everywhere the consequences of science press in on us and influence our lives. It is small wonder, then, that it is the object of deeply-held views. There is one stereotype in our culture that idealises science, glorifies it as a human triumph, celebrates it with optimism and enthusiasm as the onslaught of human rationality upon ignorance and powerlessness. Moon-shots, superwheat and robots, these are the scientific and technological fruits of our capacity to master our environment. What we need is greater expenditure on science, more investment in technology and our prosperous future as citizens of the world is assured. Yet there is another, darker, stereotype – the Frankenstein fear of a monster out of control. Traditionally appearing as a mad but brilliant scientist who creates something horrific out of the bodies of his victims, this terror of science run amok has in the last three decades assumed a more depersonalised form. Fear of nuclear war or irretrievable damage to the global environment and a wish to return to the earth and to roots have widely replaced the 'Strangelove syndrome'.

What, then, is the truth? Is the scientist a beneficent genius in a gleaming laboratory? Or is he or she a malevolent crackpot bent upon the destruction of the world? Perhaps these are silly stereotypes. Indeed, let us agree that they are. But the cultural pervasiveness of deeply optimistic or profoundly pessimistic scenarios for the future of mankind, scenarios in which science and technology almost invariably play a major role one way or another, suggest that stylised thinking about science as a source of wonders or a source of horrors runs deep in Western thought. They also suggest a failure to come to terms with science, a failure to assimilate it critically, a failure to treat it matter of factly.

It is perhaps unsurprising that such pervasive cultural themes should find their echoes in academic writing. Philosophers are

1

predominantly concerned with the celebration of science. Its methods or findings are systematically represented as especially rational or particularly well-founded in empirical reality. Or, more subtly, parts of science are seen as distinctively rational and empirically secure. The job of the philosopher then becomes that of a judge who sorts through the heap of self-styled 'science' and allocates each finding, theory or method to the truly scientific or the clearly unscientific. However, philosophers are not alone amongst academics in celebrating the rational and denouncing that which is not. In the past the history of science has often been written as the struggle of geniuses to overcome the prejudices of their forefathers – look how well someone like Galileo fits that bill, at least at a distance. Sociologists, too, have jumped on the celebratory bandwagon by picturing science as an ivory tower protected, but not always successfully, from the prejudicial influence of surrounding society by a chain-fence of scientific norms. The predominant academic response to the popular-cultural theme of optimism has thus been to develop a picture of science as something special, special with respect to its method, special with respect to its findings, but above all special because polluting and mundane external prejudices and influences are, or can be, or should be, held at bay while the sacred business of increasing knowledge continues.

But if a part of the academic community celebrates science, there is another part that echoes the pessimism found in other parts of popular culture. There are, for instance, sociologists or social philosophers who detect a fundamental incompatibility between the technical and instrumental goals of science and technology on the one hand and the fulfilment of the human potential to interact as free individuals on the other. These writers argue that our society is one that pushes the technical and the instrumental and correspondingly devalues or even renders impossible the pursuit of creative and non-exploitative interaction. Then there arc others who do not necessarily see an incompatibility between science and equality *per se*, but argue that science as at present constituted in an inegalitarian society cannot but stifle the potentialities of most human beings.

There is much to be directly learned from both sides of this academic coin. There is, however, a further and less direct lesson to be drawn. This is that culture – including academic culture – has not quite come to terms with science. Why does so much writing celebrate it as special? And conversely, why does so much denounce it? Why is there such a general concern, albeit a concern concealed behind the technical apparatus of academic argument, to prove that science is special – specially good or specially bad?

It is our contention that social scientists should be particularly interested in this phenomenon. It is, after all, the role of the social scientist to understand and explain interesting features in social structure and culture. But to study cultural – including academic – attitudes to science it is first necessary to form a judgement about the nature of science itself. And this is something that social science has found it hard to do. Thus, not only are there analyses *of* science that either celebrate or denounce it, but in addition social science analyses themselves display a tendency to mimic or reject what are taken to be scientific forms of investigation. Thus, as C. Wright Mills observed, there are those who adopt the paraphernalia of statistics and 'unprejudiced' observation because this looks 'scientific' and they would like social science to emulate the natural sciences. But conversely, there are those who reject statistics and causality for precisely the same reason. Social science, they argue, should be different from natural science – more humanistic or liberating. Truly, in social science, we have not yet come to terms with natural science. We have not yet decided how it works or what our attitudes to it should be.

In this book we attempt to fill this gap. It is thus a book about natural science, about how it is practised, and about how it changes, that has been written with the special interests of social scientists in mind. But it *is*, it needs to be emphasised, very much a book about natural science. It is only in the last part of the book that we concentrate primarily upon the special problems of social science. Why do we spend so much time on natural science? Why do we not discuss its nature in a couple of preliminary chapters before turning rapidly to social science?

Our answer to this is that a profound and thoroughgoing analysis of what it is to *practise* natural science cannot adequately be put across in a couple of short chapters against the kind of background of celebratory or denunciatory polemic which we have described above. On the other hand, however, such an analysis is required if we are to come to terms not only with science itself, but also with the reasons for such polemic and its influence upon our own practice. Our primary aim, then, is to build a picture of the practice of science that is realistic. Only as a subsidiary theme do we discuss the implications of this picture for practice in the social sciences.

What, then, is the nature of the scientific beast? How can we escape the polemic? Here we – all of us – are in a lucky position. We are fortunate because in parts of the history, philosophy and sociology of science during the last two decades there has developed a quite coherent, matter of fact and non-polemical picture of the nature of natural science. Small parts of the work in this tradition are quite well-known to the general reader. Thus, terms from T. S. Kuhn's *Structure of Scientific Revolutions* achieved wide currency in social science and beyond during the 1960s and 1970s, albeit often in a devalued or distorted form. Much, however, remains relatively unknown either because it appears uninteresting or obscure to the general reader, or, in a few cases at least, because of its technicality. There are, of course, occasionally difficult technical issues that need discussion. In general, however, the matter of fact picture of natural science that has grown up since 1960 is remarkably simple and straightforward once rival polemical views and presuppositions are put on one side.

Let us give an example of this. The celebratory picture of science usually assumes that rational knowledge is incompatible with the operation of psychological or social influence. It assumes, in other words, that insofar as social or personal prejudices for instance, enter into scientific observation, the results risk being distorted – that is, the scientist will see things that are not there. There are certain celebrated cases in the history of science that tend to bear this out. Thus a Frenchman called Blondlot achieved notoriety just after the turn of the century by detecting a new kind of (non-existent) radiation rather like X-rays as a result of the excessively enthusiastic use of unsatisfactory observational techniques. Bias and social prejudice *can* undermine observation. But do they have to? The answer developed in this book is a resounding 'no'. Social commitments can sometimes distort observation, but on the other hand, all observation depends upon and would be impossible without social commitments. The reasons for making this claim are discussed in some detail in later chapters. Briefly, however, the argument is that there is so much that *might* be observed in the world that it is absolutely necessary to limit perception to certain connections. We cannot possibly attend to everything – all we would see would be a meaningless confusion of idiosyncracy if we did. It is, however, *social commitments*, transmitted by such figures as parents and teachers, that select for us the things to which we should attend. Whether in science or in everyday life, as a general rule we adopt these cues as our own and ignore most of the observations that we might make of the objects that pass before our eyes.

This is a very simple principle, but one with profound consequences. It suggests, for example, that science is neither more rational nor closer to reality than other forms of thought. It also, conversely, suggests that it is not inimical to humanistic interaction. Rather it suggests that all forms of thought select from what is observable and construct observations on the basis of that selection. It suggests, in other words, that there is no fundamental methodological distinction between science and common sense of the kind assumed in the polemical views mentioned above.

It can be seen that a simple principle about the nature of observation has the effect of undermining the standard polemical views. It has the effect of saying that all knowledge with empirical import is essentially similar. This, however, cannot be all the story. No theory of knowledge which failed to notice that there are, indeed, differences if only in content between natural science and other forms of belief could possibly be viable. In fact the matter of fact approach has no difficulty in explaining such differences. It says that they result from the operation of different socially generated interests. In a differentiated society there is a wide range of specialist interests – there are those who are interested in football scores just as there are those who are interested in molecular genetics. It is, accordingly, only to be expected that there will be different, sometimes overlapping, indeed sometimes incompatible, forms of knowledge in a society. This is explained by the different observational selections and constructions made in different social milieux.

The claim about social interests has many fascinating impli-cations. One of these is that the ivory-tower conception of science so favoured by those who celebrate it cannot be sustained. Science is not directed by 'disinterested intellectual curiosity'. Rather it is directed by a wide range of different interests. It very much reflects and partakes of the society of which it forms a part. This means that some aspects of the 'debunking' polemic of those who are opposed to science and its applications turn out to contain more than a grain of truth. Scientific apologies for nuclear power or claims about the inadequate nature of the evidence connecting the burning of fossil fuel with acid rain are most certainly to be understood in part by noting that certain powerful commercial interests lie behind them. On the other hand, it also means that those who oppose nuclear power or advocate controls on sulphur dioxide emission at power stations by using scientific knowledge are doing exactly the thing of which their opponents are being accused. All knowledge – not simply other people's knowledge of which you happen to disapprove – is directed by social interests of one kind or another.

Analysis of conceptual change in science, as elsewhere, thus becomes a task for social science and in particular for that branch of the social sciences called the sociology of knowledge. The task is to understand the growth of all forms of knowledge by detecting the social interests that underlie it. This, however, tends to put prescriptive philosophers out of business. Science is no longer seen as advancing rationally, or simply under the impetus of neutral observation. But it also has the effect of putting polemical and moralistic accounts of science out of business quite generally. Anyone who works from the assumption that science is different in kind from other forms of knowledge has no role to play in this new, matter of fact and empirical approach. Pollution rhetoric – 'science is polluted by society or science pollutes society' – has no place.

It turns out that pollution rhetoric is widespread in social science and therefore, after first establishing in Parts I–III the nature of science and knowledge in general, we consider in Part IV of this book some of the forms taken by pollution rhetoric. Consider the following claims: primitive thought is less rational than ours; primitive technology is not as good as ours; common sense is more superficial than scientific thought; ideology is distorted knowledge; relativism is self-refuting because it claims to be preferable to other forms of knowledge. These have in common, first, that they are widespread in social science and second, that they depend for their force upon pollution rhetoric. In each case, translated into a social science analysis, they assume that good, right, rational or coherent beliefs must be conceptually unlike their opposites. They assume, more particularly, that the former must be explained in terms of one kind of principle (perhaps correspondence to reality) whereas the latter are properly explained by the operation of the prejudices and biases of social interests. This is where the matter of fact view of science most obviously obtains purchase on social science practice. Asymmetrical explanations of social phenomena – those that fail to explain those phenomena in terms of the same kinds of causes – are untenable if the style of analysis preferred is here adopted.

But it obtains purchase in other ways too. There are those who think that they can mimic science if they use statistics or computer programmes. There is, indeed, nothing inherently unscientific with such methods – many scientists use them and use them effectively. But the idea that quantification confers scientific status is mistaken. *Per se* it has nothing to do with science. Conversely, those who believe that social science explanation should be different in quality from that in the natural sciences are being equally unrealistic. They too are working in terms of a stereotype of natural science that has little to do with the way in which this is really practised. They too are assuming things about the nature of causality and comparative analysis that come from an outmoded and normative philosophy of science rather than from a detailed understanding of the way in which natural science is practised.

Our book, then, starts unpolemically but moves in the direction of polemic. Why does it start unpolemically? And why does it so move? Both questions are easily answered. It starts without polemic because it aims to be descriptive. There is so much interesting work in cognitive psychology, in the sociology of science, in anthropology and in the history of science that bears upon the nature of science and other belief systems. This is work that simply tries to *describe* how knowledge looks, how it functions or how it changes. It would be a shame for a textbook on the nature of science and its implications for social science not to rest upon a firm base of excellent empirical work. Indeed it would be foolish, for this work easily leads the reader to the contemplation of issues that are normally regarded as the necessary preserve of those who have been through professional training in philosophy. We might, if we were being slightly tongue-in-cheek, say that the early chapters of the book thus constitute a philosophy of science but without the philosophy and we might go on to say that philosophy of science without the philosophy turns out to be much more interesting, stimulating and empirical than the old variety. This is because the old variety tended to be self-citing, one philosopher referring to another in a seemingly endless

chain of 'Jacob begat Isaiah' without ever pausing to touch
ground in science itself. Of course we exaggerate somewhat.
Nevertheless the empirical basis of most of our text represents a
quite deliberate decision to pay heed to discoveries in the
empirical sciences in preference to standard modes of philosophical discourse. The result is that we pay precious little
attention to many issues that are of standard concern to
philosophers, but our anxiety on that score is small since there are
many good textbooks on the philosophy of science and social
science to which the rare student who is interested in these issues in
their technical form may turn.

Our non-polemical opening is thus achieved by deliberately
refusing to adopt what could have been a thoroughly polemical
path. The controversial nature of our claims about science should
not be denied. But how are they controversial? They are
controversial precisely because they are matter of fact, empirical,
down-to-earth and, most of all, they are non-evaluative. They do
not judge whether science is a force for liberation or oppression.
They do not attempt to demonstrate or illustrate the truth of one
or other of these propositions. Neither do they attempt evaluation
in any other way about science or common sense. They are
directed, insofar as this is possible, by an interest in finding out
what is going on in science that is divorced from concerns to
moralise or draw global conclusions about how society should be
organised. We agree, of course, that lack of overt political
commitment is out of fashion in many reaches of social science,
just as the failure to moralise is rejected by most philosophers.
Nevertheless, the absence of such evaluative concerns conveys
certain advantages. Specifically, it eases the search for very general
explanations because it does not, as we indicated above, distinguish on *a priori* grounds between what is approved and what is
disapproved, and then proceed to try to explain them in different
ways. At any event, this is the course that we have adopted in this
text.

But if we avoid global judgements, how do we become engaged
in polemic in later sections of the book? The answer is that a
matter of fact empirical approach directed by an interest in
understanding how and why science works generates findings that
turn out to be at variance with the claims made by those who start
off from different, globally evaluative, presuppositions. At this
point technical controversy if not polemic becomes inevitable. But

notice one thing about this controversy. Evaluations from the matter of fact stance adopted here never involve judgements about the validity of bodies of knowledge or practices that are being explained. We do not take sides on phrenology, on nuclear power or the Zande poison oracle. To do so would be quite improper given our commitment to symmetrical analysis. We only argue technical questions with other social science approaches which make assumptions that are incompatible with our own. In general, in fact, we only enter controversy with those social science approaches that wish to make judgements of validity about other bodies of knowledge as a preliminary to explaining their generation. The fact that these judgements are widespread is regrettable. It means that most of the last part of this book is controversial – indeed, in places, polemical. But unlike its opponents, it is not globally moralistic about science. The latter is treated as a cultural phenomenon, an important one to be sure, but one that works like any other.

Part I

People and their Knowledge

In Chapters 2 to 8 we outline the basic properties of knowledge in a manner broadly consistent with Mary Hesse's network theory of science. It is important to understand, right from the outset, that we are not talking about knowledge 'out there', detached from human beings and their experience. Far too often knowledge is treated as if it had properties and a life of its own. Our conception of knowledge is severely practical. We are concerned with knowledge as it is handled and utilised on a day to day basis by human beings. We are therefore, not only concerned with scientific knowledge (though this is enormously important). For us, the know-how to write cheques, follow animal tracks, travel the subway or eat a meal also counts as knowledge. When we talk of knowledge, then, we are really talking of human beings. We are talking about how human beings make sense of their world. We are, indeed, talking psychology, at least in the first instance.

In Part I of this book, then, we start with speculative psychology and talk about the basic mental operations in terms of which people construct their cognitive maps. We indicate that people often learn about the world not directly, but rather indirectly, from cues given off by other people. Our argument is that the form taken by our knowledge thus depends both upon the way in which our minds process experience (the psychological) and upon the information that actually comes to us. With the latter we move from the psychological to the natural and the social (though in saying this we do not mean that we see either the social or the psychological as unnatural).

Our approach is descriptive. We *describe* the way in which people acquire and adapt their knowledge. We differ, then, from many of those who study knowledge – particularly high status scientific or social scientific knowledge – whose aim is prescriptive: to make judgements about the optimum way of acquiring good knowledge and to draw a boundary between the good and the bad. So far as we are concerned, *all* knowledge is 'good' knowledge because, however mistaken we may personally believe it to be, we assume that it has been generated by the same kinds of psychological, natural and social processes that generate any other knowledge. To repeat, then, our aim is descriptive. On the other hand, our description of knowledge has inevitable implications for other theories whenever the latter can be shown to rest upon unrealistic assumptions about how people operate in the natural or social world. In Chapter 8 we allow ourselves a short detour to discuss the implications of network theory for three positions in the philosophy of science. This is, however, the only chapter where we depart from our practical and down-to-earth mode, and may be ignored by those who have no interest in the philosophy of science.

2 Classification

We start with an assertion: human beings have the capacity to classify phenomena into groups. In principle every moment is novel, every situation is something that we have never encountered before, each object is slightly different. But in practice we do not see the world that way. We actually see the world as peopled by familiar objects, objects that we classify unproblematically and without question into conventional groups. There are men and women, girls and boys, birds and animals, fish and fowl. The capacity to classify is something that we all possess and it is something that we do routinely.

How is it that we classify? The answer (we have already given it) is that we have the capacity to classify. We have the capacity to notice similarity and difference. When we fix our eyeballs on objects some look similar and some do not. There is a psychological assumption here: we are wired up to notice objects that are similar in certain respects. For instance, it is the case that certain visual stimuli trigger responses in and are recognised by certain parts of the brain. One part of the visual cortex responds to vertical stimuli, a slightly different part to stimuli that are ten degrees from the vertical, and so on. Other parts of the visual cortex respond to movement, yet other parts to colour. Somehow – and the full mechanisms are not yet understood – the brain groups these different primitive responses, stores them and recognises the 'same' object when it reappears in a different context. Furthermore, it does this in a way that is typically below the level of consciousness. This is a process that the great German psychologist, Helmholtz, called 'unconscious inference'. He wrote that:

> The psychic activities that lead us to infer that there in front of us at a certain place there is a certain object of a certain character, are generally not conscious activities, but unconscious ones. In their result they are equivalent to a conclusion.[1]

FIGURE 2.1 *The relationship between the angle of a line and the number of times a single cell fires*[2]

Or, as Richard Gregory, a contemporary psychologist puts it, 'perception is a kind of problem solving'.[3] Simple visual experiments can show us that we group objects together in accordance with a variety of principles. For instance, we make use of proximity, similarity and, perhaps at a higher level of complexity, we 'see' things that simply are not there. Thus, though the details of how we classify are imperfectly understood, it is most certainly clear that we classify, order and sort below the level of consciousness. We are wired up in such a way that the stimuli which impinge upon our eyeballs are simplified and reduced to some sort of order before we even 'see' them.

Now consider two corollaries of this. The first is the converse of the psychological assumption. It is that there *is* a material world, a real world that emits stimuli that trigger off a response in our visual (etc) cortex. If this account is correct then we are committed to a particular version of materialism. We are committed to saying something to the effect that the real world is perceptually lumpy: it offers purchase for the brain, the eyes and the ears. It emits stimuli that are detectable as movement, noise, shape and structure. It is in fact the case that the nervous system depends upon such external stimulation. Experiments on sensory deprivation show that human beings deprived of all such stimuli rapidly lose sense of time and orientation. We exist in a perceptually lumpy world, then, and are dependent on that lumpiness for our sanity.

To this materialistic corollary we must add a second: it is certainly the case that some stimuli are more noticeable than others. Figures 2.2, 2.3 and 2.4 informally demonstrate this to be the case.[4] We notice sharp edges and angles. We classify according to shape, colour and proximity, among other things.

FIGURE 2.2 *Association by proximity*

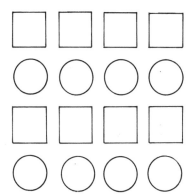

FIGURE 2.3 *Association by shape*

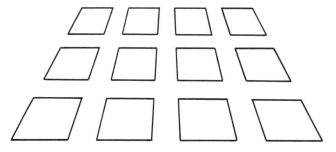

FIGURE 2.4 *The detection of a plane which is not there*

Now let us think for a moment about the classes into which we group stimuli. Consider the shapes depicted in Figure 2.5. Any normal user of the Roman alphabet will immediately recognise what it is that these eight symbols have in common despite the very considerable differences that there are between them. The set of representations depicted in Figure 2.6 are probably even more generally interpretable as having something in common. Are these classifications – the decision to classify each of the first set of symbols as the letter 'E' and each of the second as a 'ship' or a

18

Figure 2.5 *Shapes with something in common*

Figure 2.6 *More shapes with something in common*

'boat' – natural? The answer has to be that they are not. Unlike the *propensity* to classify which we have just discussed, the *actual* classifications adopted appear to be *conventional*. The native Mandarin speaker will not recognise the similarity between the different objects that comprise the first group of representations. And someone who does not know about ships or boats would make heavy weather of the second grouping.

When we talk, then, of classification, we are talking of two different but related things. First we, are talking of an inbuilt psychological propensity to order and sort, to reduce to a relatively simple order, and second, we are talking about learned preferences for grouping the products of classificatory propensities into conventional classes.

We will consider the conventional aspects of classification at much greater length later. But first we want to say something about the form of knowledge that is mobilised when we recognise similarity. Look back at Figure 2.6 and consider the first two representations only. These have something in common, even though the nature of their similarity may be somewhat clearer in different circumstances. A and B in Figure 2.7 have in common that they are boats and differ from C and D which we group together and classify as locomotives. Now that we have named these classes notice that we actually recognised the similarities and differences before we wrote them down or said them to ourselves. Indeed, proper usage of the words, the spoken labels, depended upon a recognition of similarity and difference rather than the other way round. But what was it that we noted as being similar in the case of A and B? And where was this knowledge located?

We want to suggest that it is not necessarily clear what there was in common between them. Indeed, to be literal for one moment, they are in each case nothing more than lines on a sheet of paper. But even if we choose not to be literal, if we think of coasters, tugs and Viking longboats that we have seen at one time or another, it still is not necessarily clear what it is that they have in common. You may want to say something like: well, they all float on the surface of the water and carry people or cargo. This is correct, but it doesn't solve the problem which is unsolved in two different ways. First, it seems to be the case that we can *recognise* boats or ships without having to go through a mental checklist of this sort. In other words, verbal accounts of what these objects have in common, though possibly correct, seem to come after the event

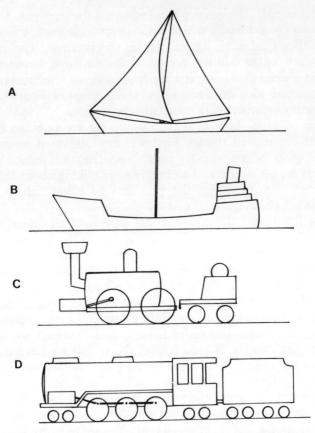

FIGURE 2.7   *More shapes with similarities and differences*

when we are asked to justify or make public our use of classification. And second, it may well be the case (though this does not necessarily follow) that your description of the features shared by recognisable 'boats' is in any case inaccurate. Consider the vessel depicted in Figure 2.8. This is a craft that floats on the surface of the water and carries people and cargo. That is to say, it fulfils our definition of a boat. It is found in the North Sea oilfields, and is used as a supply-tender and fire-fighting rig. But, though it strains our conception of a 'boat' it must be one if our definition is all that there is to it. In Figure 2.9 we draw a further craft which fulfils our criteria, but is definitely not a boat but a raft. Just as

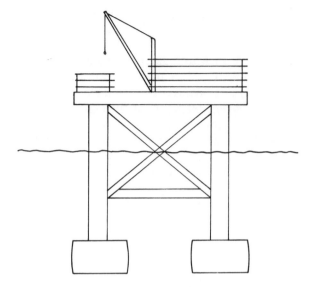

FIGURE 2.8 *Is this a boat?*

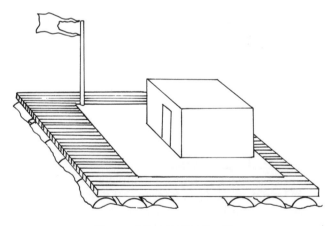

FIGURE 2.9 *Another boat?*

there are vessels that seem to accord with our definition which we do not count as boats, so there are things that we call boats without difficulty, but which have never been near the surface of the water and which are incapable of carrying people or cargo.

Think for instance of all the pictures of boats, or think of models of boats that are to be found in museums or in bottles on old-fashioned mantelpieces.

The point that we wish to make here, then, is that recognition (that is to say, immediate visual classification) can be achieved even though we do not necessarily have a clear and explicit idea about *what* the different members of the class have in common. Presumably they are similar in certain respects or we would not be able to recognise them as 'the same'. That is to say, if our drawings are to be recognised as boats they have to share something in common with boats that we have seen in the past. But *exactly what that similarity is for the purpose of recognition and whether all boats are similar in the same respects are both open questions.*[5] It is clear that the knowledge which allows us to notice and recognise such similarity and thus to classify it, is in large measure located below the level of consciousness. We are not in this case suggesting that it is wired into the hardware of the brain. The capacity to recognise objects as boats is quite clearly a learned skill. But it is learned in such a way that it sinks below the level of consciousness and influences immediate perception. Deliberate cogitation about classification only occurs in anomalous cases: is a North Sea supply vessel a boat or not? Most of the time recognition just happens, and we see . . . a boat.

There is another point that must be briefly made. When we notice similarity (similarity with respect to what we are not sure) and classify we lose information. This follows directly from our original suggestion that human beings are designed in such a way that they notice similarity between different objects and events. If we call a phenomenon a 'beautiful sunset' we lose the specificity of that particular evening, the company, the scenery and our emotional state. Even if we specify these four variables our description of the scene remains incomplete. 'When you say that the girl was lovely, what do you mean?' If you are sceptical about the loss of information that arises in the natural process of classification, then try describing your lover's looks. It is, of course, finally impossible. By treating unique events (and all situations and events are unique) as instances of general classes we have lost something. Of course, if we are interested enough in the phenomenon under study we can classify it very minutely. But finally even the description of the lover runs dry. One has to know him or her to know how they really are.

In this chapter we have characterised classification:

1 This is something for which human beings have a natural psychological capacity.

2 Part of this capacity is built into our brains. We notice and associate certain kinds of stimuli.

3 We do this unconsciously, using stimuli which come to us from the outside world.

4 Part of the capacity is learned. There are culturally prescribed classes into which we slot phenomena.

5 This too is normally an unconscious phenomenon.

6 It depends on the recognition of similarity between objects, though the nature of that similarity may be obscure.

7 All classification involves loss of information.

3 Inference

Now consider a second, and similar, human capacity: the ability to relate different objects together, to associate them. Thus, we not only classify, order and sort our lumpy environment, but we tend to see the classes as coming together in packages. One potent way of learning to see these connections is by experiencing them as temporally adjacent. If y closely follows x, if, for instance, pain follows the investigation of fire, then it doesn't take us very long to construct a link and to suppose that fire is painful. Much of our learning is of this sort. We see classifications as being sequentially related, as being connected in one way or another. Another way in which we link classifications is to notice that they are spatially adjacent. Husbands go with wives, small boys go with dirt and noise. To repeat, we are endowed with a natural capacity to link classes of events together, to cross-classify.

As a matter of fact this capacity is no different from that discussed in the previous chapter. It rests upon the same kinds of operations. In particular it rests upon a tendency to notice similarity, to notice what goes with what. Flames, we learn in the first instance, go with burns, if we get too close. This association is reinforced the next time we get scorched by approaching fire too closely. In making these connections we are noticing two kinds of links: the first instance of fire is seen as being similar to the second instance of fire. This burn is perceived as being similar to that burn. But the spatial and temporal relationship between fire and a painful burn is also noticed. We indicate these links diagrammatically in Figure 3.1. The capacity to cross-classify, to associate, is evidently identical with the capacity to notice similarity and erect classification. It is something that human beings can do and it is something that they can do automatically if necessary, below the level of consciousness. Actually, there is one respect in which this example is somewhat misleading. It is quite unlikely that we would learn that fire is hot and painful without having the matter drawn to our conscious attention. Nevertheless, a large part of our

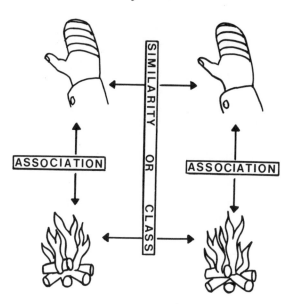

FIGURE 3.1 *Two kinds of links*

tendency to reduce the world to an orderly place operates below the level of consciousness. And even those associations, like the fire–pain link, which *initially* enter in part through conscious attention tend to sink, as it were, below the level of consciousness. Think of the skills involved in driving a motor car, of changing the gears and of avoiding other traffic as we make progress down a road. We know (we do not think about it, we *know*) how to change gear correctly and in the direction for which we are aiming. We *know* that a certain set of manipulations will lead the engine to cease labouring and give the vehicle a new surge of power. We *know* that the truck that is approaching us will in fact pass us on the other side of the road. We have learned, by association and inference, that these are the typical links between classes (or, if you prefer to think of it this way, the manner in which certain phenomena typically behave). And we know about these links in general without having to think about them. We go, as it were, on autopilot.[1]

So far we have considered the direct acquisition of association only. That is, we have supposed that for any individual the only way of learning about associations is via immediate physical experience. In fact, of course, we often classify and make connections between classes without having directly experienced the lumpiness of physical stimuli and their association. Consider, now, the following type of injunction often enough addressed by parents to their children. 'You musn't eat earthworms, they'll make you sick!' We can draw this out as in Figure 3.2. What is the child to make of this? Indeed, what reason does the adult have for saying it in the first place? First let us consider the conditions of the intelligibility of such a statement. For it to mean anything at all the child must know about eating, earthworms and sickness. We may suppose that if the issue arises at all, then the child has been exposed to a set of phenomena that are classifiable as, on the one hand, eating, and on the other hand, earthworms. That is to say, tacitly or otherwise, the child is capable of noticing similarities between what we call earthworms – and likewise for the case of eating.

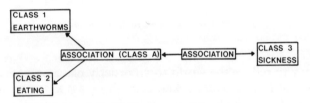

FIGURE 3.2   *Associations with earthworms*

What of the third 'primitive' class – that of sickness? Here the matter may be a little more difficult. It is likely, though not certain, that the child will have been put to bed at one time or another with a variety of physical symptoms and told that it was sick. In other words, the classification will have been learned via the guided detection of similarity in just the way that the class of 'earthworm' was learned. But suppose, for the sake of argument, that this is not the case, that the child has never been sick. Assuming, as is probable, that it nevertheless has some conception of sickness, this will have been learned indirectly via the association of classes that lead, in the end, to physical events that are recognisably similar. This is an important point. Not all learning need be via direct empirical experience, suitably structured. Much learning takes place via chains of terms that, in the end, have empirical implications. In the example that we have taken, that of sickness, it is possible to construct such hypothetical chains:

'What's sickness, Daddy?'

Father sighs, looks heavenwards, and responds:

'Well it's when you're put to bed because you feel ill. You know, like when Granddad was poorly last year.'

Father's response here chains the term or class 'sickness' to a variety of other classes which, he hopes, either have direct empirical referents for the child or can be indirectly linked to terms which do have referents. 'Bed' and 'Granddad' clearly have such referents, and he is hoping that 'illness' and 'poorly' will not provoke further interrogation. A possible further response from the child might be:
'You mean, like when the rabbit died?'

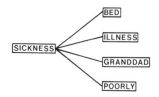

FIGURE 3.3   *Associations with sickness*

This poses interesting problems for the father, because death is not synonymous with sickness, though it sometimes follows it. It shows that the child is making at least some of the correct classificatory associations, though it is misconstruing their nature somewhat. The question of the proper relationship between terms is something that we will pick up in Chapter 4. Here, however, the important point is that the child has learned the proper use of a class or term by means other than direct physical association and detection of similarity. Though the term now has a physical referent for the child – who will be able to use it appropriately from now on – it was learned indirectly via the association of classes.

Having established that the term 'sickness' is now clear for the child, we next need to note that the classes of 'earthworm' and 'eating' are brought together in the exhortatory sentence. This is unproblematic. We may, if we wish, treat this as the creation of a new class (Class A in Figure 3.2) though in the present context this is of no great importance. At any rate, the phrase 'eating of earthworms' now covers a rather specific set of real or possible events, events bound together by the same kind of similarity relations that held the 'primitive' classes together. The intelligibility of the command now ensured, we are in a position to reconsider its empirical status. Remember that our interest is the following: that we can learn to make connections between classes without directly experiencing the lumpiness of physical stimuli. Do we *know* that the eating of earthworms causes physical sickness? The almost certain answer to this question is that we do not. We have never tried and we have never known anyone who has. Indeed, casting around we may remember that at times of great hunger people have, indeed, casseroled earthworms without appearing to have suffered unfortunate consequences. Nevertheless, most of us adhere to a version of the theory that earthworms are inedible. In the late 1970s, McDonald's hamburgers suffered a severe drop in sales in certain cities where rumours circulated that the 'meatiness' of the hamburgers was sustained by the addition of earthworms. The association – that earthworms make you sick if you eat them – is widespread, but more or less empirically ungrounded.

At this point it is important to emphasise that the foregoing is a lesson about learning – not primarily about the truth or otherwise of classificatory links. What we should be taking from this example is the following: human beings can learn to use terms or classes and make connections *between* classes without directly relating those classes and associations to what we have called 'physical lumpiness'. It suffices that such links be *indirect*. The important point, then, is that if terms and associations between terms are to have meaning – essentially if they are to be usable – they have to be linked directly or indirectly to an empirical referent which is sustained by an unverbalised sense of similarity. Another way of making this point is to note that it is quite impossible to learn French from a French-French dictionary. To learn the meaning of French words we either have to interact with a French speaker who points out objects and names them or we have to have recourse to a dictionary where approximate English equivalents – terms which already have a direct or indirect empirical referent for the learner – are indicated.[2]

The lesson that should *not* be drawn from our earthworm example is that terms or associations between classes learned indirectly are less true or reliable than those learned by means of direct physical experience. Many associations learned by the latter route are false. Barnes cites a meeting between his daughter and a parrot:

> Although its vocabulary was limited the parrot could talk. Several times it bade us 'Goodbye', to be bade 'Goodbye' in turn by our delighted two-year-old. Thenceforth her encounters with parrots have involved cries of 'Goodbye', and puzzlement at the lack of response. Only slowly has she abandoned the expectation that parrots just do say 'Goodbye'.[3]

Clearly the child was able to detect similarities between certain lumps in the physical environment which we call parrots and on the basis of an association between one such parrot and its utterances, developed an expectation – albeit false – about the future behaviour of such lumps. Direct physical experience may, and indeed often does, mislead.

Conversely, however, indirectly learned associations may (unlike our earthworm example) be perfectly acceptable. Most inhabitants of the British Isles are aware, for example, that vipers have a dangerous poisonous bite and are, for this reason, to be treated with respect. Yet relatively few of the inhabitants have ever seen a viper, let alone been bitten by one and suffered the consequences. The point, then, is that classifications and associations are learned both directly and indirectly. The distinction, though noticeable, is of no relevance in determining the truth or otherwise of what has been learned.

We have been talking in this section about inference, the way in which human beings connect classes together. Before moving on it is worthwhile making one point that has so far only been implied. We have also been talking about *prediction*. When classes are established and inferentially linked together human beings have taken the moves that are necessary for predictions to be made. In our examples we have seen the following predictions: 'Fire burns' (read 'future fires will burn you if you get too close to them'); 'eating earthworms causes sickness'; 'parrots say goodbye'; 'vipers bite dangerously'. Trivial though these particular predictions are, a quick thought experiment immediately suggests that much of our routine and daily knowledge is precisely of this kind. Note, again, that much of it is implicit, tacit, below the level of consciousness. We do not have to remind ourselves that earthworms are inedible when we turn them up while digging the garden. It is only under exceptional circumstances that we do anything other than leave them alone.

In this chapter we have outlined some of the attributes of cross-classification:

  8 Human beings are capable of associating classes together in a manner identical to their ability to notice similarity between the objects that go to make up a class.

  9 Much of this cross-classification operates below the level of consciousness – again it is perceptual.

10 Cross-classification can be learned either directly (via empirical association) or indirectly (via linkages with other already usable classes).

11 Even indirect learning has in the end to be tied down to the empirical via chains of classificatory associations.

12 All directly or indirectly learned associations may be either true or false.

13 Cross-classifications may take the form of predictions.

4 Networks

THE RELATIONS BETWEEN TERMS

So far we have traced the way in which human beings notice similarities between lumpy phenomena in the environment and proceed to classify such lumps as 'the same', after which they draw links between those classes. We have seen that many terms used in such classification have a direct empirical referent and that all terms have at least an indirect empirical connection. We are, in other words, dealing with knowledge, with mental maps about the real world, and not with word-play. Naively, we may say that the knowledge built up in the course of such classificatory activity may or may not be correct. Presumably, from the standpoint of any given individual it must, however, at least be workable. The workability of the generalisation 'parrots say goodbye' was rather too low· for it to survive, whereas the workability of the generalisation 'eating eathworms causes sickness' is higher. It is higher because it does not lead to action that is difficult to reconcile with the generalisation. These are matters to which we shall return at a later stage. In this chapter we wish to consider the question of cross-classification in a little more detail. What conditions our cross-classificatory activity? And what consequences does this have for our empirical classifications – those built up on the basis of directly detected similarity relations?

The first thing to note is that once we start the activity of cross-classification this has a strong tendency to ramify and link together large numbers of previously unrelated classes. This point, which should be intuitively obvious, can be illustrated by means of one of our previous examples. Consider once again the links that were built up or utilised in the explanation that followed on from the pronouncement 'eating earthworms makes you sick'. Figure 4.1 shows some of the more immediate links that arise in the course of this conversation. The nature of these links varies – this is something that we will consider later. But what we should also

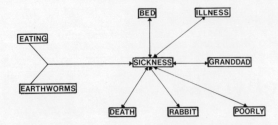

FIGURE 4.1   *Links between sickness and other classes*

note is that this network can be extended in at least two ways. On the one hand further connections may be established – indeed undoubtedly exist – between classes in the network. Figure 4.2 depicts the links that the child might forge between the class of death and other terms in the network. Death goes, as it were, with illness, for the rabbit was ill before it died. But Granddad was ill too, so perhaps he died or might die. People who go to bed may be ill and illness can lead to death. People may die in bed. And now there is a new immediate cause of sickness (which can lead to death): the ingestion of earthworms.

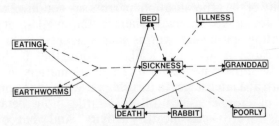

FIGURE 4.2   *Links between death and other classes*

This is just one way in which such a network may ramify (and notice that there are many other connections that might be made that we have not drawn in). The term death may be (and doubtless is) also connected with other, additional classes. Some possibilities are depicted in Figure 4.3. Each of these new classes is associated with many further terms. The result is impossibly complex, impossible to map for any individual, but may in principle be pictured as a network where there are indefinitely many connections between the nodes that make up the classes. As

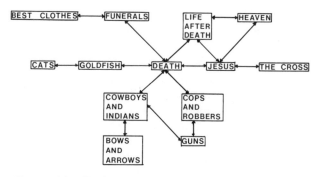

F<small>IGURE</small> 4.3 *Further links between death and other classes*

individuals – for instance the hypothetical earthworm-eating child – move through each day they make use of this network, the similarity relations and the links of association, to make sense of the perceptually lumpy phenomena that they encounter. That is, they use this network to impose some kind of order on what they see and to make predictions on the basis of that order. To recapitulate, some of this sensemaking and inter-connecting is deliberate and conscious, but a large part of it, though learned in the first instance, sinks below the level of consciousness and is built into our everyday perceptions.

DIFFERENCES BETWEEN NETWORKS – OR WHY WE DON'T ALL BELIEVE THE SAME THING

What can we say about the structure of this network? How are the connections and cross-classifications ordered? The elements of an answer become clear when it is recognised that one of the basic themes that lies behind the action of classification and cross-classification is a drive for simplicity. On the whole human beings prefer an *economical* account of phenomena. They avoid needless elaboration. Caution must be exercised in making this claim. A drive for perceptual and predictive economy does not automatically lead to a set of connections that are uniform for all human beings, or there would be complete agreement about the nature of the world rather than the actually observable diversity.[1] But if the structure of an economical network of classes is not unambiguously given by the natural world, how, then, does the principle of economy work? The answer is that human beings try to construct classes that are as general as possible and seek to link those classes together by means of associations that are also as widespread as may be. There is, in other words, a drive for generality and inclusiveness. One might rephrase this psychological propensity by saying that human beings are lazy. If one generalisation will do, then do not use two. If a new instance, another perceptual lump, can be fitted into an existing class, then do so. Do not make a change for the sake of change.

Consider now the following example taken from an imaginary taxonomic zoology. Xaanthi, the intrepid Martian taxonomist, has been on earth for three weeks.[2] He has established to his satisfaction that a useful distinction can be drawn between 'animals' and 'plants'. Turning his attention to 'animals', he starts to collect instances. Figure 4.4 shows four classes which he quickly builds up on the basis of substantial similarity. Furthermore, cross-classification reveals that for certain purposes it is possible to economise in this description of instances of a species by grouping them together. Instances of 'elephants' and 'mice' walk, live on the land and have warm blood, whereas those of 'sharks' and 'catfish' live in the water, swim, and have cold blood. Xaanthi is excited by this set of connections and proposes the generic names 'mammal' and 'fish' for the two natural kinds. This can be depicted economically in network form, as in Figure 4.5. The classes of 'fish' and 'mammal' are very general and inclusive. The associations between the classes are also general.

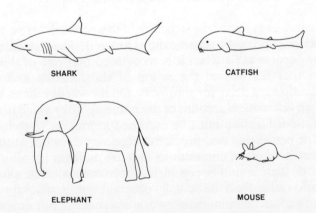

SHARK   CATFISH

ELEPHANT   MOUSE

FIGURE 4.4   *Four classes built up on the basis of substantial similarity*

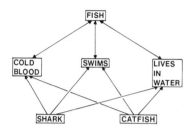

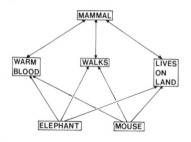

FIGURE 4.5   *Tentative animal taxonomy*

They permit certain kinds of prediction. Thus if Xaanthi comes across an instance of an animal that walks on land he can predict that it will be warm-blooded. Furthermore, as time passes, he builds up an impressive array of instances of species that confirm these generalisations about classes. Examples of 'herrings', 'gold-fish', 'trout' and 'sturgeon' are all discovered and found to conform to the classification. So too are 'lions', 'tigers' and 'giant pandas'. Notice how economical Xaanthi's classification has become. Instead of detailing the habitat, blood-temperature and mode of locomotion of dozens of species, it suffices to classify them as being 'mammals' or 'fish' and the work is done.

Now, however, Xaanthi encounters a problem. He comes across a further creature, something that he calls a 'whale'. His taxonomy suggests that since it swims it has cold blood. The problem, of course, is that its blood is warm. The theory of animal taxonomy that Xaanthi has carefully erected is now in jeopardy. In terms of his theory the 'whale' is an anomalous creature. What should be done about this? One possibility is to ignore it – to argue, for instance, that its sighting was unreliable. This has often been done in practice. For instance, eighteenth-century French scientists dismissed reports that stones fell to earth on the grounds that this was impossible, and that the witnesses were of doubtful standing.[3] The other possibilities are to accept that instances of 'whales' do, indeed, occur. Thus, the 'mammal'/'fish' distinction might be preserved and a new genus, that of the 'whale' inserted. Such a three-class solution is depicted in Figure 4.6. Then again, the 'mammal'/'fish' distinction might be preserved, and the attributes of each class changed. Thus the whale might be included in either the class of 'fish' (Figure 4.7) or 'mammal' (Figure 4.8). Though, given present day European taxonomic conventions we are inclined to want to allocate it to the class of 'mammal', there is *in the abstract* no reason why one solution should be preferred over the others. Indeed, there is no reason why the animals concerned should be classified in one or other of these ways at all. Plausible alternative classifications could perfectly well be erected to take account of such attributes as edibility, degree of dangerousness, size, nature of skin or fur, climatic zone preferred or whatever. The general point here is that there is nothing about the phenomena themselves that strongly dictates how the network should be elaborated or altered. Other, practical, considerations enter into the choice of solution adopted.[4]

"FISH"	"WHALE"	"MAMMAL"
COLD-BLOODED	WARM-BLOODED	WARM-BLOODED
SWIMS	SWIMS	WALKS
LIVES IN WATER	LIVES IN WATER	LIVES ON LAND

FIGURE 4.6   *Three-class solution to the anomalous whale problem*

Let us suppose, however, that Xaanthi persists with a two-class taxonomy in which the 'whale' is grouped with 'mammals' (as in Figure 4.8). That is to say, he decides that blood-temperature is a more important attribute than habitat or mode of locomotion. Now he makes a series of further discoveries: that there are other warm-blooded creatures which swim in the sea – for instance 'dolphins' and 'porpoises'. The list of 'mammals' grows again. In addition, he discovers that they all breathe air, whereas cold-blooded 'fish' breathe water. The attributes of the class of 'mammal' are therefore adjusted again, as are the species so classified. Then he encounters 'lungfish' and taxonomic confusion

"FISH"

SWIMS
WARM OR COLD-BLOODED
LIVES IN WATER

(SHARK; WHALE)

"MAMMAL"

WALKS
WARM-BLOODED
LIVES ON LAND

(ELEPHANT; MOUSE)

FIGURE 4.7 *Two-class solution to the anomalous whale problem (whale = 'fish')*

"FISH"

SWIMS
COLD-BLOODED
LIVES IN WATER

(SHARK)

"MAMMAL"

WARM-BLOODED

(ELEPHANT; MOUSE; WHALE)

FIGURE 4.8 *Two-class solution to the anomalous whale problem
(whale = 'mammal')*

reigns once more. This is an anomalous creature, cold-blooded, water-breathing *and* able to breathe in air. The same problems of adjustment confront Xaanthi now as they did before in the case of the whale. Is the 'lungfish' a genus all by itself? Is it to be treated as a 'mammal' (in which case the attributes of 'mammals' will have to be altered)? Or is it better seen as a 'fish' (which also involves some adjustment)? Xaanthi decides on the grounds of blood-temperature, the ability to breathe in water and the fact that its lungs are poorly developed, to allocate the 'lungfish' to the class of 'fish'. Further investigation strengthens his conviction that this decision was wise when he discovers that all creatures classified as 'mammals' bear their young live – something which fish do not. His triumph, however, is short-lived. On a visit to Australia he encounters the air-breathing, warm-blooded, egg-laying 'duck-billed platypus'. At this point Xaanthi is recalled home by the irate grant-giving subcommittee of the Martian Academy of Sciences. Their irritation has arisen because Xaanthi does not seem to have made any progress. His attempt to construct general classes and associations between those classes has apparently encountered disaster. An economical network, a lazy Martian's predictive guide to the anatomical and behavioural characteristics of the fauna of earth, has not been developed.

This example not only illustrates the search for generality that underlies the construction of classificatory networks (a search that is common to laymen as well as to taxonomists). It also suggests that classes and the links between classes in any given network are inherently revisable in the light of experience. The boundary between the classes of 'mammal' and 'fish' altered a number of times in the course of Xaanthi's adventures. And in case the reader is tempted to think that at least the names of the species have an intrinsic stability, it would be as well to remember that these too are open to revision. 'Elephants' are divisible into 'Indian' and 'African' subspecies, and where do 'mammoths' and 'mastodons' fit in? 'Camels' may be distinguished from 'dromedaries', and so on. So though some kind of intrinsically detectable similarity lies at the root of species identification, the *particular similarities picked out* depend on other criteria. This is, of course, a corollary of a point which we made earlier: that classification involves us in a loss of information. To classify in one way involves us in noticing and emphasising the similarities that underlie that classification and in ignoring or at least de-emphasising those that underlie alternative possible classification. Books in libraries are normally classified by subject matter or author, and rarely by size, date of acquisition, or the colour of the cover.[5] Such other similarities may be attended to if we have some special reason so to do, however. So it is with animals and species. There is an animal found in parts of New Guinea which Europeans call a 'cassowary' and which they treat as a species of 'bird'. In everyday language we would say that it looks like a small 'ostrich'. European taxonomy takes broadly the same view. For the Karam of New Guinea, however, it is not a 'bird' at all. It is something different. For the Karam what we call 'birds' and 'bats' belong to the genus '*yakt*', whereas the cassowary is a '*kobtiy*'.[6] There are reasons for such differences which we need not consider here. What is, however, important is that the lumpy perceptual raw material is susceptible to imputations of similarity and difference in more than one way. Such raw material does not by itself impose a single possible classification. It offers us a variety of possibly detectable similarity relations and in our classification we pick up one, whereas the Karam pick up another.

This is an extremely important point and it is one to which we shall return on a number of occasions in order to strengthen and broaden it. However, an analogy may be helpful at this point. We draw this from the psychology of perception by considering examples of well-known figures that are susceptible to more than one interpretation. Look at E. G. Boring's ambiguous figure

FIGURE 4.9   *'Bird' or 'kobtiy'?*

(Figure 4.10). Is she a gay and beautiful young girl dressed up for her first ball? Or is she a forbidding and ugly old harridan, wearing a wrinkled and dirty shawl? Is the nose a nose or is it a cheek? The picture is susceptible to either interpretation and we tend, as our eyes wander from place to place, to flip from one to the other. The same point can be illustrated by looking at the famous Necker cube. Which corner is it that you see, sticking out of the page in your direction? Is it A or B? Either interpretation is possible. The perceptual lumpiness that presents itself to our senses may be constructed, for these ambiguous figures, in this way or that. More or less at will we may see an eye or an ear. With the identification of species we do not have that freedom to choose between alternatives. There are very good reasons for this – reasons which we shall consider when we come on to discuss the acquisition of 'ways of seeing'. But the variation between the various classifications and taxonomies that we find, both between cultures (think of the case of the cassowary) and within the same culture but over time (see our oxygen and phlogiston example in Chapter 18) suggest that perception and classification, even for apparently stable objects, is not given in the lumpiness of the

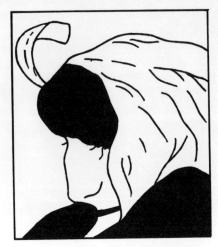

FIGURE 4.10   *Young girl or old hag?*

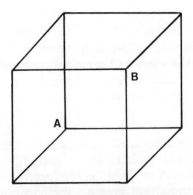

FIGURE 4.11   *The Necker cube*

natural world alone, but rather in an interaction between nature
and accepted ways of seeing, an interaction that exploits some and
ignores the rest of the many similarities offered to us by nature.

MEANING, INTENSION AND EXTENSION

We are now in a position to consider the vexed question of
meaning – what it is to say that a term has a given meaning. It is

vexed because it is perhaps the case that more philosophical ink has been spilled over this question than over any other. We do not need to consider such philosophers' problems in detail for our present purposes and readers who have a particular interest therein are urged to consult appropriate specialist texts.[7] Nevertheless, the network theory of knowledge leads quite naturally to a particular understanding of 'meaning', and we will consider this briefly.

Consider once more the problems that Xaanthi encountered in his attempt to erect a terrestrial animal taxonomy. The problems grouped themselves into two kinds. First of all, there were those questions concerning the types of animals that might properly be described as 'mammals'. Instances of 'elephants' definitely fell within this class and 'sharks' did not, but he was faced with a series of decisions about such species as 'whales', 'lungfish' and 'duck-billed platypuses'. He was concerned, then, with the class of animals to which the term 'mammal' might appropriately be applied. The class of objects covered by a term is sometimes called its *extension* by philosophers and we will adopt this usage here.

The second class of problems (and one related to the first) concerned the similarities and differences taken to be important in deciding whether a given animal should be included within or excluded from the class of 'mammal'. Warm-bloodedness was held to be an important similarity throughout, but Xaanthi decided early on that terrestrial habitat might safely be ignored. These decisions – in this case those concerning the properties of 'mammals' – are sometimes called the *intension* of a term by philosophers. Again we will adopt this usage.[8]

As we have mentioned, philosophers have spilled much ink over the question of meaning. Some, for instance, have sought to show that the meaning of a term is nothing more than its extension – the class of objects to which it applies. Most, however, have found this definition unsatisfactory on the grounds that it 'misses out' on something, or more formally, that two terms may have the same extension but 'mean' different things. In the case of network theory this is so. A change in intension does not necessarily reveal itself in a corresponding change in extension, for attention to different similarities and differences may lead to identical classes of objects. Thus, the *importance* of intension can be a little difficult to see in practice unless there is a simultaneous change or difference in extension. If we disagree only about the intension of a term, but not about its extension, then in practice we will have no difficulty in using the term in a way that extracts practical agreement all round. Indeed, disagreements about intension may simply not be apparent under such circumstances – it will appear as if there is agreement not only over extension but intension too.

On the other hand, it will not do to define meaning in terms of extension alone. Aside from the feeling that we are 'missing out' on something we may, more formally, say that terms are related together in the network and are thus in some sense dependent upon one another for meaning. The term 'mammal' is not simply dependent on the objects that it properly describes, but also on its boundary relations with such neighbouring classes as 'fish' and 'reptiles'. Accordingly, it is necessary to argue that meaning depends upon both extension and intension, for it is intension that relates to and defines such boundary relations.

Consider the importance of intension for Xaanthi's efforts. The intension of 'mammal' changes in the course of his investigation from 'warm-blooded and terrestrial' to 'warm-blooded, placental and equipped with well-developed lungs'. Thus 'mammal' is definitionally linked with a series of other terms – from 'lungs' to 'warm-blooded' – in a variety of ways. These definitions, which define the boundary relations between 'mammal' and 'fish' are *also* susceptible to changes in intension and extension – changes that might (or might not) influence the extension of 'mammal' or 'fish'. Thus, without quibbling, we may imagine discussion about what constitutes 'warm-blooded'. Many kinds of 'reptiles' which, we may agree, cannot be counted as 'mammals', in practice adopt styles of life which ensure that their blood-temperature is approximately $37°$ C, for it is at this temperature at which they operate most efficiently. (Consider, here, instances of 'crocodiles', 'marine iguanas' and probably also 'dinosaurs'.) Meanwhile many 'mammals' routinely allow their blood-temperature to fall way below $37°$ C (for instance during hibernation). It is possible to rescue our conventional distinction between 'mammals' and 'reptiles' by, for example, insisting that the heat be metabolically generated, but this is not the important point. What is important is that, in the course of such manoeuvres the intension of the class of 'mammals' is being altered and adjusted. The meaning of the term, properly applied, is being resited in the course of a process that may be described as tinkering with the network.

In case this is not absolutely clear, it is perhaps worthwhile making it explicit that the meaning of a term is thereby susceptible to change, not only if the term itself is linked to an altered network in a somewhat different way, but also if there is a change in other parts of the network. Adustment of the term 'warm-blooded' affects the class of 'mammals' just as it affects the classes of 'fish', 'reptiles' and, for that matter, what is to be taken as 'warm'. It may help if we mix metaphors and note that adjustment of one part of a network has implications for other parts just as a stone dropped in calm water has spreading implications for the motion of the water elsewhere in the pool.

In this chapter we have explored some of the implications of cross-classification, using a network metaphor, one which stresses the interconnectedness of classes and have defined meaning in terms of intension and extension. We have stressed that such interconnectedness almost always leads to misfits and via an imaginary example we have outlined what it means for classes when human beings attempt to iron out those misfits. In the following chapter we look in more detail at certain aspects of those connections.

In this chapter we have suggested that:

14 Cross-classification leads to a densely interrelated set of classes which, following Hesse, we call a 'network'.

15 Despite the complexity of networks these are ordered by a search for simple, economical and general classes and interconnections.

16 This does *not* imply that there is a single 'best' classification for all individuals.

17 In the search for economy of classification misfits occur.

18 In the attempt to eradicate misfits, all terms and links in a network are at risk for alteration.

19 This includes terms with a direct empirical referent, because such terms rest upon a small selection from an indefinite number of possible similarity relations. Other similarities might be chosen.

20 It follows that empirical descriptions are not dependent on nature alone (though nature makes them possible).

21 The meaning of any term depends, in addition, upon its position in a network, both with respect to the objects referred to by that term (extension) and the properties with which those objects are seen as being similar (intension).

22 Agreement about extension does not entail agreement about intension .

23 The extension and intension of a term are both susceptible to alteration as the result of changes elsewhere in the network.

5 Links Between Classes: Economy and Coherence

ASSOCIATION OR LINKING

We have already shown that the way in which the terms or classes in a network relate together are such that disturbance at any one point in the network is likely to have implications for classes elsewhere. But what is the nature of such links? In earlier chapters we have been deliberately vague, using such terms such as 'association' without specifying precisely what this intends. What then can be said about such associations? Here we deal with the *quality* of such links. In a later chapter we will consider the fact that such links vary in strength.

Association may take a variety of forms. Turn back to the Martian taxonomy example in the previous chapter and consider one of the associations we hypothesised, that between the classes of 'mammal' and the property of 'warm-bloodedness'. What status does this relationship have? Without extending this hypothetical example beyond reasonable lengths we cannot really say. However, on the face of it, it does appear to be something like a definition, perhaps a tautology, of the form 'All bachelors are single'. Elementary textbooks of philosophy are fond of pointing out that this pair of terms is definitionally related. If somebody is revealed as a bachelor then it is no further discovery to establish their marital status as single. So, it would appear, is the case with the relationship between the classes of 'mammal' and 'warm-bloodedness'. The situation, however, changes when the network is elaborated, as it was in our example, into the set of links indicated in Figure 5.1. Here the relationships are more complex. Out of such a triangle a definition can be extracted: 'A mammal is a warm-blooded creature that breathes air by means of well developed lungs'. On the other hand it might also, under the right circumstances, act as a predictor. Thus, one can imagine coming

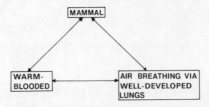

FIGURE 5.1 *A network about mammals*

across the corpse of a large animal which proved, on investigation, to have well-developed lungs. Assuming that no other class of animal had well-developed lungs, we would be warranted in making the assertions first, that we had discovered a mammal and second, that the creature, when alive, had warm blood. In other words, here the associations act as an *indicator* and a *law-like statement* respectively. Now consider the remarkable discovery that may be summarised in the further network displayed in Figure 5.2. The fact that warm-blooded air-breathing creatures bear their young live is precisely that: an *interesting empirical discovery*, and one that becomes more certain as more corroborating instances are uncovered. Over time such a discovery, an empirical generalisation, can alter in status. Thus one can imagine the 'bearing young live' criterion becoming the defining characteristic which determines membership of the class of mammals.

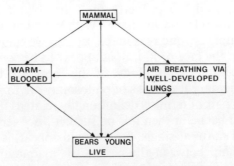

FIGURE 5.2 *A network about mammals*

Though this example is, of course, hypothetical, such shifts in the status of associations and terms occur routinely in practice. The status of the Marxist claim that class conflict is basic to capitalist society is a case in point. Starting life as a supportable empirical generalisation, it achieves a law-like status in Marx's own writing and that of some of his early followers. More recently it has been transformed into something close to a definition so that empirical findings are substantially irrelevant to its status. And now certain Marxists, though a minority, are in the process of abandoning any version of this claim at all. Lest it be thought that we are unfairly picking on Marxism, we should add that similar shifts occur routinely in the sciences. Newton's second law of motion, that 'the rate of change of momentum is proportional to the applied force, and takes place in the direction in which the force acts', though it took many years of empirical and theoretical research to achieve, now has the status of a logical and irrefutable truth in the context of classical dynamics. The same can be said for the chemical law of fixed proportions. Before Dalton it was an erratic factual finding of doubtful empirical status. After Dalton it became a part of the definition of a chemical compound, being thereby ascribed an untestable status.[1] Thus, though the distinction between discovery, empirical generalisations, laws and definitions are obviously of great practical importance, it should not be supposed that they are immutable, or finally distinct. The network theory supposes that, like classes themselves, such associations are mutable, and this is, of course, what we discover in practice.

We should also remind ourselves that links between classes may, as it were, be tacit and perceptual. Cognitive psychology again has a range of elegant experiments to show how classes can be perceptually associated – indeed associated with such strength that even prolonged exposure to anomaly does not necessarily break down expectations. Consider the anomalous playing card in Figure 5.3. It is anomalous because, though it appears to be a five of hearts, in fact the hearts are not red but black. Bruner and Postman[2] report an experiment in which subjects were allowed brief glimpses of playing cards and asked to identify them. The cards shown were a mixture of the normal and the anomalous. When subjects had only a brief moment for identification they nearly always named the cards, whether normal or anomalous, without hesitation. The card in Figure 5.3 would, for instance, have been described as a five of hearts. When subjects had longer to study the cards, they began to detect that something was 'wrong' though it was often difficult to work out exactly what this was. Though a minority of subjects were never able to handle the

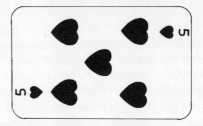

FIGURE 5.3 *The anomalous playing card*

anomaly, most of them, after two or three such cards had been accurately described, were untroubled by the further presentation of anomaly and rendered subsequent accurate descriptions. Thus we find that, for this case at least, tacit perceptual associations were susceptible to being overturned in most cases if undermined by experience (just as the expectation that parrots say goodbye was similarly abandoned), but we also find that such associations nevertheless help to structure perception until suspicion is roused that something is wrong.

THE ECONOMY OF LINKS

Having seen that the links of association are diverse, and noted that they are susceptible to change in status, or can even be overthrown, we are now in a position to consider a very fundamental question: what do human beings do when they notice an association that appears to have empirical status? This is an exceedingly complex question and an answer depends on a wide variety of factors. In part, for instance, it depends on whether or not that association is important to the person concerned. Unimportant associations may be ignored or forgotton. Those associations that have relevance for action ('Eating earthworms makes you sick') are not, however, ignored. Rather, they are linked with other similar associations, and a tie of some generality is forged. This, of course, is just another guise for the drive for conceptual economy that underlies the production of networks, a principle of economy that has, as a consequence, the tendency to create associations of increasing simplicity and sometimes, at least, of predictive power. The *form* taken by this tendency to cognitive laziness is highly variable. An association can vanish, as it were, into the tacit and perceptual (remember the problems of driving a motor car and making sense of the movement of other vehicles). It can take the form of general predictions or laws, or it can take the form of definitions. In addition, it would be wrong to suppose that all empirical associations are assimilable as further instances of already existing patterns of general association. Misfits may occur. Our Martian taxonomy example, as well as the playing card instance already outlined reveal that it may be difficult to find a consonance between old associations and new empirical links. The Martian taxonomy example revealed some of the network adjustments that can occur when an inconsistency becomes noticeable – an inconsistency that spoils the economy and generality of the network.

The tendency to economy, to see new links as being like old, is absolutely fundamental to this understanding of human cognitive activity. It is a principle which, though variously applicable in practice, can always be found at the centre of seeing, perceiving and thinking. The principle of economy is one of the most important ordering features of a network of associations. We may therefore describe it as a *coherence condition*: it helps to determine what goes with what and what form the network will take. Now, however, we should reiterate a warning that we made earlier. The operation of the coherence condition of economy on perceptually lumpy phenomena does not *uniquely* determine the form that a network will take. This is the case for several reasons. First, as we noted earlier, human beings experience different phenomena and therefore notice somewhat different regularities. Second, they have different interests. This leads them to attend to different regularities. This is a matter that we will discuss in a later chapter. But third, and this is most important for our present purposes, in their search for similarity and economy people have different socially-structured similarity relations upon which to draw. The cultures into which they are born have, as it were, prepackaged, and in many cases divergent, similarities to which attention is properly to be directed.

In a later chapter we will fill in a missing piece of this jigsaw, and discuss socialisation and pedagogy. Here it is simply enough to note that, for whatever reason, human beings in different societies have very different conceptions of their natural and social environments. We have already briefly mentioned the case of the cassowary, and we will illustrate such divergences at greater length for the case of the natural sciences when we come to discuss the case of phlogiston and oxygen. It is, however, extremely easy to illustrate the disparity that exists for conceptions of social structure.[3] Butler and Stokes, for instance, in their study of the voting patterns of the British electorate[4] discovered that some (not all) Labour voters have a very different conception of social hierarchy from that of most Conservative voters. About half of the Labour voters (who tend to have a relatively low socioeconomic status) have a more or less clearly articulated class view of social structure. They say things like 'Labour's for the working man. The Conservatives have only ever looked after the rich'. This class conflict view of hierarchy is widespread. In addition, further Labour voters have a conception of working-class solidarity, though without the element of conflict. Such voters say things like 'The Labour party has always seen the working class right'. Such class conflict or class solidarity views are rare among Conservative voters who tend, if they accept the existence of hierarchy at all, to see it as a continuum rather than as a dichotomy. The two views are depicted in Figure 5.4.

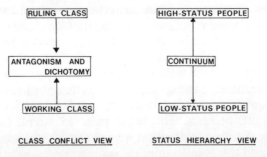

FIGURE 5.4 *Two views of British social hierarchy*

We are not, here, concerned with the origins of such mental maps, though intuitive explanations spring to mind. What is important is to note that as models of society they are radically different.[5] Many other examples of such differences could, of course, be found. Remember, now, that the principle of economy suggests that human beings will try to use existing classifications and classificatory links to explain new associations or phenomena. This is an aspect of the propensity to see objects or events as similar to prior objects and events. If human beings have very different social and natural networks it will therefore come as no surprise if they associate what the outsider might take to be the same phenomena with different classes and network links. This may be easily illustrated. For instance, it is a fact that about two-fifths of the British working class votes Conservative. Why should this be? The class-antagonistic voter is able to proffer an explanation on the basis of fear, self-delusion or ideology. For the status-hierarchy voter it is a welcome sign that some of the lower status ascribe their relative lack of success to personal lack of performance rather than to imagined class disadvantage. Furthermore, it is not immediately possible to show that either of these explanations is incorrect. Thus, the class-antagonist can point to the Conservative inclinations of large sections of the popular press and indicate that, given such an ideological climate, it is unsurprising that forty per cent of the working class does not understand its real political and social interests. The status-hierarchy theorist can point to the isolated cultural milieu of certain low-status groups and explain class-consciousness in terms of locally dominant subcultural norms.

To recapitulate, what we are arguing is that the coherence condition of economy does not, in conjunction with perceptually lumpy phenomena, lead to a unique solution in the form of a universally agreed network. Different experiences, different interests and, most important for our present purposes, different social maps or networks combine to lead us to a wide variety of solutions, not only in conceptions of social life, but in the networks of association as they apply to natural phenomena.[6] There are many such examples of the modelling of natural explanations on social metaphors. The similarity between Darwin's theory of evolution by natural selection and the theory of classical liberal economics has often been noted.[7] Rudwick suggests a link between the conception of geological time which, of course, expanded greatly in the nineteenth century under the influence of uniformitarian geological theory, and the notion of the existence of unlimited banking credit.[8] Law has shown an exact analogy between nineteenth-century American liberal thought and an atomistic theory of geological sediment structure which developed in the United States at that time.[9] The suggestion, then, is that in a variety of ways, the culture in which human beings operate suggests a variety of further coherence conditions over and above the search for economy. Or, more precisely, it structures how the search for economy will be achieved. Models that are developed in one area of experience (for instance the social) will be applied to other areas such as the natural because it is economical to do so. If associations can be ordered via such models, then the latter will be used. And yet more direct coherence conditions will be available. Members of one society will tend to explain events with reference to God. Others will construct alternative explanations on the basis of class or national destiny. In other social environments simple causal explanations will be modish. With such ready-made cultural resources, it is small wonder that human beings, in their lazy search for economical explanation, have a tendency to take over conventions (conventions which have, after all, presumably worked perfectly well in other contexts) and use them to explain new or puzzling phenomena if they possibly can.

Though this should by now be clear, it is worthwhile making explicit one implication of the position outlined above. This is that *all knowledge, including scientific knowledge, is constitutively conventional.* That is to say, it is a cultural *construct.* It is not unambiguously determined by nature. Rather it results from an interaction between perceptual lumpiness, the coherence conditions with which we have been naturally endowed (that is, the propensity to seek economical associations) and the coherence conditions which are made culturally available to us, for instance in the form of preferred models. Thus empirical knowledge, knowledge of events in the world, is *also* conventional knowledge. There is no inherent tension between empirical knowledge and social convention. Empirical knowledge cannot be other than convention. Though this is, in fact, common sense and arises naturally out of the position that we have developed, it entails a variety of consequences that are both unusual and controversial. It suggests, for instance, that the distinction between science and ideology may well be untenable, or at the very least requires reformulation.

In this chapter we have suggested that:

24 Association between classes can take a variety of forms: definition, law, empirical generalisation, empirical finding, indicator or tacit perceptual assumption.

25 These forms are not rigidly distinct. One type of association may turn into another if the conditions are right.

26 *Coherence conditions* are the principles by which a network is ordered and structured.

27 The most basic coherence condition is *economy*. Human beings try to simplify their mental maps by detecting similarity between new experience and old classes. Thus, they try to maximise the ordering power of their existing networks.

28 Naturally misfits may be perceived. Then network change (either to the old classes or the new phenomenon) may take place.

29 The coherence condition of economy does not determine a unique network for all human beings because the latter experience different biographies, have different interests and have different explanatory principles made available to them in the course of socialisation.

30 Such socially transmitted explanatory principles are also coherence conditions. They include preferred models and modes of explanation.

31 It follows that all knowledge, including scientific knowledge, is constitutively conventional.

6 Links Between Classes: Strength

PERSONALIST PROBABILITY

In Chapter 5 we considered the quality of links between classes in a network and suggested that this varies considerably. So far, however, we have not considered another way in which the association between classes may vary. This is the *strength* of any given link in the network. In the first part of this chapter we consider the problem of induction and attempts to measure 'rational degrees of belief' in terms of the so-called theory of personalist probability. In the second part we informally introduce questions of probability and utility.

Suppose that people were inductive-learning-machines – that is, they went about making general claims on the basis of having observed particular instances.[1] Suppose, then, that people behaved like Xaanthi. He claimed, quite generally, that 'all animals that bear their young live are warm-blooded' having studied cases of animals that proved both to be warm-blooded and to bear their young live. Philosophers have been very uneasy about induction. The philosophical problem of induction, if it is a problem, arises from the fact that a generalisation so created goes beyond the facts. Claims about future warm-blooded animals cannot be *deduced* from discoveries about past warm-blooded animals.

Some philosophers have sought to understand science in a way that avoids induction altogether. Others, however, have sought to explicate the concept and develop theories about how well-supported a generalisation might be taken to be, given a body of evidence that tends to sustain it. These 'confirmation theorists' have encountered a number of philosophical difficulties which need not detain us here.[2] Yet, for obvious reasons, the network theorist cannot afford to avoid the issue altogether. Since the links in the network – or many of them at least – are inductive

54

generalisations and since the aim is to develop an understanding
of the way in which knowledge is generated, some attention must
be paid to the degree to which different links in the network are
secure and the processes by which they gain or lose that security.
In other words, some attention has to be paid to the way in which
people learn about their environments, how they build up their
knowledge and their attributes as inductive-learning-machines.[3]

An obvious way to express the strength or security of network
links is in terms of probabilities: the probability that one class
(warm-bloodedness) will be associated with another (bearing
young live). However, if this is to be applied to network theory in
order to understand the way in which human beings learn, then it
has to reflect the *subjective* degrees of confidence that people
attach to different relationships,[4] rather than to any putative
'objective' and abstract relationship between classes. This avenue
of thought has been investigated by 'personalist probability'
theorists, who have sought in a variety of ways, to understand
how people do (or should) allocate degrees of confidence or
confirmation to given relationships. Many such theorists have
made use of Bayes's theorem,[5] a statistical expression that
describes the effect of new evidence on the degree of probability of
a hypothesis which had been allocated a previous probability on
the basis of old evidence. Informally, Bayes's theorem may be
treated as saying three things about the probability of a hypothesis after the addition of new supporting evidence. The first is
that this probability directly relates to the probability of the
hypothesis *before* the addition of the new evidence: in other
words, the more probable it was before, the more probable it will
be afterwards. Second, it also relates directly to the probability of
the new evidence, given that both the hypothesis and the original
body of evidence are true, and third, it relates *inversely* to the
degree of probability of the new evidence given the truth of the
original body of evidence. This last has the effect of tempering
the importance of new evidence if that evidence would have been
anticipated in the absence of the hypothesis in question, but,
conversely, of increasing its importance if it would not otherwise
have been strongly anticipated.

Bayes's theorem is, then, a possible expression of the human
capacity to learn from the environment in the light of past
experience. It needs, however, to be remembered that it is a
hypothesis only. Mary Hesse, who has discussed Bayesianism at

some length, supplements it with other statistical expressions. The point is that social scientists are far from a general model of learning, even if some kind of inductive process seems to be centrally involved. It is also the case that the *interpretation* of Bayes's theorem (and related expressions) is controversial, even for those who are prepared to accept personalist probability theory and ignore important technical problems (for instance, concerning the measurement of prior probability). Thus Mary Hesse sees it as providing a possible model for rational degrees of belief. Rationality is definitionally related to betting behaviour, specifically to the maximum odds a bettor would accept on the occurrence of an event, this being in turn related to the proposition that no rational person will bet in such a way that an opponent who knows more than him will always be able to win, no matter what the outcome. Thus Hesse distances herself both from 'objective' probabilities and from what she calls 'merely subjective degrees of belief'.[6] She is precisely concerned with what she calls 'rational degrees of belief'. However, despite this, it has been argued that Hesse's theory is primarily descriptive rather than being normative.[7] It is not appropriate to pursue the details of this argument here; all we need to note is that since we are concerned in the present text with *describing* knowledge rather than *prescribing* behaviour, personalist probability theory and Bayesianism will be useful insofar as they turn out to be generally applicable to the construction of all belief or knowledge.

PROBABILITY AND UTILITY

If, indeed, human beings may be seen as inductive-learning-machines, then, as we have just noted, they may be treated as generating networks whose links can be posed in terms of probability. Consider the network depicted in Figure 6.1.

The first thing to note is that the strength of the link may depend on the direction in which one chooses to move through the network. There is a probability, $p = 1$, that a mammal will be an animal, for according to the theory all mammals are animals. The probability that an animal will be a mammal is smaller, $p < 1$, for an animal stands a chance of being a fish rather than a mammal. If all animals are either mammals or fish, then of course the joint probability 'this animal is a mammal' and 'this animal is

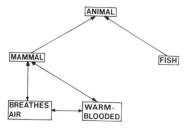

FIGURE 6.1 *A network about some animals*

a fish' will be $p = 1$. In some cases, however, the probabilities are identical from whichever end of the link one starts. The probability that a mammal will breathe air is $p = 1$, and the probability that an air-breather is a mammal is also $p = 1$. This and the value of some other links are indicated in Figure 6.2.

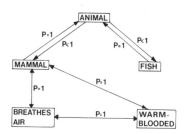

FIGURE 6.2 *A network about some animals with probabilities*

Now notice something else. Only a small proportion of the possible links between classes have actually been drawn in. A full network would, of course, look like Figure 6.3. The probability of many of these new links, though not all, is zero. There is no chance that fish breathe air, or are warm-blooded. If it is a mammal, it cannot be a fish. On the other hand, if it breathes air or is warm-blooded, then it is certain to be an animal, $p = 1$, and so on. In principle, with the establishment of a network of classifications, every point can be connected with every other and, ignoring the *quality* of the link, can be expressed in terms of one or two probability relationships. Of course, this does not mean to say that we actually attend, either consciously or unconsciously, to most of the possible associations. Here again the coherence

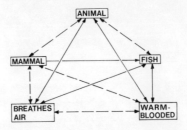

FIGURE 6.3   *All possible links between five terms*

condition of economy comes into play. Unnecessary links are not constructed and examined. That would lead to unnecessary work. Thus it makes sense to distinguish between such links as 'spaceships are fried eggs' and 'fish are warm-blooded'. Though the association of the class 'spaceship' with that of 'fried egg', like that of 'fish' with 'warm-blooded' is extremely unlikely – that is to say, the probability of such a linkage approaches zero – the utility of the latter far exceeds that of the former. One can fairly readily imagine practical circumstances in which the relationship between fish and warm-bloodedness might be useful ('You mean it had warm blood when you caught it? Then it can't be a fish'). In the present world, however, though spaceships form part of the same network as fried eggs, their relationship is not such as is likely to be of any use. The possible links remain inactive, unactivated and, for all intents and purposes, non-existent.

Probabilities may take any value between $p = +1$ which represents tautology, definition, invariant empirical link, complete correlation, to $p = 0$, which represents a hypothesis or relation that has no probability at all. $p = +1$ and $p = 0$ are depicted in Figure 6.4 which represents most of Figure 6.3. However, we frequently encounter situations where the probability of the association is not so clear-cut as in the above case. Consider, once again, the case of Martian taxonomy. Imagine a situation where mammals are defined as warm-blooded creatures that bear their young live. For the purpose of simplicity, imagine that this definition is based on a study of the three species, elephant, camel and whale. Without using Bayesian statistics it is possible to illustrate informally what might happen to the probability values with the discovery of the egg-laying duck-billed platypus. The relationship between warm-bloodedness and

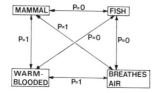

FIGURE 6.4 *All possible links between four classes*

the bearing of live young is affected. Assuming that each species carries the same weight in terms of the calculation of probabilities, the probability that warm-blooded creatures bear their young live sinks to $p = 0.75$. This is indicated in Figure 6.5. Meanwhile, the similar association in relation to fish (if it lays eggs then it will be cold-blooded) is likewise affected. And since a definition of 'mammal' based upon a combination of warm-bloodedness and the bearing of live young will no longer serve, it follows that qualitative and quantitative adjustment is required there too. If, for example, it is decided that, henceforth, mammals will no longer be defined as creatures that bear live young, then this too becomes a problematic relationship (and corresponding associations for the class of fish also require adjustment). The redefinition of 'mammal' is depicted in Figure 6.6. Notice that

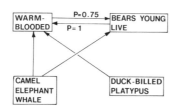

FIGURE 6.5 *A network which includes the duck-billed platypus*

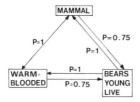

FIGURE 6.6 *A redefinition of the term 'mammal'*

there is nothing fixed, even now, about these probabilities. The discovery of llamas, mustang, and hedgehogs will increase the value of the probability association between 'bears young live' and the other two classes. Again, a subsequent decision to exclude the class of 'duck-billed platypus' from the class of mammal on the grounds of further zoological investigation and instal it in a class of its own would render all the associations equal to unity ($p = 1$) and restore the possibility of a definitional relationship between mammalhood and the bearing of live young.

It should not be supposed that those associations close to plus one (complete identity) are in any way privileged. Though definitions and tautologies usually rest upon an association of $p = +1$, perfectly respectable empirical and theoretical generalis-ations may have a much lower probability: to take but two instances, weather forecasts and public opinion polls. There is also a question of terminology. Certain events are uncertain: for example, an outcome of the toss of a die or the spot where a photon will fall on a screen in Young's double slit experiment. Despite the uncertainty of any such event, the probability that any given outcome will occur is, however, calculable. It is on this long-run and statistical predictability that gambling and quan-tum mechanics each rest. The distribution of events is, as it were, knowable with complete certainty.

In this chapter we have suggested that:

32 The links in a network vary in strength. This strength may for certain purposes be measured as the prob-ability of that link.

33 Confirmation theory has attempted to quantify that probability. In particular, personalist probability theory proposes that the strength of a link be treated as the rational degree of belief in that link.

34 This may be calculated in a number of ways, though Bayes's theorem has been particularly useful in at-tempting to mimic the acquisition of knowledge by a 'human learning-machine'.

35 Given two classes, A and B, the probability that A is associated with B may or may not be the same as the probability that B is associated with A.

36 Probabilities may take any value between plus one (identity, invariant empirical link, complete correlation) and zero.

37 Over time the links between classes may vary in terms of probability.

38 All classes in a network may, in principle, be linked with all others.

39 However, a principle of economy is at work here. Links are not actually constructed unless they are of some use.

40 The utility of a link between classes is partially independent of its probability value(s).

7 Workability and Truth

AN ANALOGY WITH VISUAL REPRESENTATION

At several points in previous sections we have used phrases such as the *utility* or *workability* of a network. The careful reader will have noticed that in so doing we are using a notion that, while of great importance to the network theory, has not yet been explicitly introduced. In this chapter, then, we sketch out what we intend when we use such notions as workability.

We can profitably start, once again, with a visual example. Most readers who have ever visited that city will recognise Figure 7.1 as a representation of the London Underground System.[1] Our question is: is it accurate? Is it a true representation of the underground railways of London? One is tempted to say that it is, indeed, accurate, even true. But is this right? What does it mean to say that it is true?

Consider, first, the signalman who routes the trains through the system. It is intuitively obvious that this representation must be imprecise from his point of view. This is because, for instance, it fails to show which lines are single track and which double, where the different lines are physically connected and similar details. Similarly, the engineer commissioned to build the Jubilee line would have found this map inadequate. For though he knew the line should run south from Baker Street to Bond Street, Green Park, and so on, the map would not have told him how the tunnels should be aligned, how deep they should be drilled or a host of other necessary facts. Even the traveller, new to London and hence unaware of its topography, might be forgiven for making the assumption that a journey between Baker Street and Watford would take only twice as long as a journey from Piccadilly Circus to Paddington.

Clearly this map is not a proper representation of the London Underground System *except for certain purposes*. It has, in fact, been specifically designed with one major purpose in mind: to

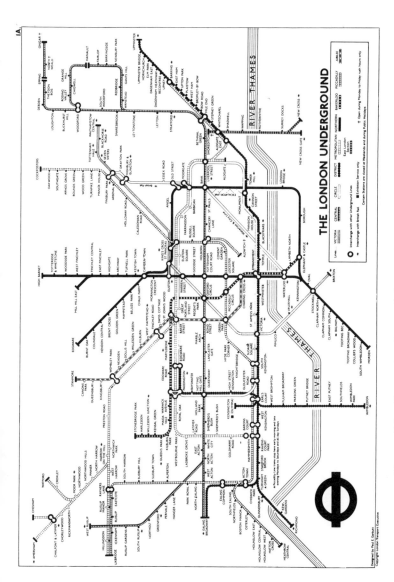

FIGURE 7.1 *Conventional map of the London Underground System*

allow travellers to plan routes through the system with the greatest possible efficiency. If you are at Euston and you need to get to Victoria the map suggests that the most efficient (though certainly not the only) route is by way of the Victoria line. And when the system is running properly, this reading of the map is right.

To jump to the end of our argument, our conclusion is that networks, like maps, are not true, if by 'true' we mean that they correspond precisely to reality. It only makes sense to say that they are true if by that we mean that they are *workable* or *usable*. The map of the Underground is eminently workable for certain purposes. The average traveller can afford to treat it as true because it is a workable aid to puzzle-solving. But as our examples of the signalman and engineer quickly showed, it is not workable for other purposes. The map does not relate to reality sufficiently for them. Rather, it is a useless distortion.

It is possible that some readers may feel that, in choosing an example as obviously conventional as the London Underground map we may have loaded the dice in our favour. Could there not be maps or other representations which depict the original with greater veracity than this? Look, now, at Figure 7.2. This is

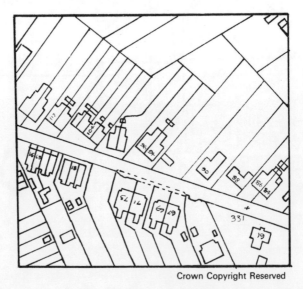

FIGURE 7.2   *Detail from United Kingdom Ordnance Survey map*

redrawn from a detailed map by the United Kingdom Ordnance Survey, a survey which is widely recognised for its veracity and accuracy. It is the kind of map which surveyors and town planners use. It is also very workable if you live at number 104 and need to find number 61. If, however, you want to lay a drain or site a new dwelling it is only *relatively* workable because, despite the degree of detail, it still excludes such relevant items as drains, telephone lines, trees or the height of buildings. It is totally unworkable if your interest is in the style of architecture, the distribution of the flower borders, or the political affiliations of the inhabitants. And its unworkability is not merely a question of lack of detail. The very detail given makes it quite unusable for many purposes. Even if one obtained all the relevant sheets at this scale and fitted them together, it would be a most inefficient type of map to use for planning a route by road from Piccadilly Circus to number 84. A small-scale route-planning map would be better for this purpose and the Ordnance Survey indeed markets such a map.

Even photographs, seemingly a direct copy of the object being photographed, may be assessed in terms of workability. This may be illustrated by Figure 7.3 which is drawn from a photograph of a motor car (for technical reasons we are unable to bring you the photograph itself). This is no more 'true' of that motor car in every sense than the preceding maps were 'true' of the features they covered. The difference here is that if one stood at the point where the picture was taken one would see something like Figure 7.3. But the workability of the depiction depends upon one's interest in the vehicle. An engineer from a rival car firm would, for instance, find the photograph relatively unworkable. He would need engineering drawings and details of performance, perhaps something like Figure 7.4, though this also conceals a great deal. Insofar as the photograph appeared in an advertisement which was designed to persuade potential consumers to purchase the vehicle, we are probably warranted in assuming that the advertisers take it that the depiction is workable for this specific purpose. But we can easily think of purposes for which it is unworkable.

CORRESPONDENCE AND WORKABILITY

There is a wide variety of lessons that we may draw from the discovery that all visual representations, even naturalistic photo-

66

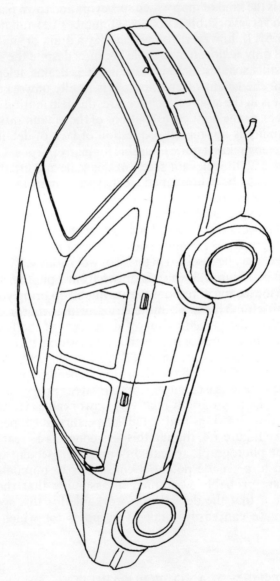

FIGURE 7.3 *A picture of a motor car*

67

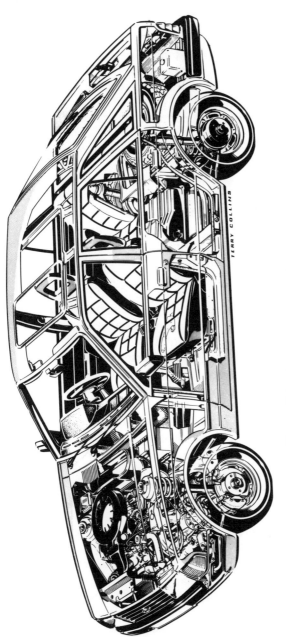

FIGURE 7.4   *A cutaway picture of a motor car*

graphs, may be assessed in terms of workability. It is, for instance, noticeable that workability depends upon the capacity of the viewer to 'decode' information from the representation.[2] However, what is of importance in the present context is that there is a direct analogy between the workability of a pictorial representation and the workability of networks of classes. A network cannot completely represent what it stands for. It cannot, in other words, *correspond* to reality in every respect. It can only represent what it stands for *for particular purposes*, or under the auspices of a particular set of interests. Consider, once more, the case of Martian taxonomy and remember how it was built up. It depended, in the first place, on the recognition of similarity between instances. This beast is similar to that beast and so on, and they will be classed as 'elephants'. The Martian taxonomist was concerned with a special kind of workability. He was concerned with distinguishing the various species into more inclusive classes ('mammal' or 'fish') in a way that allowed him to make certain kinds of predictions, for instance, 'if it bears its young live, then it will have warm blood'. The classification of species proceeded then, not because 'elephants' naturally go with 'whales' but because, for certain purposes they may be treated as 'the same'. The taxonomy attended to certain features (blood temperature, for instance) in ascribing similarity and ignored other features such as habitat. The crucial thing to note, then, is that similarities are noted, classes built up and links erected between classes in accordance with the *purposes* for which a taxonomy is being made. As a description of the animals of the earth, the above classification is of no use if the interest is rather in the extent to which they are a danger to life or have economic value for man.

Why are networks built up for one purpose likely to be of no use in the pursuit of alternative goals? The reason for this is easily given in network theory. It is because networks and knowledge involve simplification. They involve the *selection* of a small number of similarities and associations from among a vast range of possibilities. They involve, as we noted in Chapter 2, a loss of information. There are many other things that one might have chosen to say about the animals or the motor car but they were not said. From the standpoint of this network it is information lost. Whether or not the loss of information is a serious matter entirely depends on the workability of the network that has actually been built up. Information-loss was of no importance to the Martian taxonomist until the advent of the duck-billed platypus. Then, with the resulting loss of simplicity, it became clear that amongst the information lost (or perhaps, more precisely, never noticed) there might have been alternative similarities which would have permitted a simple and predictive classification to be erected.

Let us briefly illustrate this with a real example, one which has already been mentioned. How should the creature that we, in English, call the 'cassowary' be classified?[3] Is it, or is it not a 'bird'? As we indicated earlier, for the Karam of New Guinea this is not a '*yakt*' which is a class that covers most of those creatures that in English we call 'birds' or 'bats'. Rather it is a '*kobtiy*'. When the Karam are asked why it is not an instance of a bird, they give a variety of reasons. For instance, they say that, unlike other birds, it has no feathers, but has hair. Certainly a European can agree to this extent. It lacks stiff, quill-like feathers. Instead it has limp, soft feathers. Again, the Karam note that the head of the *kobtiy* is all bone and no brain – a matter of some importance to them given their predilection for eating the brains of the animals that they hunt. Again, a European would have no difficulty in agreeing that the brain-to-bodyweight ratio of the cassowary is disappointingly small. In addition, the Karam give further responses which suggest that, in some ways, they see *kobtiys* as being like human beings. Overall, then, for whatever reason, the Karam maximise the *dissimilarities* to be found between a '*yakt*' and a '*kobtiy*'. Furthermore, we can assist them by finding further disanalogies, as shown in Figure 7.5.

'YAKT'	'KOBTIY'
FEATHERS	FEATHERLESS
NO HAIR	HAIR
BRAIN	NO BRAIN
HEAD NOT BONY	HEAD BONY
CAN FLY	FLIGHTLESS
SMALL & MEDIUM SIZE	LARGE SIZE
SMALL LEGS	STRONG HEAVY LEGS

FIGURE 7.5 *Disanalogies between a 'yakt' and 'kobtiy'*

On the other hand, the European too, rests his case for the bird-status of the cassowary on sets of similarities and dissimilarities. Like other instances of birds it is a warm-blooded vertebrate with a covering of feathers. Its forelimbs, like those of other 'birds', have been transformed into wings. Furthermore, it is relatively closely related to 'ostriches', 'rheas', 'kiwis' and 'emus', because these too are flightless with breastbones that resemble a flat, bottomless raft (see Figure 7.6).[4]

'BIRDS'

WARM-BLOODED
VERTEBRATE
FEATHERS
FORELIMBS ARE WINGS
LAY EGGS

'RATITAE'

FLAT KEEL-LIKE
BREASTBONE
FLIGHTLESS

FIGURE 7.6 *Birds and ratitae*

Both classifications, the European and the Karam, result in loss of information. Yet both are workable from the standpoint of their respective cultures. To say that one or the other is true (or false) is simply wrong. Each classification selects from the (dis)analogies that exist, naturally, between instances of birds, cassowaries and men. Social coherence conditions assist in making that selection.

This has a variety of philosophical implications, the most important of which is this: in the philosophy of science and social science there are two basic approaches to the notion of truth. There is what is called 'correspondence theory'. Though this is variously formulated and tends to vagueness, it generally asserts that true knowledge is that which may be attached to relatively stable observation via definite 'rules of correspondence' and that, under these conditions, true knowledge 'corresponds' to reality. Then there is the 'pragmatic' or 'instrumental' theory, which asserts that true knowledge (or at least that which is taken to be true) is that which works most satisfactorily. It is obvious that the network theory lies on the instrumental or pragmatic side of this divide, for according to the theory, no knowledge can completely represent reality. We have to be a little careful here. Knowledge may appear or be treated *as if* it completely represents reality from the standpoint of the network theory. This is because, for practical purposes, it predicts reality or allows human beings to interact satisfactorily with their environments. It is therefore no criticism of the network theory to show that human beings *think* that their knowledge corresponds to reality, because this merely shows that they have never had any practical problems in using it. Furthermore, they are, in one sense, right. Nothing about the network theory denies that knowledge is empirical. Maps and theories are not dreams. They *do* tell us a lot about the perceptual lumpiness we will encounter if we use them for the purposes for which they were constructed. In this strictly limited sense, then, it is perhaps not unreasonable to say that networks correspond to reality, but from a particular point of view only.

One last remark. What of the term 'truth'? We will consider arguments that science moves towards the truth in a later chapter, so our remarks here are of necessity preliminary. Our view is that the term 'truth' is so closely associated with the correspondence theory of knowledge that it would be better abandoned. As we have seen, no theory can be true if by this is meant that it completely represents reality. A preferable strategy is to talk instead, as we have done, of the *workability* of knowledge. In the last instance, however, this is little more than a verbal quibble. If it is clear that the term 'truth' implies workability rather than correspondence, then no harm has been done.[5]

---

41 The adequacy of a map or plan depends upon the purposes for which it is used. There is no such thing as a completely accurate map for all purposes.

42 Even apparently accurate photographs vary in the extent to which they are workable from any given standpoint.

43 The same is true for networks. They do not completely represent reality. Rather, they depict it for certain purposes.

44 The reason for this is that the construction of networks rests upon the selection of a small number of similarities and associations from the vast range of possibilities. There is always a loss of information.

45 The loss of information involved in network construction means that if the network is used for other purposes it is likely to prove inadequate.

46 The network theory is thus in accord with instrumental or pragmatic rather than correspondence theories of knowledge.

47 Given that the term 'truth' is closely associated with correspondence theory, it might, on balance be better to abandon its use.

8 Philosophies of Science and the Network Theory

PRESCRIPTION OR DESCRIPTION

In what we have so far written we have attempted to *describe* how knowledge is built up, whether this be everyday, social scientific, or natural scientific in nature. In doing so we have built on three basic assumptions. It will be worthwhile to remind ourselves what these are. First, we have adopted a *materialist* stance. That is to say, we have assumed that there is a material world which makes itself known to us via what we have described as 'perceptual lumpiness'. Second, we have made a *psychological* assumption about human beings – that they are capable of noticing similarities and associations between these perceptual lumps, and have a propensity to create economical classifications. And third, we have indicated (though we have yet to consider the matter in detail) that the forms taken by classification are influenced by social *convention*. Though our aim is a *description* of the generation of knowledge, our exploration of the implications of these three assumptions is in sharp disagreement with certain widespread accounts of the nature of scientific knowledge.

By and large, these alternative accounts are motivated by a concern with *prescription* rather than description. That is to say, these philosophies of science have sought to establish procedures or rules of method by which *good*, *true*, or *workable* knowledge might be built up. They have sought, that is, to distinguish between good and bad knowledge in terms of the methods used in its construction. They have then sought to advise natural and social scientists about the proper methods for the establishment of good (or at least the best possible) knowledge.

An excellent example of prescription in philosophy of science is to be found in the writing of K. R. Popper who developed a well-known theory that distinguishes between scientific and non-scientific knowledge in terms of a number of conventional criteria.[1] For Popper a statement must be *falsifiable* if it is to be scientific. Thus, the two claims 'Class contradictions within capitalism will lead to revolution and the subsequent rise of communism' and 'When zinc is added to sulphuric acid, then hydrogen is given off', are both, on the face of it, scientific statements because one can imagine ways in which they might be tested. This is not, however, the case for: 'In the beginning, God created the heaven and the earth'. This is not a scientific statement in Popper's view, because there is no way in which it could be empirically tested and thus falsified. To say that it is not scientific does not, of course, mean that it is actually false. It might very well be true, but it is certainly beyond the pale of empirical science.

Falsifiability is not the only criterion that *demarcates* between science and non-science for Popper. It is, in addition, necessary for the scientist or social scientist to adopt a policy of attempting to falsify the claim. And if he or she succeeds, the claim must be abandoned forthwith and a new and more testable (that is, more general) hypothesis must be erected in its place. Thus, though the statement about revolution and communism mentioned above is falsifiable and hence, in isolation as it were, scientific, in fact Popper argues that the attitude of Marxists is such that it has ceased to be scientific. This is because, in the face of apparent falsification, they have hung on to this and other predictions and attempted to save them with subsidiary hypotheses of one kind or another. Thus, in the absence of successful communist revolution in advanced capitalist societies, and given the *presence* of such revolution in such precapitalist societies as Russia and China, the scientific Marxist should have abandoned his hypothesis and searched for a more general alternative – one that encompassed the empirical findings and was susceptible to further test.

Though parts of this Popperian view may remind the reader of our discussion of changes in Martian taxonomy, the important point is to note that it is explicitly *prescriptive*. Words like 'should' crop up time and time again. Our account of changes in Martian taxonomy was, on the contrary, *descriptive*. We described those changes without attempting to suggest what should or should not take place. Our later discussion of the move from the phlogiston to the oxygen theory of combustion will be in the same descriptive mode. Though in some later chapters we will enter prescriptive debate here and there, our overall object is to *describe* the way in which knowledge is constructed.

How then, can our description of the growth of knowledge be in conflict with prescriptive accounts such as that of Popper? Might not our disagreement simply reflect a divergence in goals? Though this is in part the case, our disagreements with Popper (and other philosophers of science) are not simply a reflection of differing aims. They arise, in addition, because if the network theory of knowledge is realistic, then Popper's theory (like many others) is based upon a correspondingly unrealistic conception of the nature of knowledge. Interestingly, then, a matter-of-fact description leads us inevitably in the direction of prescription.

OBSERVATION AND NEUTRAL OBSERVATION LANGUAGES

The major areas of disagreement between the network theory and alternative philosophies of science are two-fold. The first concerns the nature and status of observation. The second, which is linked to the first, concerns the relationship between general theory on the one hand, and observation on the other. Let us start with the status of observation. We have seen that all observation statements (that is to say, all empirical classifications) are affected not only by detectable similarities in the lumpiness of nature, but also by decisions about which similarities should be noted and which should be ignored. In other words, we have seen that observation depends not only on nature, but also on the operation of coherence conditions and among these coherence conditions we have noted the importance of culturally transmitted convention. This means, if we might put it informally, that there are no 'raw data'. All data are 'partially cooked'. When philosophers talk about this issue, they use a special term. They argue about whether there can be such a thing as an uncooked 'neutral observation language'. The network theory asserts that there is no such thing as a neutral observation language. Thus in the event of a disagreement between competing theories, the data are partially related to those two theories and the possibility of a neutral description, detached from theory, and available for adjudication in the dispute is not available.[2] There can be no empirically privileged statements and no neutral observation language. There is no direct access to reality in public knowledge. To anticipate the example of the Priestley–Lavoisier oxygen–phlogiston debate, though we find the two principals undertaking many of the same physical manipulations, we also find that they describe their results in quite different language. For Priestley, burning objects gave out phlogiston. Burning stopped if the air became 'phlogisticated' – that is to say, saturated with phlogiston – for the air could only absorb so much of this substance. For Lavoisier, burning objects took up oxygen out of the air. If burning stopped in an enclosed space, this was because the oxygen was exhausted. Though it is, of course, possible to redescribe these physically identical experiments by noting that a lighted taper goes out after burning for a short period of time in an upturned bell-jar held over water, this description does not solve the problem either. This is no more a neutral description than those of Priestley and Lavoisier. Coherence conditions enter equally into its construction. Neither is it empirically privileged. It gives us no greater access to what is 'really' going on in some final sense than either of the other descriptions. In fact, on the basis of the data we have given above, there is no reason to prefer any one of the descriptions over the other two.[3]

The absence of a neutral observation language has several implications. The first is that, even if a theory proves inadequate, it is impossible to abandon it and all its related classifications in one go. This is because the only thing that makes interaction with the world possible is (theoretically influenced) classification. One has, as it were, to stand in one part of the network in order to restructure another part. A metaphor – that of Neurath's raft – is useful here. If you take the raft apart completely you fall into the water and there is no raft left. On the other hand, piecemeal reconstruction is perfectly possible and over time the entire structure can be reshaped. No particular part of the network – including observation statements – is immune to this process, for observation statements, it should be remembered, depend upon coherence conditions. If there is any doubt about this point, the reader should refer back to our discussion of the Martian taxonomy example in Chapter 4.

The second implication of the non-existence of a neutral observation language or atheoretical classification is that those philosophies of science that assume this to be a possibility find themselves in difficulty. That is to say, those philosophies of science that are sometimes loosely called 'empiricist' are unworkable.[4] Furthermore, those natural or social scientists who conceive of themselves as collecting 'raw data' are obviously mistaken.

J. S. MILL'S INDUCTIVISM AND K. R. POPPER'S FALSIFICATIONISM

An example of a philosophy of science that encounters difficulties given the theory-laden nature of observation, is J. S. Mill's inductive method. Mill took the view that a scientific theory was justified only if the evidence collected in its area of relevance supported it inductively. He further argued that theory was generated on the basis of inductive inference. But the problem is: induction from what? It is necessary, in Mill's theory, for objects in the world to be detectable as 'the same' or 'different'. This is because generalisation is possible only if differences and similarities are detectable. Consider, for a moment, Mill's 'Canon of Difference':

> If an instance in which the phenomenon under question occurs, and an instance in which it does not occur have every circumstance in common save one, that one occurring only in the former, the circumstances in which alone the two instances differ is the effect, or the cause, or an indispensable part of the cause of the phenomenon.[5]

This is easily exemplified. Consider the difference between the following two chemical events:

Zinc + Sulphuric Acid + Air ⟶ production of hydrogen gas

Zinc + Air   ⟶ nothing new.

The difference in circumstances between the two cases is, obviously, the presence of sulphuric acid. The 'phenomenon under question' (to use Mill's language) is the production of hydrogen gas. Similar social examples are easily found:

Capitalism + Vanguard Communist Party ⟶ Communist revolution

Capitalism   ⟶ nothing new

Hence, in accordance with the Canon of Difference, sulphuric acid, or the Vanguard Communist Party, must be the 'effect, or the cause, or an indispensable part of the cause of the phenomenon'. The problem, however, is that the various 'circumstances' or 'phenomena' which are reported above are not, of course, classifiable in terms of criteria of similarity provided by nature alone. The choice of which lumps to classify together as similar and which to distinguish as different, or indeed irrelevant, depends upon coherence conditions which arise in part from cultural conventions. The difference between J. S. Mill's theory of induction and the Hesse network theory can be conveniently depicted diagrammatically, as in Figure 8.1.

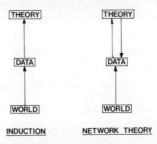

FIGURE 8.1 *Induction and network theory compared*

Though Mill's theory of induction is now over a hundred years old, the inductivist thinking which it represents is commonly found in the social sciences. To take a familiar, though by no means contemporary, example, Durkheim's *Rules of Sociological Method*[6] expresses a broadly inductivist programme. Indeed, Durkheim cites Mill extensively. Thus, the investigator is instructed to collect social facts and to build them up into patterns that permit generalisation. But what is a social fact? Durkheim writes as follows:

Since objects are perceived only through sense perception we can conclude: Science, to be objective, ought to start with concepts formed independent to them, but with these same perceptions. It ought to borrow the materials for its initial definitions directly from perceptual data. . . . Science, then, has to create new concepts; it must dismiss all lay notions and the terms expressing them, and return to sense perception. . . .[7]

The problem is that Durkheim assumes that initial definitions may be constructed directly out of perception without the operation of coherence conditions. However, as we have seen, this is simply not possible. Furthermore, in practice Durkheim naturally makes use of material that has been generated in the course of interaction between perceptual lumps and coherence conditions. For instance, it is well known that Durkheim claimed that suicide rates in Catholic communities were lower than those found in Protestant communities. He used this finding to support his claim that insufficient integration led to higher suicide rates. However, it has often been suggested that the difference in statistics is as much due to different everyday classificatory practices (suicide being a greater sin for Catholics) as to any real difference in suicide rates.[8] It is obvious, then, that the operation of everyday coherence conditions is likely to interfere with Durkheim's inductive methodology.

Similar problems affect Popper's falsifiability theory.[9] Here scientific knowledge is not seen as being built up inductively. Rather, Popper recommends that the theory should be created in bold imaginative leaps that go beyond the data. As we noted earlier in this chapter, the scientist is then enjoined to attempt the falsification of the theory by checking its empirical predictions against the data. But, as we have seen, there is no such thing as raw data. The network theory suggests that the data are constituted in part via the operation of coherence conditions. Furthermore, we can assume that the construction of the data relates, however remotely, through the network, to the theory that is to be tested. Given Popper's concern with falsifiability this is potentially rather serious. Clearly a conjecture can never be checked against the real world directly – it can only be checked against other more empirical parts of the network. In practice Popper and his pupils – for instance Lakatos – have readily agreed that the data are in part constituted by theoretical coherence conditions and have reformulated the testability criterion by suggesting that theories are tested against other theories rather than against raw data.[10] The situation, then, is this: if there is a misfit between theory and (theoretically constructed) data, then the scientist has to decide which is at fault. Is it the theory that he set out to test, or the theories that assisted in the generation of the data? The problem is that Popper's criteria of demarcation give no guidance to the scientist as he makes his decision. They simply do not work on the ground.

Consider the following example. Newton's laws of motion and the theory of gravitational attraction taken together with initial conditions more or less account for the motion of the planets around the sun. Imagine (as actually happened) that observation of the motion of the planets reveals systematic though small departures from the predicted movements. Calculations undertaken in accordance with the laws of motion and the theory of gravitational attraction indicate that the existence of an as yet undiscovered planet of a given orbit, mass and position, would explain the difference between observation and prediction. Telescopes are directed at the predicted position of the new planet, but nothing is seen. Does it therefore follow that Newton's laws of motion are in error? The answer, of course, is 'no'. This is because there are many other laws, empirical generalisations and initial conditions involved in the test. An error in any one of these would also lead to the non-appearance of the new planet. To name but a few possibilities, we have the laws of optics, the nature of perception, the absence of intervening opaque objects in the atmosphere or outer space and the albedo of the new planet. The data can be seen as the product of an interaction between all these and limitless other factors. To say the least, it is clear that the criterion of falsifiability offers little guidance to the scientist under these circumstances.

Does this mean, then, that Mill and Popper are entirely wrong? The answer, of course, is 'no'. Mill's theory was, as we saw, inductive. It assumed that it is possible to group objects together according to relations of similarity and association. The network theory makes exactly the same assumption. It is taken for granted in both cases that human beings have a capacity to order and sort their environment. The difference is this: Mill does not consider the fact that it is possible to order and sort the perceptual lumpiness offered to us by nature in many different ways. In order to cut down these possibilities we need the coherence conditions that are offered to us by culture. It is such social coherence conditions that allow us to attend to certain similarities only and which permit classification and association to take place.[11]

Talk of coherence conditions drives us, inevitably, in the direction of theory. Think once again of Martian taxonomy. The distinction between mammal and fish was something that varied over time. It was also put at risk whenever an anomalous creature appeared. Was a whale a mammal or a fish? The empirical classification was dependent on theory. That is, it was dependent on decisions about what constituted a sufficient similarity to allow a creature to be included in the class of mammals.[12] Legs and terrestrial habitat were held to be inappropriate. Blood-temperature and the bearing of live young were held to be sufficient, despite the fishy disanalogies also exhibited by the whale. But here, although there are differences, we can see how Popper's theory of science, despite its prescriptive interest, relates to the network theory. Popper, it will be remembered, says that it is vital for the scientist to make bold theoretical conjectures that may be tested against the data. We have seen that there are problems with a naive conception of 'data'. Leaving these on one side, however, Popper is right in at least one important respect. He is right to stress that science involves a process of checking theory against data. Seen from the standpoint of network theory, we need to say that it involves comparing one part of the network with another. It involves checking a relatively theoretical section of the network with a different, relatively factual part. Note the term 'relatively' here. We have already seen that there can be no absolute distinction between theory and data, for data is con-structed via the operation of (more or less) theoretical coherence conditions.[13]

The strength of Popper's view of science lies, then, in its stress, albeit partially misunderstood, on an active role for theory. Explicit scientific theory constitutes a part of the coherence conditions of a network, selecting between the various possible perceptual similarities. Perhaps we could put it like this: science does not proceed by induction alone; it proceeds by a judicious mixture of induction and theoretical guidance. Mill and Popper have got hold of opposite ends of the same stick.[14]

DICTIONARY THEORIES OF SCIENCE

To conclude this chapter we want to return to a point we made earlier. It will be recalled that in Chapter 3 we argued that all terms are inevitably tied, whether directly or indirectly, to the recognition of empirical similarity. No class or vocabulary can, as it were, freewheel in mid-air. We noted, in support of this point, that it is impossible to learn French from a French–French

People and their Knowledge

dictionary. The above discussion about theory and its relation to data can be seen as a further exemplification of this point. Even the most abstract and theoretical term has indirect empirical implications. However, many of the more formal philosophies of science, though they in general concede this point, nevertheless make a distinction in kind between theoretical and empirical predicates. Thus N. R. Campbell distinguished between a system of axioms on the one hand and the application of those axioms to physical reality on the other. For Campbell the axioms had no direct empirical referent. To be applied to the world they required translation by means of a dictionary of 'correspondence rules'. In effect, then, he was proposing a three-level model of science. An example of this approach is given in Figure 8.2. For Campbell a theory comprised both formal terms and axioms on the one hand and the dictionary on the other. The axiom system was, so to speak, independent of the dictionary and empirical observations. The virtue of such a procedure is that it allows for the easy introduction of methods of formal analysis: it is possible to show quite easily for the axiom system presented below that it is internally consistent. The disadvantage of such a procedure is, however, equally clear. It may be a good way of testing the internal consistency of well-structured and relatively stable scientific theories, but it doesn't help much in an analysis of the complex processes that lead to conceptual change. For this reason, such 'two-language' theories[15] are not particularly useful in most *descriptive* (as opposed to *prescriptive*) contexts. This observation can be sharpened up if we remember that the network theory draws no distinction in principle between the status of different classes and associations. What is a discovery at one time

(1) *Terms and axioms*	(2) *Dictionary*	(3) *Empirical observations*
All xs are t	x = animal	Elephants and whales
All xs are either p or q	p = mammal	are both physically
No x can be both p		mobile, warm-blooded,
and q	q = fish	and air-breathing
All ps are r	r = warm-blooded	
No qs are r	s = air-breathing	Sharks and catfish
All ps are s	t = physically	are both physically
No qs are s	mobile	mobile, cold-blooded, and water-breathing.

FIGURE 8.2 *An example of Campbell's 'dictionary theory' of science*

(consider 'Mammals bear their young live') may become a definition or tautology at a subsequent time. The network theory is a 'one-language' theory where the associations between classes are widely variable in quality, both at any given moment and over time. Its virtue, by comparison with formal two-language conceptions of science is that it offers us a way of thinking about how knowledge is put together and undergoes change.

In this chapter we have explored some aspects of the relationship between network theory and the philosophy of science:

48 Our account of the generation of knowledge, unlike that of most philosophies of science, is descriptive in intent.

49 Nevertheless certain implications of the network model suggest that some features of prescriptive philosophies of science are unrealistic.

50 Thus, the network theory suggests that all data are sensitive not only to perceptual 'lumpiness' but also to the operation of coherence conditions.

51 This is incompatible with those philosophies of science – for instance, Mills' inductivism and some versions of Popper's falsificationism – which rest upon the contrary assumption that data can be constructed in the absence of coherence conditions.

52 In practice a test of theory against data must be seen as a test of one kind of coherence condition (theory) against another (theoretically-selected perceptual lumpiness).

53 The network model also suggests that it is impossible to abandon all knowledge simultaneously, though radical but piecemeal reconstruction of the whole is quite possible. This is incompatible with Popper's insistence that falsified theory be rejected outright.

54 Despite its failure to consider coherence conditions, Mill's theory of induction is correct in one important respect – its stress on the importance of the detection of similarity and association.

55 Likewise, Popper's theory which stresses the role of theoretical activity (as opposed to induction) is also correct in this respect.

56 Finally, network theory suggests that two-language conceptions of science which draw a basic distinction between terms and axioms, dictionaries and empirical observations, overstress such distinctions. In practice, though distinctions such as these do exist, those who are primarily concerned with the description of conceptual change are better advised to treat them as practical differences which may change over the course of time.

Part II

The Acquisition of Knowledge

In Part II we move from the formal analysis of network properties to a study of the acquisition of networks and to the problem of socialisation. Our argument, in consistency with what was outlined in Part I, is that many of the coherence conditions that structure our networks are generated socially and are transmitted to us via authoritative cues. For purposes of convenience we distinguish between three distinct aspects of knowledge: knowledge as perception, knowledge as manipulation and knowledge as theory or metaphor. These are not, however, principled distinctions. The three faces of knowledge overlap and intersect one another: networks are holistic phenomena. An important point, one on which we have already touched in Chapter 7 is that knowledge is *practical*. An occupational hazard of those who study knowledge is that they allow it to become detached from practice and achieve an independent life of its own. In order to counteract the danger of such reification we start with types of knowledge that are so practical that we do not, for the most part, even talk about them. We consider here the way in which perceptual and manual skills are acquired. Only then do we come to relatively explicit theory, to 'talked-about' knowledge.

9 The Acquisition of Social Coherence Conditions: Perception

In previous chapters we have often referred to the role of social coherence conditions. These, we have suggested, are absolutely essential in determining the choice of similarity relations, given that the environment provides a more or less unlimited range of possibilities. Social coherence conditions were mentioned in other contexts, for instance, in the case of the indirect acquisition of classes and links. We noted that it is not necessary for the perceptual lumps that are associated in a network to be learned from direct physical experience. Most British adults know that vipers have a dangerous bite, though few have observed anyone, let alone themselves, being bitten. So the acquisition of social coherence conditions is clearly indispensable if the network theory is realistic. How, then, are social coherence conditions acquired?

A proper answer to this question clearly requires a full-blooded theory of socialisation, something which we are not yet, as a discipline, in a position to provide. Knowing, however, that it involves, in essence, the acceptance of guidance about which similarities to notice and which to ignore, we can at least sketch the outline of an answer. First, and most important, we can be sure that no network can be transmitted in the abstract. Just as it is impossible to learn French from a French–French dictionary, so the central and most crucial part of socialisation involves, not the learning of names, but the grouping of objects into classes, the discrimination *between* classes and the determination of the proper relationships that exist between classes.

LEARNING TO 'SEE'

By far the largest – and in many respects the most important – part of this process is perceptual. The capacity to *see* rightly lies at the bottom of successful learning. One of us remembers, with painful clarity, an elementary biology lesson. Microscopes had been set up and their proper use had been demonstrated. Leaves of a water-weed had been distributed and placed in the proper position for observation under the microscope. Lights had been properly directed and the microscopes had been focused. Then we looked through the lenses and tried to see the cells and the circulating chlorophyll which, we were assured, should be there for observation. We fiddled with the focusing, worrying that if we extended the object-lens too far the slide might get broken. (We were assured that dire consequences would shortly follow in any such eventuality). We were a little concerned that we seemed unable to see anything. Our worry was compounded by the fact that other members of the class could be heard expressing interest and pleasure at what could be seen down their microscopes. We tried refocusing again, and some vague, bubble-like images appeared momentarily, only to vanish again with a slight movement of the eye. Further attempts at focusing produced more bubbles and then an indescribably confusing complex of lines and blobs. At this point the teacher appeared. Had we seen the chlorophyll in the cells?

'No', came our answer back.
'You mean that you can't see the green blobs moving around?'
'No sir.'

The teacher pressed his eye to the microscope, briefly touched the focusing, and retreated to the front of the room with an irritated expression on his face. At the next moment he was announcing to the class that he simply could not understand why some of us were unable to see what was staring us in the face. And, more helpfully, he was drawing up on the blackboard a representation of what we *should* be seeing (see Figure 9.1). At this point, recognition was instantaneous. We were able to match what was erratically visible down the microscope with what had been drawn on the blackboard.

There are five main lessons that we wish to draw from this example. The first is to indicate that it is a perfect paradigm case

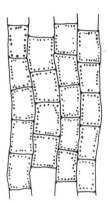

FIGURE 9.1 *Representation of plant cells*

for the acquisition of social coherence conditions in this respect: there is an authority, in this case a person rather than a textbook, which provides an unchallengeable definition of the right way of looking at things. Why is it unchallengeable? Though this answer begs more questions than it answers, for the moment we will simply note that it was rather clearly *not* in the interests of a schoolboy to disagree with the biology teacher about anything very much and in particular about the nature of the microscopic world. If the teacher said that plant-cells have a certain sort of aspect and if there was anything in the perceptual environment that a schoolboy could see that was interpretable in that way, then the boy did so rather quickly.

The second point is that, as we have already suggested in other chapters, 'seeing' is not something that human beings can do automatically from scratch and without any guidance. There is substantial evidence that this is, indeed, the case. Certain specialist groups are exceedingly good at noticing and connecting together visual and other stimuli which are unnoticed by average westerners. Wine-tasters, whisky-blenders and the Arthur D. Little 'taste panel' in Cambridge, Massachusetts, are all practised at esoteric activities which demand advanced and apparently acquired sensory discrimination. Art experts are able, at a glance, to distinguish genuine Vermeers from the often very skilful fakes produced by Van Meergeren.[1] Radiologists can 'read' chest X-rays in short order. And, to turn to a tactile medium, midwives are able to determine the 'lie' of the unborn child in the womb by prodding the belly of the expectant mother. If they are to be believed, the acquisition of this skill is almost like learning to see plant-cells down a microscope, for, after relatively little success for a period, the 'touch' comes all at once.

A third and extremely important point is that once perceptual similarities and differences have been properly established, it is almost impossible to undermine them. Our perception of the everyday world achieves a solidity and stability that is altogether massive. Even in less everyday situations such as the biology class, it is now entirely impossible for us to look down an appropriate microscope and avoid seeing the cells. Perhaps more interestingly, it is almost impossible to remember why it was we could not see them until we were given appropriate social cues. In retrospect, all that we can say, rather lamely, is that we had no idea of the size of what we should be seeing.[2] Claims, then, that 'seeing' has to be learned should emphatically not be read as claims that perceptual classification, once acquired, may be willed away, even under the auspices of some new authority. Perception, once acquired, becomes largely automatic and extremely obstinate in its persistence.

The fourth lesson that may be drawn from our example – and we have already briefly mentioned it – is that cues from authority are only likely to be entertained and permanently accepted if they are workable. In this context, it is quite clear what counts as workability: the perceptual lumpiness must licence what authority tells about the proper way of seeing. Random or arbitrary commands will not influence perception, because there will be no appropriate raw material upon which to build stable perception. Consider the pattern of shapes shown in Figure 9.2. What is it? What should you see? If we tell you that it is a woman wearing a fancy hat, then you *may* succeed in seeing it that way, but it is improbable that you will maintain this as a stable perception. If we tell you, on the contrary, that it is upside-down so you should turn the page round, and then that there is a rider and horse, you will most likely have no difficulty whatsoever in seeing that rider and horse – and seeing it again the next time you look at the diagram. Authority, then, cannot act in or on a vacuum. It needs perceptual lumpiness upon which to get to work. Those social psychological experiments[3] which reveal that the majority of subjects resists group pressure to 'see' lines as longer than they really are, though not directly applicable to our present discussion

FIGURE 9.2   *Enigmatic shapes*

which is about *learning* to see, again tend to underline the conclusion that local authority cannot impose a way of seeing that is not sanctioned by a wider social group.

SEEING BY DOING

Another point that arises out of the biology-class example is something which leads us to our second major topic: the role of the practical and concrete. First, let us remind ourselves that in order to learn to see plant cells it was necessary to try looking down the microscope for oneself. No amount of reading about it in books or seeing it in pictures, would do. True, these (and the guidance of the teacher) might offer invaluable clues. But in the end the neophyte botanist had to look down the microscope, fiddle with the focusing and make the connection for himself. We want to argue that *all* learning is similarly practical, though for the case of abstract classes that are learned indirectly, we shall need to adopt a rather counter-intuitive conception of what we mean by practical. Postponing the case of such abstract knowledge, we now consider those cases that incur physical involvement.

Consider the following example, again drawn from real life. It is summer. We are on a hill in Vermont and are climbing steeply up the edge of the forest. There are birds in the trees, but what kind of birds? One of us is a European. He has a reasonable knowledge of the common birds of Europe. The other is a native New Englander, but city-born. He knows a pigeon and a house-sparrow apart, but knows little of the woodland birds. A particular bird appears. It moves quickly in and out of the foliage, stops for a moment on the trunk of a tree and then vanishes from view. What species is it? The European instantly recognises the family. The bird must be a nuthatch, from the family *sittidae*. How does he know this? The answer, of course, is that there are similar-looking birds in the Old World. He has come across them in the woods of England. Though he does not know exactly what species the bird that they have just seen is – it had, for instance, a white breast, whereas the one to which he is used is chestnut coloured – he detects, on the basis of his familiarity with the latter, a *family resemblance*. He advises the New Englander to look up 'nut-hatches', and they discover that it is a white-breasted nuthatch, *sitta carolinensis*.

FIGURE 9.3   *Nuthatch*

Of the *sittidae*, Roger Tory Peterson's *Field Guide to the Birds* writes:

> Small, chubby tree-climbers; smaller than a Sparrow, with a long bill and a stubby tail that is never braced against the tree woodpeckerlike as an aid to climbing. No other tree climbers attempt to go down tree-trunks headfirst, as these little birds habitually do.[4]

Of *sitta carolinesis*, he writes:

> Nuthatches are the 'upside-down birds'. The White-breasted
> Nuthatch is known by its black cap and its beady black eye on a
> white cheek. Similar species: Red-Breasted Nuthatch has
> eyestripe. Chickadees have black bibs.[5]

He also provides a picture.

Peterson's description is characteristically skilful. For complete
beginners he defines size in relation to a bird they would almost
certainly recognise – the sparrow. He points out distinguishing
features and distinguishes it from other tree-climbing birds,
including other nuthatches. What he says can be summarised in
two informal networks (Figure 9.4).

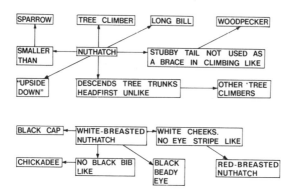

FIGURE 9.4   *Attributes of nuthatches after Roger Tory Peterson*

For anyone who knows how to recognise a nuthatch already,
this is an excellent description. But, leaving aside the reference to
sparrows, how useful would it be for a beginner, someone who
had never seen woodpeckers, or chickadees? Some of the
referents should be known to most aspirant bird-watchers: for
instance, the conception of tree-climbing. But how about 'long
bill'? What is the distinction between a long and a short bill? And
how 'stubby' does a tail have to be before it *really* becomes
stubby?

How, then, does one learn the distinction between nuthatch,
woodpecker, flicker, chickadee, brown creeper, and warbler?

Verbal descriptions based on known referents are obviously very helpful. So are the pictures. But in the end one has to take one's binoculars and go out into the woods to see if one can make one's classes match up with the perceptual lumpiness offered by nature. And, furthermore, it helps greatly if one can have recourse to a real live expert, someone who, like our European, can say that 'yes, it is indeed a nuthatch'. It is by actively birdwatching, by collecting real live visual impressions of nuthatches, that one moves away from the static and largely inoperable knowledge of the book to an instant capacity for recognition. For the *real* expert can tell in a single short glimpse of retreating tail feathers what bird he has seen.

A final note about the role of the bird book. This is, of course, very useful for all but the most expert and inexpert birdwatchers. The expert knows all that it has to tell him. The complete beginner has insufficient referents to make the terms usable. We remember trying to introduce a friend of ours to the delights of amateur ornithology. She looked in the front of *A Field Guide to the Birds of Britain and Europe* and read the following in the section entitled 'How to Identify Birds':

What is its size?

First acquire the habit of comparing strange birds with some familiar 'yard stick' – A House-Sparrow, a Blackbird, a Pigeon etc., so that you can say to yourself 'smaller than a Blackbird, a little larger than a Sparrow', etc.[6]

What, she wanted to know, is a blackbird? And how large is a pigeon? To extend empirical knowledge one has to start with an empirical referent, even though it may later turn out to be the case that some of this initial knowledge is unworkable. This is because it is not possible to identify relevant similarity relations if no usable models are available. However, once beyond the stage of the complete beginner, the learning process picks up. The book draws analogies, similarities and differences which are useful to the user because the new classes are being built up on the basis of old classes that are themselves usable.

To summarise the point that we have been making with our ornithological example: learning involves practical recognition – something that can only be learned by 'doing'. Theoretical knowledge of the characteristics of birds does not imply (indeed will almost certainly not lead to) an ability to recognise the species on the wing. Though the learning of names is a useful guide to the recognition of species – it permits easy written and verbal communication – naming is idle unless it engages, directly or indirectly, with perceptual lumpiness. Why do we say indirectly? This is because a name may represent a class which we have not seen. We have not, for instance, been lucky enough to see a bearded reedling. This is a small titmouse-like bird which inhabits reed-beds in the Old World. Peterson, Mountfort and Hollom offer a description of the type with a picture. They connect it in terms of similarities and differences with such other species as the titmice, reed-buntings, reed-warblers and so on, these being birds which we are able to recognise in nature. We anticipate, and we are probably right, that we *would* be able to recognise it if it were to fly into our field of vision. So, though it is a term without direct referent, it is sufficiently closely connected with perceptual lumpiness to be readily usable. In saying this we are, of course, doing no more than developing one of the themes that was introduced in Chapter 2 where we wrote that even indirect learning has to be tied down to the empirical via chains of classificatory associations.

If knowledge involves practical recognition, then it can be no surprise to discover that scientific knowledge is of the same order. Thomas Kuhn in his *Structure of Scientific Revolutions*[7] makes exactly the same point, arguing as we have throughout our exposition of the network theory, that knowledge has to be connected with the real world. He talks of 'acquired similarity relations'[8] and describes the way in which scientists learn to see similarities between different events by means of authoritatively chosen examples. We will discuss scientific socialisation in more detail in a later section, but it will be worthwhile to take a quotation from Kuhn in order to illustrate the point that we have made in a scientific context:

Galileo found that a ball rolling down an incline acquires just enough velocity to return it to the same vertical height on a second incline of any slope, and he learned to *see* that experimental situation as like the pendulum with a point-mass for a bob.[9]

57 Learning involves the discrimination of perceptual objects into classes.

58 Authority provides cues about conventional discriminations (though authority in turn is built upon the basis of workable perceptual cues).

59 Perceptual grouping ('seeing') is not something that is given in the perceptual lumpiness of the world alone.

60 Once a usable perceptual classification has been established it is remarkably difficult to break this down.

61 It follows that the sense of perceptual stability which we all routinely experience does not necessarily constitute evidence against the existence of a learned component in perception.

62 Cues from authority will only be entertained and permanently accepted if they are workable: perceptual lumpiness must endorse what authority tells is to be seen.

63 Since classes group perceptual phenomena, learning must forge a link between perceptual lumpiness and class. It is intensely *practical*.

64 Learning new classes depends upon extension from classes that are already practically usable.

65 Thus certain classes may be 'empty' without direct empirical referent, but still usable.

66 Finally, scientific knowledge and learning is like all other knowledge. It too is intensely practical.

10 The Acquisition of Social Coherence Conditions: Manipulation

ACTION

In Chapter 7 we suggested that the structure and stability of a network is a function of its workability. One that is subject to change is, correspondingly, one that has proven unsatisfactory in practice. There is, in other words, a strong relationship between network structure and utility and this relationship is usually tested in the course of action. Networks are not idly created. They have some practical relevance – they are used by human beings to guide their interactions with the environment – including the social environment.

But if networks are to guide action, then there must be knowledge not only of the outside world, but also of one's own actions, their relationship with external events and, most crucially, an ability to monitor and control one's own motor actions. How far the network metaphor may be profitably pressed in an analysis of motor skill is a moot point, but one that is not directly relevant for our present purposes. Here we want to suggest first, that motor skills are closely related to perceptual networks, second, that the former are, or rest upon, a particular kind of knowledge and third, that they are acquired, in a manner analogous to perceptual knowledge, by an interaction between perceptual lumpiness (partly within the body) and authority-given cues about which associations between those lumps should be attended to. We start with an example.

A few years ago one of us attended a weekly evening class on woodworking. We were told that there would be no formal instruction. Rather, we would each build an artefact under the informal guidance of the teacher. We each chose a project and wood was purchased. We then set about sawing and planing this wood to shape. As we proceeded with this task we discovered two things. First, that sawing and planing are both skilled activities. And second, that we were not particularly accomplished at either. Consider, for instance, the art of planing. Our planks of wood, though beautifully smooth, tended to be thicker in the middle than at either end. This is a very elementary mistake, something that is automatically avoided by any competent woodworker. It arises because at either end of the wood being planed, the plane is not supported for its full length. The incompetent finds that as he presses down, the unsupported end of the plane has a tendency to drop and the bowing we have described results.

In the abstract the solution to this problem is clear enough, and was easily demonstrated to us by our teacher. At the start of a plane-stroke it is necessary to press down most strongly at the front of the plane. At the end, conversely, one needs to press on the back. In this way the greatest downward pressure is exerted on that part of the plane which is supported by the wood. The error and its solution are depicted in Figure 10.1. But, though the principle was easy, the practice was a great deal more difficult. Even after a number of attempts we were not as good at it as our teacher. Our wood was slightly bowed or warped. And this, of course, is not the only skill involved in successful planing. Sharpening the cutter is an art for it is important to make sure that this is held at a particular angle to the surface of the grindstone. There is a whole set of techniques related to the diagnosis and correction of wood that winds down its length. And there are special circumstances in which the back iron has to be properly placed.

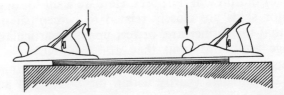

FIGURE 10.1   *The correction of an error in planing wood*

Take the case of the back iron as a second example. This is a piece of metal that backs onto the cutter of a plane. Figure 10. depicts it in its proper place, back to back as it were, with th

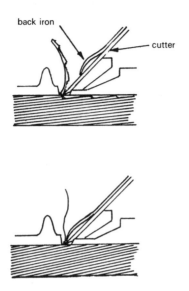

FIGURE 10.2 *Placing the back iron in a plane*

cutter. The back iron is important, under certain circumstances. For instance, if the grain of the wood is at a small angle to the direction of motion of the plane, then the cutter, which is, of course, taking a shaving off the surface, tends, as it were, to 'dig in' down the angle of the grain. Its tendency to do this is exacerbated by the fact that a sliver of wood, that which has been shaved off, rises up the cutter exerting its own upward pressure. In such circumstances the back iron is placed such that its end is very close to the end of the cutter. (See the second part of Figure 10.2.) This has the effect of breaking off the shaved sliver of wood, which thus ceases to exert its former tearing pressure.

We have now presented two examples of problems that can easily arise for the person who has little experience in operating a plane. There are, of course, many others. We have described how the expert woodworker circumvents such problems. We are now in a position to see what is involved. First, think what counts as workability here. The answer is obvious. The person planing wishes to produce a result that avoids both bowing and tearing. Now think about the role of perception in relation to workability. It is vital, of course, that the fault be perceived – and perceived as a fault. In the case of tearing this is relatively unproblematic. It is

normally obvious here, even to the most inexperienced, that
something is awry. This may not be so immediately obvious in the
case of bowing for, in the absence of knowledge of its possibility,
there is perhaps little reason to check that the surface of the plank
is not curved. Here the intervention of authority may be
important. The perceptual lumps that correspond to a curved
surface are there to be found, but their detection depends upon an
appropriate manipulation of the plank of wood in relation to the
eye. (Obviously one has to take a line of sight along the surface if
one wishes to discover whether or not the surface being planed is
satisfactorily flat.)

Having perceived that a fault has occurred, its rectification
involves the acquisition and application of certain motor skills,
some of which we have already indicated. Here instruction is also
very important. 'You press here and here' says the teacher. 'You
release the back iron by loosening the screw that holds it to the
cutter.' In telling the novice what needs to be done he makes use of
classes which he assumes to form part of the usable network of the
former. Once again, then, knowledge is important. Sometimes it
is easier for the teacher to *demonstrate* the appropriate action
rather than describe it. This makes little difference in principle
though it may be important in practice as we shall suggest later in
this chapter. The success of a demonstration depends on the
ability of the novice to detect the salient features of the action by
means of conventional perceptual classification. In other words, it
depends upon prior knowledge.

Finally the novice has to learn to correct the fault for himself by
replicating important aspects of the motor skills of the teacher.
This is something which depends upon practice – and how much
practice depends, among other things, upon the extent to which
similar acts have been successfully mastered in the past. Moving
the back iron into the appropriate position is, for instance,
relatively easy for anyone who knows how to use a screwdriver.
On the other hand, the prevention of bowing in the course of
planing is somewhat more difficult in practice, however easy it
may be to describe the theory.

Like the acquisition of a network of perceptual terms, the
acquisition of appropriate motor skills rests upon practice.
Neither perception nor action are abstract. It is not possible to
learn how to see or do with recourse to verbal categories alone.
Though the latter can be important, they have, as it were, to be
tried out. Perceptual links have to be detected. Association

between motor activity and a given outcome has to be noticed. The skills necessary for a desirable or workable outcome have to be demonstrated and then exercised. Skill, then, rests upon or is itself constituted by a form of knowledge, knowledge about how to manipulate the body in order to achieve a given goal.[1] If it involves something more than perception, then it is, at the very least, intimately related to it. Perception rests upon manipulative skill – the capacity, for instance, to set up the necessary relationship between the wood and the eyeball. Manipulative skill in turn depends upon perception: perception of what is happening to that part of the environment that is being acted upon. Arguably, skilled movement might be understood in terms of educated perception, for it depends upon more than the ability to detect, create and recreate at will certain states of perceptual lumpiness within the body. However, as we earlier suggested, nothing stands or falls with this argument, so we do not develop it here. The important point is that skill is a form of knowledge or 'know-how', it is practical, it can only be learned in practice and, as with other forms of knowledge, authority and convention play a vital role by offering cues about which objects and actions properly go with which.

THE ROLE OF THE TACIT

Now consider in a little more detail the role of talk in the transmission of skill. We suggested that the former may, on occasion, be less efficient than physical demonstration, though in fact the two are probably normally used in conjunction, with talk directing the attention of the novice to particular phenomena and demonstration offering a model for how the action is to be done. Many people, however, have a tendency to uprate the importance of talk in the transmission of knowledge and, correspondingly, to down-rate physical demonstration. Likewise, some commentators place undue stress on formal and explicit knowledge at the expense of tacit, perceptual and manipulative skill. Since such commentators – who, understandably, are often academics who have, of course, made an investment in explicit verbal dexterity – often point to the natural sciences as an example of the predominant importance of the formal and overt aspects of knowledge, we will conclude this chapter with a recent historical example taken from a branch of physics which very persuasively shows the importance of the tacit transmission of knowledge.[2]

The Transversely Excited Atmospheric Pressure CO_2 laser (henceforth the TEA laser) is a form of laser that many scientists thought would prove impossible to build. However, a Canadian team succeeded in building one that did indeed work. But how had they managed to do this? Despite the fact that descriptions of the machine were published in the scientific literature, it did not prove easy for teams at other locations to replicate the experiment and to construct a working TEA laser. In fact, and this is the point of the story, only those scientists who spent some time in the Canadian laboratory where the success had been achieved proved capable of successfully building their own version of the laser. This was not primarily because the first team had been secretive. It was because they could not say exactly what it was they had done that had led to their success. Knowledge, a network of associations and actions, was available to them – the proof lay in their ability to construct a working TEA laser – but they could not verbalise that knowledge to the extent that it was successfully transmissible as talk. The skill had to be passed across in the course of demonstration. The situation was like that of learning to plane. Showing was more efficient – in this case infinitely more efficient – than telling.

Several writers have stressed the craft nature of scientific knowledge. Michael Polanyi looks upon science as a set of skills where what he calls 'tacit knowledge' is transmitted in a process of direct modelling as from master to apprentice[3] and J. Ravetz has argued a similar line.[4] This position – which we in general endorse – has a number of implications. We will mention one. If certain kinds of knowledge require personal contact for effective transmission then it follows that such 'craft' knowledge cannot be distributed by more impersonal means. Some kind of master–apprentice relationship is important. Polanyi, in talking of science, seems to think that *all* scientific knowledge is of this form. We have our reservations about this, for we believe that some scientific knowledge is, in fact, successfully transmissible without demonstration, resting as it does upon workable categories that are already available to the recipient via generally available learning.[5] Nevertheless, the writing of Polanyi and Ravetz is important in so far as it redresses the balance between implicit and explicit. The centre of gravity of the cognitive content of science lies below the explicit and in the tacit.

67 The workability of knowledge is typically tested in the course of action.

68 If knowledge is a guide to action, it must classify not only perceptual lumpiness in the outside world, but also perceptual lumpiness in the body and determine the relationship of the former with the latter. In addition it must include the ability to monitor and control internal perceptual lumpiness (action).

69 There is thus a close relationship between perception and action. Action depends upon perception and may in turn make it possible.

70 As in the case of simple perception, the provision of authoritative cues is important in the classification and association of perceptual lumps and actions.

71 It is often easier to demonstrate action rather than to describe it.

72 In some cases it is not possible to describe a skill fully. Direct modelling may be necessary. Polanyi rightly stresses the role of direct modelling in the natural sciences with his notion of 'tacit knowledge', though it is certainly the case that some knowledge can be transmitted without such direct modelling.

73 As is the case for perception, the only way of acquiring such a skill is through practice.

11 The Acquisition of Social Coherence Conditions: Metaphor and Theory

ON SIMILARITY AND METAPHOR

Having considered knowledge at a tacit and a manual level, we now wish to explore the notion of theory within the network model. The reader will recall that network theory rests upon the assumption that human beings are endowed with the capacity to notice similarities between perceptual objects and associations despite the fact that, formally, all objects and associations of objects are unique and never repeated. A network of workable classes is built up by ignoring the visible differences between cases and by assuming that it is the similarities which should be exclusively attended to. Objects are treated as 'the same' even though, in strict terms, they are different.

Consider the case of the ships or boats which we discussed in Chapter 2. We saw there that we had no difficulty in classifying our drawings, even though when we came to examine how this was achieved it turned out to be a relatively complex operation. No simple definition of 'ship' or 'boat' seemed to distinguish between those objects which we unproblematically described in this way and those which we equally unproblematically defined as members of another class. And when we look back at the drawings it is clear that these members of the class of boats are, indeed, different in important respects. This one is a Viking boat, that a galleon, and so on.

When we say that an object is a boat, one way of describing what we are doing is to say that we are making a *hypothesis*. We are saying that in ways of which we are not necessarily entirely clear, the new object looks to us to be like past objects that we have classified as boats. We are saying that we will treat it *as if* it is the same as those past objects. We will assume that from a practical or workable point of view it may be treated as if it has the attributes of past boats. The network theory, then, leads us to the following rather important conclusion: *all knowledge is constitutively metaphorical.* It is metaphorical for the reasons we have just been suggesting. It is metaphorical because it tells us to treat objects or associations *as if* they were the same as prior objects or associations. Given all that we have said about the palpable dissimilarities that always exist between objects on the one hand and the loss of information that follows from the unavoidable act of classification on the other, it is clear that the search for complete identity, the supposition that objects can be the same in every respect is unrealistic.

Many of our classifications are perceptual and by now completely automatic. For this reason the reader may have difficulty in seeing that from the standpoint of the network theory there is less than complete identity between the objects so classified. But the network theory nevertheless leads us inexorably to this conclusion. All classifications and associations propose a similarity which is provisional. The workability of all classes and associations is hypothetical. What we are doing when we use them is to say 'let's treat the new experience *as if* it is like past experiences that we have so classified'. We are attempting a *metaphorical extension.*

This is an important point, so we are going to explore its implications by way of a scientific example. We have chosen this because it is easy to see that metaphorical transfer or extension has taken place. It is correspondingly easy to see the importance of metaphor for the explanation of novel events. The weakness of our example, to which we shall return at the end of this chapter, is that since the metaphor is relatively easily seen, the sceptical reader may be tempted to concede only that metaphor can be a useful aid to the growth of knowledge, rather than actually constituting that knowledge itself. Accordingly, our example must itself be seen as a metaphor, a metaphor for all knowledge, however literal and secure that knowledge may appear to be.

THE CASE OF JOHN DALTON

Our example concerns the rise of chemical atomism under the influence of John Dalton.[1] Dalton was born in 1766 and brought up in the English Lake District. His early scientific work was in meteorology, and as a result of this he became increasingly interested in the nature and properties of gases. Then, between about 1800 and 1807, he turned his attention to chemistry and developed a quantitative method for the analysis of chemical combination. Specifically, he proposed that atoms combined in certain definite ratios and as a result of this hypothesis he was able to propose a list of atomic weights. We will now outline Dalton's career in a little more detail to emphasise the continuity between his earlier work on gases and his later, and absolutely fundamental, work on chemical combination. The fact of this continuity will allow us to see that he used his theory of gases as a metaphor for thinking about chemical combination.

In 1793 Dalton published his first work – a book called *Meteorological Observations and Essays* – in which he catalogued and discussed many meteorological phenomena. Though he cast his net wide, including studies of barometric pressure, temperature, wind, thunder and the *aurora borealis*, it is his work on rain and water vapour that is of most importance from our point of view. To put the matter simply, his problem was to find out what happens to water when it evaporates and correspondingly, what happens for rain to appear in the atmosphere. The dominant theory at the time suggested that the relationship between water vapour and air was chemical and depended on short-range attractive and repulsive forces. For a variety of experimental reasons Dalton was not, however, content with this theory. Instead he took a different and much more 'mechanical' approach, supposing water vapour to exist separately at all times rather than combining chemically with other atmospheric particles. He thus looked upon the atmosphere as a mixture, where 'aerial fluids' of different kinds diffused among one another without interacting chemically or, indeed, exerting pressure on each other. Thus, he wrote that:

> When a particle of vapour exists between two particles of air let their equal and opposite pressures upon it be what they may, they cannot bring it nearer to another particle of vapour.

It is this idea, the notion that gas pressures are independent, which is of most importance for our present purposes. Moving forward to 1801 we find him making explicit that in a gas mixture the pressure exerted on the particles of one gas results from the action of other particles of that gas alone. The particles of other gases have no repulsive action on those of the first gas. Or, to put the matter in a nutshell, only like can (and does) repel like. Figure 11.1 is adapted from one of Dalton's works, *A New System of Chemical Philosophy*. Here the circular atoms of azote and hydrogen are pictured as being surrounded by repelling atmospheres of 'caloric'. The repulsive forces of the caloric surrounding the azote (or as we would now say, nitrogen) press against those of the neighbouring azote atoms, thus holding the individual atoms apart. However, they do not touch and thus repel the similar forces that surround the hydrogen atoms. Dalton's conception of the way in which only like can repel like is illustrated in Figure 11.2 which is also redrawn from Dalton, though this time from a paper which appeared in 1801. Here the individual gas atoms are held apart by their atmospheres of caloric – a process that is illustrated in the top four boxes which contain pure samples of each gas. The difference between this and the previous diagram is simply that the caloric has, in this case, been left out. In the lower of the diagrams the gases are mixed. It can readily be seen that they have no effect on one another. What determines the position of any given atom is its relationship with other identical atoms alone.

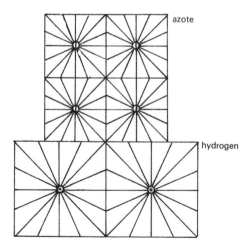

FIGURE 11.1   *Atoms of azote and hydrogen with their atmospheres of caloric*

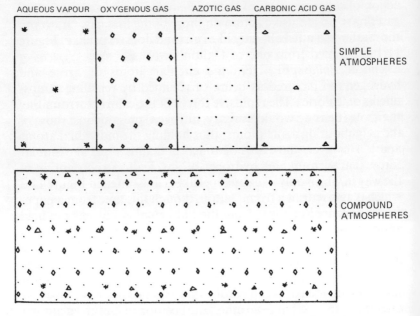

FIGURE 11.2   *Simple and compound atmospheres after Dalton*

Thus we can say that, in contrast to the chemical affinity theories, Dalton's investigation of gases was structured by a mechanical conception of pressure and repulsion. In 1802 he extended this way of thinking to the study of the solubility of gases in water. Carbonic acid gas, he wrote:

> is held in water, not by chemical affinity, but merely by the pressure of the gas . . . on the surface, forcing it into the pores of the water.

But there were problems. Though his friend, William Henry undertook experiments which showed that at a given temperature the mass of gas absorbed by a given volume of water is directly proportional to the pressure of the gas, something which fitted neatly with the mechanical conception of atomic relations that lay behind Dalton's approach,[2] an outstanding puzzle remained: why was it that water did not admit the same volume of different kinds of gas when temperature and pressure were held constant?

This question led Dalton to think about the particles that made up the gas. Perhaps they were different from each other in some important way. Perhaps, for example, they were of different weights. And perhaps some of the gases were composed of compounds of particles. If this speculation was correct, then a given pressure would push a larger mass of heavy or compound gas than of a light or simple gas into the pores of the water. But how might the relative weights or probable combinations of atoms be determined? Here, once more, Dalton's mechanical conception of like repelling like came to the rescue. He assumed that when atoms of two elements (call them *A* and *B*) come into chemical combination it is the mutual repulsion of like for like which determines the form that this combination will take. He then assumed that atoms could be pictured as small spheres of roughly the same size. Spatially, up to twelve atoms of *B* can touch the surface of *A* at the same time (see the first part of Figure 11.3). However, this ignores the mutual repulsion that exists between the atoms of *B*. Such a combination was therefore most unlikely. Since like repelled like, if it was known that chemical *A* combined with chemical *B*, then the most likely combination would be simple: one atom of *A* with one atom of *B*. In this way, atoms of *A* and *B* would be as far as possible from other identical atoms. If two compounds of *A* and *B* were known, then the most likely formula for the second compound would be two of *B* with one of *A*, or *vice versa*. In this way identical atoms would be as far from each other as possible. This reasoning could, of course, be further

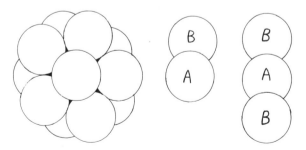

FIGURE 11.3 *Spatial arrangements of atoms. The first group shows how twelve spheres can touch the surface of another (hidden). Groups two and three illustrate the most probable stereo-chemical combinations according to Dalton's chemical atomism*

extended. Thus Dalton's line of argument led him to presume that if one compound of *A* and *B* were known, the chemical formula would probably be '*AB*'; if two were known, their formulae would probably be '*AB*' and '*AB*₂' (or '*A*₂*B*'); and so on. Furthermore his theory enabled him to predict how the atoms would be arrayed spatially.

Figure 11.4 is redrawn from a later paper by Dalton which appeared in 1835. On the top row we can see some of the individual atoms. Lower down Dalton depicts some of the spatial formulae of simple compounds of those elements.

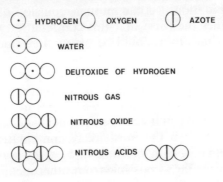

Figure 11.4   *Daltonian atoms and compounds*

As a consequence of this approach Dalton was thus able to draw up a list of possible combinations of two (or more) different types of atoms, with an indication as to which would be the most probably discovered in nature. For instance, if only one combination of hydrogen and oxygen were known, then this would probably have the formula '*HO*' (see Figure 11.4). Of course, we now believe that this is incorrect, but our views on this are not immediately relevant. The point, rather, is that Dalton had established an eminently workable way of depicting atomic combination. However, we have not yet indicated the real triumph of this approach. Such simplifying assumptions permitted Dalton to calculate a list of *relative atomic weights*. Thus, knowing that eight ounces of oxygen combined with one ounce of hydrogen, it was a simple matter to calculate their relative weights as eight to one. Giving hydrogen a notional weight of one, then an oxygen atom had a weight of eight. Furthermore, there was no reason why the principle should not be extended to calculate the relative atomic weights of a large number of elements.

Dalton's 'chemical revolution' laid the foundations of nineteenth-century chemical practice; it was quantifiable; it was practical; it suggested many fruitful lines for further exploration. His importance was not that he proposed that chemical atoms were fundamental and indivisible. It was not that he proposed them to be of different weights. It was rather that he offered a practical way of *calculating* those weights and in general an approach that could be widely used in future chemical work.

But if this was Dalton's importance, how had he been able to make such a spectacular advance? The answer, in retrospect, is simple. He had adopted a metaphor for thinking about the behaviour of gases, liquids, and solids, and he pursued the implications of that metaphor as thoroughly as possible. We can easily use the language of network theory to make this point. We can represent Dalton as saying 'let us treat matter *as if* it were the same as solid little balls which repel identical kinds of little balls'. That is to say, we can see him as asserting a similarity between mutually repulsive spheres and the complex behaviour of chemical elements of compounds. This is, of course, a metaphor. No one supposes that the atoms were *exactly* like the diagrams or models that Dalton had executed. If there were no other disanalogies, then at least there was a difference in scale.

But now consider the positive aspects of this metaphorical redescription. A metaphor brings with it, or indeed is constituted by, a whole set of possible associations or connotations. A metaphor is, itself, a network. Consider the case of the Daltonian metaphor that we have been discussing. Spheres (think of billiard balls) have weight or mass; size; certain spatially-conceivable relationships, can impart momentum to one another and have spatio-temporal continuity. When we think of spheres we tend to think of the properties of spheres that we have encountered in the past. And it is these associations that constitute the power of a metaphorical redescription. Metaphorical redescription involves the transfer from one domain to another of a whole network of classes and their associations. And this network offers a model, provides a template as it were, for thinking about the events that have been so redescribed. 'Perhaps if they are spheres then they stick together in certain ways'. 'Perhaps if they are spheres they are made of different stuff and hence have different mass'. Many of the associations will be dead ends, of course, in an exploratory metaphor. But overall they offer a *model* for thinking about problematic phenomena.

METAPHOR AND THEORY

One implication of what we have been saying is that all science is metaphorical. Additionally, however, it follows in particular that theory, any theory, is nothing other than a metaphor applied. Consider the second suggestion first.

At one level theory may be seen as a plausible story – some account that makes narrative or perhaps causal sense of a series of phenomena in a workable manner.[3] What counts as 'workable' varies, of course, from context to context. In the example of Daltonian chemical atomism that we have just discussed, workability clearly had something to do with the capacity to make predictions about relative atomic weights and, accordingly, render coherent qualitative data on chemical combinations. In other contexts a 'plausible story' does not necessarily involve such an obvious element of prediction. Thus, the Marxist theory of class does not, at least in its contemporary manifestations, make strong predictions about class warfare or the destruction of capitalist modes of production, but on the other hand it does (for those who are willing to embrace it) render a large quantity of data coherent, and offer a plausible story about the nature of events or phenomena in social structure.

In each of these cases the plausibility of the account lies in the fact that singular events – say, findings about chemical combination or the attitudes of working-class people – can be connected to a model that reinterprets them by classifying them and linking them with other classes in some kind of ordered manner. They are, in other words, plugged into a network where they can be ascribed a certain significance. Looked at in this light, then, a theory is a relatively explicit section of a network metaphorically extended to new phenomena.

The fact that this extension is indeed, metaphorical, is obvious where the two domains – that from which the theory is drawn and that of the object to be classified – have not previously been normally associated. Thus the metaphorical nature of Dalton's chemical atomism is plain to see. The metaphorical nature of description is, however, somewhat concealed in those domains where there is no other obvious way of classifying events. Thus the term 'working class' is so institutionalised (at least among some social and sociological circles) that the fact that its application to certain kinds of people is not literal but rather an extension of a metaphor may not, at first sight, be readily visible. Nevertheless, the network theory of knowledge leads us to this conclusion: namely that a description that passes as literal is simply one that has been institutionalised within a given social context. Where such institutionalisation has occurred, then the sense of novelty that people sometimes associate with metaphor is lost. All seems routine, and it is forgotten that there are, in principle, other ways of talking that would highlight other similarities and differences.

Theory, then, in this view, is the inevitably metaphorical extension of an at least partially explicit section of a network to describe, account for or explain phenomena that can be placed within the ambit of its classificatory system. It follows that everything we said of the case of Dalton's chemical atomism is generally applicable to theory: it is a model, a set of links of varying degrees of strength and quality, that provide an explanatory context for new instances; it provides a set of connotations for what would otherwise have been disconnected bits and pieces. It accordingly offers some kind of plausible story and it furthermore suggests, by means of these connotations, how, and in what directions, it might be further extended: what further bits and pieces it might connect together, what other ultimately idiosyncratic lumps in the environment might be treated *as if* they were the same in this, that or the other way. To summarise, then, perhaps the best way of expressing it is to say that theory offers a model – a way of thinking about the world – that relates instances together by means of metaphorical extension.

Turning now to the claim that all knowledge is metaphorical, we want to consider two further questions. First, there is a pervasive tendency in Western culture to assume that metaphor is 'unscientific'. It is often held that the proper place for such 'imagery' is in literature or poetry. Of course good writing often deliberately plays upon metaphor for its effect, but as we have seen, this does not mean that metaphor is unimportant for science. Rather it *constitutes* it. It therefore follows that those who attempt to distinguish between metaphor and science are making a mistake. Consider, for instance, Althusser's homilies about the necessity for Marxism to transcend the prescientific concept of 'levels' of social structure because this is a metaphor derived from another domain (for instance, the description of a multi-storied building). From Althusser's point of view it may very well be that the metaphor of levels has outlived its usefulness and ought, for this reason, to be replaced with something more workable. It is clear, however, that its inadequacy cannot arise from the fact that it is a metaphor.[4]

Second, there is the fact that a metaphor is a bridge: it is saying 'see x as being similar to y, and see them both as being similar to z', and so on. Furthermore it offers, as we have seen, a network of associations with which to think about experience. 'Mammals are warm-blooded and they bear their young live. This is warm-blooded, so we'll treat it as a mammal and assume that it bears its young live.' Now consider the case of death. This, like all other classes is given intension and extension by means of an interaction between 'raw' experience and socially transmitted cues. Pet rabbits die. Uncle Jeff dies. Death is like going to sleep. Death is followed by funerals. Death is a cause for solemnity. The class 'death' is a bridge, a bridge to other classes and a bridge between discrete events that have been directly or indirectly explained. Many middle-class young Englishmen went to war in 1914 with a noble conception of death. '*Dulce et decorum est pro patria mori.*' Most, as they watched their fellows being killed or maimed in the trenches gradually revised their view of death. It became associated with pain, squalor and loss. Its more romantic connotations were displaced. The network of knowledge about death changed. Old links were snapped and new ones forged. This was a process identical in principle, though not of course in its inhumane personal content, to any other learning behaviour – to any other metaphorical extension. We said that a metaphor bridges. In this case the metaphor of death bridged the gap between peacetime and wartime experience. For most people, in the face of daily death in the trenches, the old metaphor was inadequate. As it was altered, so this alteration had consequences for remembered pre-war experience. This was seen differently, by means of the new network. *Old* experiences of death took on *new* meanings. The pain of remembered death, the inadequacy of the patriotic sentiments, became all too clear.[5]

Our point, then, is that if metaphor is a bridge between two different areas of experience or knowledge, it does not sustain a one-way traffic only. Though all new experience rests for its structure on the metaphorical extension of class, that metaphor is in turn susceptible to alteration as a result of the new application.[6] 'Death' or 'mammal' comes to mean something different. Past instances are reclassified.

The attentive reader will have observed that in the preceding two paragraphs we have done no more than to redescribe, in a language of metaphor, something that we had already made explicit and discussed in Chapter 4. There, to quote from Propositions 18 and 19 at the end of the chapter, we argued that 'in the attempt to eradicate misfits, all terms and links in a network are at risk for alteration. This includes terms with a direct empirical referent'. We have made this point again in the context of metaphor because we want to emphasise that this revisability, what we have just described as the two-way traffic across the bridge, is absolutely no cause for concern. People sometimes worry if they notice such a two-way traffic. They feel that something less than scientific is taking place. A notorious example is the two-way traffic between the theory and practice of artificial intelligence and computing on the one hand and the theory of human cognitive capacity and performance on the other. Another is the transfer between biological and social Darwinism that took place in the latter part of the nineteenth century. A third is, perhaps, the development of common-sense notions of labelling into the deviancy theory of labelling, which has been in turn assimilated back into political arguments about whether rising crime-statistics reflect crime waves or not. We do not wish to comment on the fecundity or otherwise of the metaphors or networks of associations that are being revised in the course of these particular exchanges, but there can be no objection to such revisions in principle. Neither can there be any question of science or social science being of necessity 'polluted' by transfers between each other or to and from common sense. As we have seen, all knowledge involves transfer and revision.

ON PREDICTION AND EXPLANATORY STYLE

In Chapter 8 we touched upon the question of prediction and suggested that not all theories seem to have predictive power. Rather they seem to have the character of rationalisations. They are utilised to render explicable events that have already occurred. For a number of reasons this is especially the case for the social sciences. First, the phenomena that interest social scientists are, for the most part, particularly complicated. It has proved extremely difficult for the principle of economy to get to work in the same way as in the natural sciences. Second, social scientists tend to study phenonena that are historically specific. Thus, though it makes sense to study the causes of, say, the First World War or, to take an ever popular example, the rise of capitalism, the predictive potential of such attempts is inevitably limited.

To say this, however, is not to deny all generality to social science explanations for it would be a nonsense to imply that they are entirely idiosyncratic. Their generality lies not necessarily in their specific applications which are often retrospective and historically specific. It lies, rather, in the network of links between classes that may be mobilised in the course of any given explanatory account. Consider the case of Weber's theory about the rise of capitalism[7] which may be expressed in the following way: a necessary but not sufficient cause for the rise of modern capitalism in the West was the development of an appropriate ethos – one of regular and rational economic activity, with the aim not of consumption but of reinvestment. Historically, as happened, this arose from a transformation of the ethos of ascetic Protestantism and not (as a hypothetical Marxist might suggest) from transformations in the economic infrastructure alone.

Here the original claim about capitalism and Protestantism is very specific. Since modern capitalism has arisen only once, and there is nothing else that can be treated 'as if' it were the same, this is very much a 'one-off'. On the other hand, it rests upon a number of more general explicit or implicit claims. Trivially, for example, it depends upon the notion that reinvestment will (everything else being equal) lead to growth. In addition, however, it rests upon assumptions about the possible role of religion in economic activity and, more specifically, on the role of *ideas* in relation to material and economic practices. Much of Weber's work is, indeed, focused on these questions, in the form not only of inquiries about Protestantism in the West, but also Eastern religious ideas and economic activity. Weber's strategy then, considered in network theory terms, is to utilise widely shared assumptions, models or metaphors (for instance about the nature of capitalism and its geographical origins) to construct specific, controversial and perhaps surprising hypotheses about historically contingent events. He utilises and reapplies elements of existing networks in novel combinations.[8] His strategy is, in fact, very like that of Durkheim in *Suicide*. The claims of the latter only constitute a plausible story against a background of assumptions, presumptively shared by suicides and sociologists alike, that people commit suicide under certain (for instance, tragic) circumstances.[9]

The same explanatory procedure underlies much more individualistic historical explanations. Consider, for instance, the suggestion that the First World War was triggered off by the assassination of Archduke Ferdinand at Sarajevo. Though the explanation is, of itself, highly specific, it rests upon a network of more or less unquestioned assumptions. It is, for instance, taken for granted that assassination is a serious event, something that might cause grave displeasure to the political allies or friends of the deceased. It is also assumed that this displeasure is such that it might, under the appropriate circumstances, trigger hostilities. The specific explanation thus trades on such general associations. It is only because it does so that it stands some chance of seeming plausible. If this seems far-fetched, then it is easy to invent alternative explanations which do *not* trade on such common-sense links, and which correspondingly appear highly implausible. As an example, consider the proposition that the First World War broke out because Archduke Ferdinand ate a bacon, lettuce and tomato sandwich in Sarajevo.

So far we have argued that even apparently specific explanations depend upon the metaphorical extension of networks or parts thereof to new domains. However, it is also worth noting that different societies have different kinds of explanatory preferences. Some like to explain events with reference to the deity whereas others adopt a strictly impersonal and naturalistic mode. Some place man at the centre of the explanatory network, whilst others put him at the periphery. Some adopt theories that explain events in terms of a future ideal state towards which the cosmos is tending, while others prefer an approach which emphasises the relationship between what is to be explained and previous events. Though such explanatory modes come and go it happens to be the case that the dominant explanatory approach for natural (as opposed to social) events in the secularised West is impersonal and causal. Natural science in particular adopts this mode. Events are explained in terms of prior conditions and as the result of the operation of naturally-occurring causes. This type of explanation has not, however, been achieved without difficulty, particularly in those areas of inquiry which relate to life and human beings. Thus, though God and man have both been displaced to the periphery of explanatory schemes in physics and chemistry for over three hundred years, this transformation is only a century old in the case of the hypothesis that is so central to biology – the theory of evolution. Our immediate reaction to this is to say something to the effect that progress is slow in coming to biology – slower than it was in physics. There are, however, a number of difficulties in taking this view which can only be mentioned at this stage. The most important is that, if theory is an explicit section of a network offering a plausible story about empirical phenomena, then what is taken to be plausible is clearly in part a matter of social convention. Thus, though we may find explanation in terms of natural selection highly acceptable, the biblical account of creation may seem (and is) highly plausible for other social groups.[10] The corollary of this is that the plausibility or work-ability of a theory is a socially-contingent matter. *The evaluation of theories as more or less workable is something that can only be done from within a given social context.* Since the establishment of *our* preferred modes of explanation will always seem to us, *from our particular standpoint*, like the triumph of reason and truth over irrationality and falsehood, we have, at least for analytical purposes, to exercise caution in our use of terms like progress. While we are concerned with explaining events we will, of course, prefer our own explanations to their alternatives. This is because we stand within a social context. When we want to stand back and see how knowledge functions and is produced, however, we have to abandon such parochial judgements. The network theory *describes* knowledge, but does not in general evaluate it as better or worse.[11]

---

74 In classifying – that is to say, in asserting a similarity – we treat new objects *as if* they were the same as old objects, even though this cannot be the case.

75 Thus, all knowledge is metaphorical. It treats different objects as if they were identical.

76 Metaphorical redescription involves the transfer from one domain to another, or from past to present experience, of a network of classes and their associations. It thus provides a model for thinking about events that have been so redescribed.

77 Theory in science and social science is constitutively metaphorical, since it involves the extension of partially explicit networks of classes to new instances.

78 The fact that knowledge in general and theory in particular is metaphorical is concealed where applications have become institutionalised. Under such circumstances people sometimes mistakenly believe that they have achieved literal description.

79 Scientific reasoning, like all other, can be seen as metaphorical redescription. Metaphor is not unscientific.

80 Thus science cannot be distinguished from non-scientific knowledge by virtue of an absence of metaphor.

81 Metaphor (the application of a network) can be seen as a bridge which carries a two-way traffic. New experience alters the extension of the terms of the network and may influence their intension. This affects the application of those terms to previously described phenomena.

82 Many, but not all, theories have predictive potential.

83 In the social sciences in particular, many explanations are best seen as rationalisations.

84 Explanations vary in their degree of generality. However, specific explanations depend on generally accepted assumptions about the relationship between classes.

85 Styles of acceptable theory vary greatly between social structures.

86 In natural science, theories are normally posed in an impersonal and causal mode.

87 The plausibility of a theory depends heavily upon what passes as an acceptable mode of explanation in a given social structure.

88 It follows that the evaluation of the workability of a theory is something that can only be done from within a given social context. The network theory itself is neutral between particular empirical theories.

Part III

Interests and the Development of Scientific Knowledge

In Part III we turn from an analysis of knowledge and its acquisition to the social processes that lie behind its uses and development. Our general argument is easily stated: knowledge changes, not under its own momentum, but at the behest of the actors who use it. They develop certain habits – habitual ways of using and extending their knowledge. They also operate in terms of certain interests. Much of Part III is taken up with an analysis of the way in which such interests affect knowledge. We do not offer a definition of the notion of interest. Such a definition would be premature, for interests are a highly-complex social phenomenon and there is no adequate theory of their generation at present available. Rather, we exemplify their operation by means of a set of examples, most of which are drawn from the natural sciences.

Why the natural sciences? The most obvious reason is that the natural sciences are enormously important in industrialised society in at least two ways. First, they constitute an economic resource, a factor of production. Second, and almost more important for our purposes, they are used as a major resource in social control. They *legitimate* actions by governments, companies, by powerful groups everywhere. A phrase such as 'scientists have shown', properly used, can silence counter-argument. In the social sciences it is common to find writers who define themselves in relation to science, sometimes against, more often for. Yet there is much evidence to suggest that social scientists, natural scientists and the lay-public alike have only the vaguest idea of what science is actually like. Indeed, more often than not, their views reflect oversimple positivist stereotypes.

We suggest that it is of the greatest importance to have some idea of what the sciences are really like and how they actually operate. Our examples allow us to obtain some purchase on the typical patterns of change in science – and they show that network theory with its fluid conception of knowledge, can be translated into practice. Here we see scientists negotiating, disagreeing, hammering out solutions, and generally trying to manipulate their networks in ways that are empirically adequate, yet at the same time serve their social interests.

We have two other reasons for using material drawn from the natural sciences. First, it happens that there is much high quality work to draw upon. The study of scientific knowledge has experienced an extraordinary flowering within the last few years. And second, we thereby prepare the ground for the argument in Part IV where we tackle head-on the relationship between science and other forms of culture.

12 Interests and Knowledge

The careful reader will have noted our use of the term 'interest' at a number of places in earlier chapters and will rightly have concluded that this concept plays an important role in the network theory of knowledge. The purpose of the present chapter is to elaborate upon this notion. We may start by recalling that we talked, earlier, of the 'workability' or 'utility' of networks and argued that this is the acid test of the success thereof. If a network allows the individual to interact satisfactorily with his or her environment, then it is upheld and reinforced. If, on the other hand, the behaviour of the environment is unpredictable from the standpoint of the network (as in the case of Xaanthi and his notion of 'mammal' or the child and the parrot) then this network is undermined and susceptible to change. However, in order to judge network workability, the individual has to ask questions of it. The network is not an idle set of terms disconnected from reality. It is a tool that may be used when the individual is trying to achieve a goal or solve a problem. It is an instrument, fashioned for certain purposes. It is a resource that allows the individual to move from A to B in his or her environment. It is, as we saw, like a map that will serve certain interests and not others.

The notions of 'workability' and 'interest' are thus closely related. With the abandonment of a correspondence theory of knowledge in favour of a practical alternative, a conception of 'interest' becomes essential if the development of knowledge is to be understood. Knowledge is developed and altered because it does things for people, it helps them to achieve their goals. To understand the extent to which people are able to align their knowledge – to agree upon the facts of the matter – it is therefore necessary to understand their interests. In the abstract we may guess that where people *share* interests, then it will be relatively easy for them to achieve conceptual agreement. This is because they are asking their knowledge to do similar things. Where, however, interests are divergent, conceptions about what is true, right and proper will vary. This is because, conversely, they are requiring different things of their knowledge. This abstract answer turns out to be correct, as can be dramatically illustrated for the case of the so-called 'race-intelligence' debate.[1]

This controversy revolves in the first instance around the American finding that white people score on average fifteen points more than black people on intelligence tests. For obvious reasons this is a controversial finding and there is, correspondingly, a wide range of views as to its significance. With considerable oversimplification it is, however, possible to group many of the protagonists together into two camps – the 'hereditarians' and the 'environmentalists' – though it needs to be stressed that there is a wide range of views within each category.

We start with the hereditarians. These tend to argue that estimates for the heritability of intelligence are quite high. Thus looking at white people alone, one finds that if those environmental factors that are known to influence intelligence are partialled out this would go only a small way to reducing the spread of IQ scores. Applying this to the difference between black and white IQ scores, and again looking at the environmental factors of known importance, they come to the conclusion that the latter would account for only a small part of the difference between the two racial groups and that there would still be a gap of eleven points between average scores. Thus, though they take the view that differences in IQ scores are a function of both heritable and environmental factors, they also take the view that the former are more important and that since this is the case there is good reason to suppose that genetic differences between the populations are of considerable importance. They add, in noting this, that given the way in which black and white populations were substantially insulated from one another for many generations, there would be nothing surprising about the discovery that there are considerable, less immediately obvious, genetic differences between the two.

Turning to the environmentalists who are, if possible, an even more heterogeneous group than the hereditarians, we find that these stress the importance of environmental factors for the determination of IQ scores, and argue that appropriate changes in environment can lead to sizeable changes in these. Thus, they note that black people in the United States have experienced a long history of multiple disadvantage. For generations they were not only economically underprivileged, but they were also slaves. Even since black emancipation these disadvantages have continued in only a slightly attenuated form. Socially, economically, culturally and educationally, as a group they continue to suffer from multiple disadvantages. Environmentalists thus argue that given this background it is wholly unsurprising that black people should score more poorly than white people on intelligence tests and that, accordingly, environmental factors fully explain the observed fifteen point difference.

Although this encapsulates in simple form some of the most important differences between hereditarians and environmentalists, the debate covers a number of other points. One of these has to do with the relationship between genetic and environmental factors. Hereditarians, in playing down the relative role of environmental factors, tend to assume that estimates of heritability would be little influenced by changes in the latter. They also tend to argue that the relationship between genes and environment is merely additive – that the environment may build (or alternatively fail to build) upon a genetic endowment, but only to a limited extent. Environmentalists take a more active view of the relationship between genotype and environment. They argue that there are interactive effects in the relationship between environment and gene which mean that high estimates of heritability tell us little or nothing about the importance of 'racial' genes for intelligence. In another environment quite different intelligence-related genes might be switched on and the pattern of IQ test scores would look very different. Against this, in turn, the hereditarians often argue that although minor social engineering is possible, we have little or no choice about the kind of industrial society in which we happen to find ourselves and that, accordingly, the observed differences are valid – and indeed that the present IQ tests (which are widely criticised by environmentalists for being biased in favour of culturally-advantaged groups) are an appropriate tool for the purpose of determining educational aptitude in an industrial society.

Not surprisingly, this turns out to be a highly politicised debate. It is not only the case that many of the environmentalists have liberal or radical views while many of the hereditarians are conservative. Perhaps more importantly, each position finds itself eagerly seized upon by liberal and conservative political audiences. Thus, hereditarians have either argued, or been treated as arguing that 'equal opportunity', 'affirmative action' and 'head start' programmes, all of which are or were designed to give culturally disadvantaged children special assistance, have failed and have failed for obvious reasons. That is, they have failed because they are based upon a flawed environmentalist assumption that the manipulation of cultural, social and other environmental factors will ultimately serve to erase the differences between the average intelligence-test score of black and white. Environmentalists and their clientele have taken a different political view. Here the importance of such programmes is stressed and though in many cases their failure is acknowledged, this failure has been attributed to their inadequacy in the face of generations of systematic disadvantage or to the fact that much more radical social changes will be necessary in order to affect interaction between gene and environment in desirable ways. The political arguments have been heated and are still continuing, albeit in somewhat more muted form.

Now let us stand back from this debate, recalling that we are not concerned here to take sides, but rather to understand how social interests influence the generation of knowledge.[2] There are two clusters of knowledge which we have labelled as 'hereditarian' and 'environmentalist'. There are, then, two 'scientific' networks which classify and link the available perceptual lumpiness in very different ways. These are linked to two political positions – 'conservative' and 'liberal' stances. How is it, then, that two such different ways of looking at the same material arose? What kind of an explanation could a social scientist suggest for the form the debate has taken?

The first question is: do the 'scientific' findings lead inexorably to a political position? If one is a committed hereditarian, is one therefore bound to be a political conservative? Likewise, if one is an environmentalist, will one inevitably be a liberal? The answer to both of these questions is quite clearly '*no*'. A committed hereditarian could perfectly well take the view that since black people were genetically disadvantaged, it was all the more important to make sure that this was not reflected in their economic or social status. Given this basic premise, it would then be perfectly consistent to advocate programmes of special education and preferential hiring.[3] Conversely, an avowed political conservative could attribute the low intelligence-test scores of black people to cultural and economic factors, and yet feel no compulsion to embark upon reforming programmes in an attempt to alter these. In principle, then, and contrary to what is widely believed, *political views do not follow from a stance on the hereditability-environmental debate. Neither do political views inevitably lead to such a stance.* Formally they are entirely independent of one another.

If the 'scientific' cannot be logically reduced to the 'political' what, then, is the explanation for the former? Can the debate be explained, for instance, by referring to the professional interests of those involved? The answer to this is 'yes, but only partially'. It turns out that the hereditarians tend to be biologists or to work on organic variables, whereas the environmentalists tend to be social scientists. A possible explanation for these tendencies would be that professional interests are involved. Academics, the argument would run, invest a great deal of time in acquiring special competences. Therefore, it is natural for them to want to maximise the scope of those competences. It is in their interests to suggest that their way of looking at things is the most satisfactory, for in this way they claim a greater status and role for their discipline. Not unnaturally, then, those who have trained in biology will emphasise the role of heredity, whereas those who have trained in the social sciences will stress the importance of environment.

There is some evidence that there were professional boundary disputes of this kind. Environmentalists sometimes suggested that they would put IQ-testers out of business, hereditarians sometimes found it difficult to obtain grants and a new specialty, that of *behaviour genetics*, came into being in the sixties which trespassed on areas previously reserved for the social sciences. All these factors can be seen as contributing to a potential clash of professional interests and to academic boundary disputes. Even psychology, which was divided between hereditarianism and environmentalism, does not necessarily constitute a counter-example, for here the division coincided with the old distinction between the 'hard' and 'scientific' on the one hand and the 'soft' and 'humanistic' on the other.

An explanation in terms of professional interests does not, however, solve another problem: the question as to whether or not a commitment to 'soft' social science or 'hard' natural science ways of thinking *preceded* the decision to enter a particular academic discipline. It is Harwood's view that the 'political' and the 'social' did indeed precede the 'scientific'. He mounts part of his case by noting that hereditarianism shares an individualistic style of thought with the classical bourgeois individualism so characteristic of American conservatism, whereas environmentalism, like at least some parts of political liberalism, reflects a holistic and 'romantic' conception of social order.[4] He also notes, however, that environmentalism had for many years been linked, if only for contingent reasons, with political liberalism. In the particular political context of the late 1950s and early 1960s, environmentalism thus provided an ideal tool for those political liberals who wished to legitimate programmes such as 'War on Poverty'. When the conservative reaction came in the late 1960s, hereditarianism was in turn mobilised as a rationalisation for reducing public spending on such programmes and as an explanation for their claimed failure. Each stance thus provided a 'scientific' basis for pursuing policies that had, in broad outline at least, been decided on quite other grounds.

The conclusion is this. Scientific networks may become rhetorical resources to be used by protagonists for political or other broad social purposes. But in order for them to operate effectively in this way, they have to be workable in two respects. First, they have to account for what are generally taken to be the facts of the matter – ideally, not only after the event but also beforehand. Preferably, then, they offer the possibility of prediction and control. On the other hand, as we have just indicated, they have to be a workable social tool with which to rationalise the preferred position and lambaste the other side. There is a close relationship between these two. If a network altogether fails from the standpoint of natural prediction and control, then it will be difficult to sustain it as a satisfactory rhetorical resource in a social context. It is therefore, important from the standpoint of broad political and social interests to maintain the *practical* workability of the knowledge in which an investment has been made. So it is with race and intelligence. Fierce arguments are sustained in a scientific mode in order to protect these related political positions. In fact, the course of the debate becomes inexplicable unless it is seen for what it is: the partial reflection of a clash of social interests.[5] Under such circumstances, the alignment of networks between protagonists and agreement about the state of the natural or social worlds is clearly impossible.

Our examination of the race-intelligence example leads us, then, to the following general conclusion. The *workability* of a network is a function of the purposes for which it is used. Analytically it may be hypothesised that knowledge is constructed and deployed for two main purposes. First, it may be used to describe, account for and explain events with the aim of interacting more satisfactorily with the natural and social worlds. This we will call *an interest in natural accounting, prediction and control* (though we should make clear that we use the term 'natural' here to encompass inanimate, animate and social). Second, it may be used for social advantage: to defend, legitimate, or rationalise a general social position which is advantageous to the person deploying or the audience using the knowledge. This we will call *an interest in social control and legitimation.*[6] The former is used before the event: it is practical knowledge and has predictive power. The latter is used after the event: it justifies and normalises. It is impractical in the immediate sense that one cannot base one's actions upon it. Rather it defends one's actions, and presents them as natural.

In practice all knowledge is guided by a concern with, or at least has implications for, both these spheres. We have seen that the different positions on the race-intelligence controversy, though ostensibly about matters of description and explanation, can only be understood if they are also seen as being directed by an interest in (political) social control and legitimation. Yet we have also seen that the workability of the knowledge, from the standpoint of the latter interest depends upon its plausibility as a tool for prediction and control. This is why there are so many arguments about 'the facts' of the race-intelligence matter. From the standpoint of social control alone, the conservative would be equally able to adopt the view that blacks have no brains at all. This, however, would be completely unworkable in terms of natural accounting, prediction and control, and its plausibility would undermine its workability in the field of social control. In case the race-intelligence controversy be thought an extreme example, it should be noted that even in cases where an interest in prediction and control is predominant, implications in relation to social position, control, and legitimation are never entirely absent. Thus, as we have seen in the present case, scientists habitually become committed to their methods and theories. This is because their social status rises or falls with the success or otherwise of their attempts at prediction and control. We discuss several further examples of this in later chapters, but the case of Dalton also underlines this point. Dalton was considered, both by his contemporaries and successors, to be an absolutely outstanding chemist. On this basis he achieved a scientific status in Britain that was second to none, though he was personally a modest man. Chemical atomism, efficacious as it was in terms of natural accounting, prediction, and control, also had the ultimate effect of conferring high scientific and social status on Dalton. His operations in relation to natural accounting had their effect on his social circumstances.

The lesson to be drawn from these examples is not that individuals have a variety of *motives* for producing knowledge, though this is undoubtedly true. It is rather that a proper understanding of the growth and alteration of knowledge must depend upon an analysis of the *field of interests* in which that knowledge is functioning. In other words, it depends on an understanding of the practical and social work which that knowledge has to do. Networks, then, are resources that are used to advance interests. Where there are common interests we may expect that so long as everything else is equal, it will be relatively easy to align those networks. People will be able to agree on the facts of the matter. Where interests are divergent, this will be next to impossible. Thus, the extent to which knowledge is shared is, at least in part, a function of interests.

This has many implications. It hints at why social science knowledge is so much more fragmented than natural science knowledge. This we briefly discuss in Chapter 23. It suggests that social interests are not irretrievably inimical to natural science or keen observation as is normally held to be the case. We have already encountered this conclusion in our earlier discussions of coherence and perception. In order to drive the point home we will further illustrate it in the next chapter. Finally, it suggests that there can be no necessary relationship between any given social interest and network. Though a stable relationship may be maintained between knowledge and social position, this will be because of the operation of a relatively stable field of interests – as has existed for twenty years between hereditarianism and environmentalism in the United States. The point of this suggestion is that, contrary to the view taken by certain Marxists, there can be no *inherently* class-oriented knowledge. The adoption of such a position displays a misunderstanding about the relationship between people and their knowledge.

---

89 Knowledge is constructed under the auspices of *interests* and may be seen as a resource designed to advance those interests.

90 The growth of knowledge can only be analysed if the field of interests in terms of which it was developed is understood.

91 Where actors or groups share interests, they have a tendency to align knowledge, and agree on the 'facts of the matter', as the same questions are being posed of the knowledge. Where interests are divergent there is a tendency to controversy.

92 At the most general level, the relationship between social interests and knowledge is contingent. There is no necessary relationship between social position and belief. However, in given circumstances social interests become linked to particular belief systems as actors buy into the latter and use them to advance their interests.

93 It is useful to hypothesise that knowledge is developed under the auspices of two interests: a practical interest in natural accounting, prediction or control; and a retrospective interest in social control or legitimation.

94 Knowledge directed primarily by an interest in social control and legitimation normally achieves its aim in part by successful prediction, accounting, or control. Knowledge directed by a primary concern with prospective accounting has additional social control implications.

---

13 Interests and the Growth of Knowledge

SCIENCE AS THE DISINTERESTED SEARCH FOR TRUTH

In the last chapter we began to fill a gap in our account of the network theory of knowledge. The theory suggests that knowledge is to be seen as a tool or instrument and does not freewheel in the abstract. It is rather constructed for a purpose – it is used to achieve goals. It was in order to specify the nature of the social uses of knowledge that we introduced the notion of interest. Though we deliberately avoided a formal definition of the term, we did, however, hypothesise that all knowledge develops under the auspices of two types of interest: an interest in natural accounting, prediction and control on the one hand and an interest in social control and legitimation on the other. Further, whatever the motives of the individual, all knowledge typically has consequences in both of these dimensions. Knowledge directed primarily by an interest in natural accounting normally has social control implications. Knowledge directed by an interest in social control is typically legitimated with reference to its supposed power of natural accounting.

In this section we want to press home a corollary of our account of the dual nature of interests. We wish to counter the widespread view that science can be seen as the disinterested search for truth – that if the scientist puts on one side all his or her prejudices and concentrates on reporting phenomena as they actually occur, then the truth will be revealed.[1] The network theory – and the associated conception of interests – suggests that there is much wrong with this pervasive image.

First, of course, we have seen that the lumps that constitute our impressions of the environment may be classified and structured in many different ways. A successful attempt to blank pre

134

conceived notions out of the mind of the observer (were such a thing possible) would not leave a residue of phenomena as they actually appear. It would leave nothing, no capacity to structure or make sense of phenomena at all. To put it in philosophers' terms, there is no such thing as a neutral observation language. In order to detect and order one's environment the observer therefore imports a network, as a set of preconceptions (or if you like, prejudices) which permit him or her to structure sensations and make sense of what is being observed. We have earlier discussed the way in which socially validated (but practically workable) cues are transmitted. In Chapter 15 we will discuss the question of scientific socialisation in greater detail. The important point to retain in the present context is that the coherence conditions that allow for an economical structuring of the lumps in nature are both socially and psychologically derived.

A second problem with the notion that science is the disinterested search for truth is that it suggests that the importation of outside social interests will necessarily subvert the truth. The distinctions that we make between pure and applied science or between science and technology, hint that pure science is in some way thought to be 'better' than applied science, which is in turn thought to be 'better' than technology. Some kind of a hierarchy based on the degree of purity of the activity seems to be a pervasive cultural theme. The network theory of knowledge suggests, however, that interests guide and direct the growth of all knowledge. We have suggested that all knowledge is a function of interests in natural accounting and social legitimation. The form that the latter takes is obviously very varied, but the model nevertheless suggests that there is nothing about the operation of external social interests that is necessarily inimical to the growth of natural knowledge. Some care is required here. It is, of course, the case that under some circumstances social interests lead to the generation of knowledge that turns out to have no long-term viability in terms of its natural accounting capacity. Examples of the latter include Blondlot's N-rays[2] and Lysenko's Lamarckian genetics.[3] In general, however, the operation of social interests leads to the careful scrutiny of aspects of nature (or social behaviour) which might otherwise have remained unexamined. In other words, it leads to the development of natural knowledge.

This is one of the lessons that might, indeed, be drawn from the race-intelligence example in the previous chapter. Unfortunately, however, we are so close to the political implications of this particular controversy that it is not possible to see the wood for the trees. In order, therefore, to make the point as strongly as possible we turn to a nineteenth century example, the case of phrenology.

KNOWLEDGE AND ITS AUDIENCES

Phrenology was at one and the same time an anatomical theory and a theory of mind.[4] Though its content varied somewhat over time, there were typically three main doctrines. The first stated that the brain is the organ of the mind; the second that the brain is a group of topographically distinct organs, each of which is the seat of a distinct mental function, and the third proposed that, if everything else is equal, then the size of the organ (that is, the appropriate section of the brain) is a measure of the power of the mental faculty of which it is the seat. It followed from this that if the surfaces of the skull and brain were parallel, it would be possible to read off the mental strengths and weaknesses of any individual by means of a simple examination of the slight bumps and depressions on the surface of the head. Figure 13.1 depicts a demonstration skull.

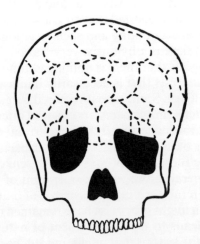

FIGURE 13.1 *Demonstration skull for phrenology*

This doctrine is nowadays unpopular, to put it mildly, and phrenology is typically depicted as a pseudoscience. It is sometimes held that, not only are its theories wrong, but also that its erroneous conclusions arose as a result of scientific prejudice and social interference in the processes of scientific observation and induction.[5] Even in the early nineteenth century in Edinburgh where it achieved some degree of popularity, it was nevertheless an object of intense controversy. Eminent philosophers and physicians engaged in public and private debate with the advocates of phrenology, and vigorous exchanges took place.

Why was the controversy so heated? One explanation rests upon the already-mentioned view that the phrenologists, unlike their opponents, were simply bad scientists. According to this view, the debate became heated because good scientists rejected phrenology whereas the phrenologists, encouraged by social and scientific prejudices, wished to avoid the socially-damaging conclusion that 'bumps on the head' had nothing whatsoever to do with mental powers. This view rests upon a version of correspondence theory and assumes, rather simply, that the doctrines of the anti-phrenologists corresponded to reality more satisfactorily than those of the phrenologists themselves. Given the doubts that surround correspondence theory, this explanation of the phrenology debates would seem to be beset by problems. An alternative explanation would refer, instead, to an array of conflicting interests within which the debate was situated. Specifically, it would trace the relatively esoteric phrenological debates back to broader political and social concerns – it would, in other words, have broadly the same structure as our analysis of the race-intelligence controversy. Let us look, then, at the context of interests in which this debate developed.

In the early nineteenth century Edinburgh was a city in a state of change. Though the most extreme effects of the industrial revolution passed it by, a merchant middle class and a restive industrial working class had nevertheless started to grow up. The new middle class participated in the cultural and political life of the city, but they were unsuccessful in their attempts to enter elite positions in such institutions as the University and the church. Though picturing society as a cosy family, the old elites nevertheless rejected the *nouveau riche* and attempted to maintain monopoly access to high status positions and knowledge. Thus, for instance, a University tradition of moral philosophy[6] was sustained in which it was stressed that knowledge of the mind was to be obtained by a highly-trained introspection. There were no short cuts into psychology, and the latter could only be properly understood after long study. Naturally this knowledge was the preserve of the University-educated elite – an elite into which, as we have already noted, the middle class found it impossible to enter.

As middle-class resentment at exclusion grew, this group established its own means of cultural and social expression. At the same time it was attracted to doctrines that tended to undermine the old intellectual and institutional pre-eminence of the elites. Thus, when phrenology came upon the scene, it was seized upon by the disgruntled middle and working classes with great vigour for at least two reasons. First, it was different from, and indeed contradicted, the elite psychology of moral philosophy. This, in and of itself, would have recommended it to the excluded middle and working classes, for it was available from non-University sources, and tended to undermine University knowledge. Second, it stressed that all that was important about psychology could be taught quickly, indeed, in a single day. The 'bumps' could easily be read by all and sundry. A long initiation into the mysteries of moral philosophy (which was taught, of course, at the University) was thus quite unnecessary.

Shapin[7] develops this line of reasoning in elegant detail. For our purposes, however, the above outline is sufficient. As in the case of the race-intelligence debates, non-scientific social interests led groups to declare an attachment to certain kinds of esoteric knowledge. The scene was thus set for a fierce controversy, one in which the root cause of the disagreement was located not within but outside the realm of the scientific. It is unsurprising, therefore, that a debate about phrenology should have flared up in Edinburgh in the first twenty-five years of the nineteenth century. The overriding interests were those of social control and legitimation: two groups were struggling to impose their view of proper social order. At the same time they sought, as we have suggested, to develop an account of natural phenomena that was realistic and workable: in other words they sought to validate their social interests by means of natural accounting. Hence the heat over phrenological matters, for much was at stake in the course of apparently esoteric debates about cerebral anatomy.

An understanding of this debate depends not so much upon an

understanding of the social origins and backgrounds of the people who produced the knowledge, although this is indeed a pointer to the broader social interests, and Shapin considers it in some detail. Rather it depends upon determining the nature of the *consumers* of the knowledge. *It is the interests of the audiences for knowledge that are most important for understanding its growth*, because in general it appears that if there is a demand for knowledge, then someone will cater for that demand.[8] The *form* that that provision will take depends upon the existing state of knowledge. It depends, in other words, upon the intellectual resources that are available at the time. Phrenology happened to be available to the middle class in early nineteenth-century Edinburgh – and was adopted as its own. Nevertheless, there are many ideas available as resources and the old notion of 'an idea whose time has come' obliquely and correctly implies that it is not so much the ideas that are important as the availability of a suitable clientele.

INTERESTS AND THE GROWTH OF EXPERT KNOWLEDGE

What was learned in the course of the Edinburgh phrenology debate? The simple answer is, a great deal. The phrenologists, for instance, undertook much detailed anatomical research. In order to illustrate this we examine a single issue – that of the size of the frontal sinuses. These are cavities that exist within the bones of the skull. Before the debate between the phrenologists and their opponents little was known about these sinuses, but during the course of the controversy they were investigated in very considerable detail. Why were they of interest to the protagonists? The answer is easy to see once it is understood that the sinuses are positioned between the surface of the brain, and that of the skull, such that they tend to reduce the parallelism between these two surfaces (see Figure 13.2). Since, as we have seen, the doctrines of phrenology depend upon such a parallelism, it was in the interests of its opponents to show that the frontal sinuses were large in size, whereas the phrenologists, by contrast, sought to show that they were relatively small. Accordingly, the anti-phrenologists proposed:

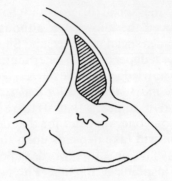

FIGURE 13.2 *A version of the frontal sinuses*

(1) that frontal sinuses were a universal phenomenon
(2) that they were a normal anatomical feature
(3) that it was not possible to determine by external indicators the actual size of the sinuses in any given individual
(4) that they obscured such a large area of the cortex that, even had the phrenologists been correct in their doctrines (which their opponents were not prepared to concede), fully a third of the organs of the mind would have been covered, and hence unreadable.

Not surprisingly, the phrenologists sought to defend themselves against these proposals and as a result of empirical study, made the following counter-claims:

(1) the skulls used by the anti-phrenologists as evidence were improperly chosen in a way that rendered them unsatisfactory data
(2) in properly chosen skulls, by contrast, the departure from brain-skull parallelism was only small
(3) frontal sinuses did not exist in small children and were very small until puberty
(4) they only became large in the elderly and diseased.

This argument persisted for a considerable period of time, and though it resulted in challenge, counter-challenge, and accusations of bad faith and fraud, was never resolved. Interestingly, from our point of view, however, it is in fact rather difficult for the contemporary investigator to award marks to either side in the debate. *This is because the protagonists knew more about the frontal sinuses than do most modern medical scientists. Gray's Anatomy*, which is the standard anatomical handbook, describes the frontal sinuses in less detail than did the principals in the debate we have just outlined which took place in Edinburgh, Scotland, in the 1820s. Insofar as it is able to adjudicate on the matter, however, *Gray's Anatomy* tends in fact to support the views of the phrenologists.

From the standpoint of the correspondence-theory version of the debate outlined earlier, this finding is puzzling. How could a practice as pseudoscientific as that of phrenology generate true knowledge, and indeed knowledge that is more detailed than that available to modern medical science? To resolve this difficulty it is necessary to say that *parts* of phrenology were scientific whereas other parts were pseudoscientific, a complex resolution, and one that fails to explain why or how such true knowledge was generated under these circumstances. The network/interest explanation for the detailed knowledge created in the course of the debate is much simpler and more straightforward. This suggests that the development of detailed and esoteric knowledge of a set of lumps in nature is likely to take place if there are pressing social interests for this development. The phrenologists and their opponents were locked in a social debate where each group sought to defend itself and to undermine the other. The potential importance of the size of the frontal sinuses has already been described. Hence it is not surprising that their size and structure should have been the object of such minute inquiry. In this view, then, interests do *not* necessarily interfere with observation. Their operation does *not* necessarily subvert the generation of practically adequate knowledge. Science is *not* best understood as a disinterested inquiry by truth-seeking intellects. Rather, interests may lead to a focus on esoteric matters that were previously of little or no interest. They may lead to the generation of new and satisfactory empirical knowledge.

---

95 The network/interest theory of knowledge suggests that science is not pure in the sense that it involves a disinterested search for truth. The search for knowledge is inevitably directed by interests.

96 Often the interests are those of important audiences. Thus experts seek clienteles for their expertise and knowledge may be constructed by experts with the interests of those clients in mind.

97 The operation of external social influences is not necessarily inimical to the production of workable empirical knowledge.

98 Social interests may lead scientists to a detailed and entirely workable study of matters that had not previously attracted attention.

14 Negotiation, Persuasion and the Power of Knowledge

PEOPLE AND THEIR KNOWLEDGE

In Chapter 12 we argued that the extent to which actors are able to agree about the facts of the matter – that is, the extent to which they are able to align their networks – depends on the extent to which their interests are aligned. In the last two chapters we have presented examples where there was a complete failure to reach agreement. In each case we explained that failure by looking at the divergent interests of the audiences at which the knowledge was aimed. We found that these came to the debates with very different social prejudices, and sought to use the knowledge in question in very different ways. Hence the accusations of bias, cheating and improper practice; hence the attempts to undermine the legitimating natural accounts offered by the opposition and hence the attempts to sustain the account of nature being used to support the actor's preferred social position.

At the same time, however, we stressed that knowledge generated under these circumstances is not necessarily bad knowledge. It may be perfectly workable for a variety of purposes. We sought, therefore, to undermine the pervasive idea that good knowledge comes only from a disinterested search for the truth. Indeed, we indicated that from the standpoint of the network/interest model it is difficult to imagine what the disinterested search for the truth would look like.

In this chapter we consider a further set of implications of the network/interest theory of knowledge – the nature of the relationship between people and their knowledge, and in particular the relationship between people in dispute and their contradictory points of view. Our argument is as follows: since networks are built up under the auspices of a variety of interests, we may expect 'the same' phenomena to be susceptible to interpretation in a variety of different ways. We may, furthermore, expect arguments to be essentially inconclusive on purely intellectual grounds. People will not adopt a position or change their views on the basis of an argument alone, however persuasively that argument may be mounted. Or, to put it another way, arguments do not, in and of themselves, have any force. Persuasion results rather from the interaction between the presented argument and the interests and network of the person who is at the receiving end. An argument thus has force when it mobilises the interests and network of the hearer, not because it is intrinsically powerful. An argument that *appears* to be powerful is thus one that is successful in that mobilisation. An argument that appears to be weak is one which is not.

This is a simple point which can be easily extracted from the examples discussed in the preceding two chapters. Despite its simplicity, it nevertheless has implications for a number of popular explanatory modes in the social sciences. Specifically, it means that any version of idealism – a doctrine that ideas have an independent power or tendency to cause actions or events – is out of the question. Our position is, in other words, materialist. It suggests that people operate with ideas, are active in relation to ideas, and have a choice as to whether or not to accept them or act upon them.

NEGOTIATIONS OVER GRAVITY WAVES

In order to illustrate the materialist implications of the net-work/interest theory of knowledge, and the rhetorical nature of scientific argument and debate, we turn now to an example drawn from physics which concerns the existence or non-existence of detectable gravity waves.[1] Conventional wisdom in physics based upon Einstein's general theory of relativity, suggests that gravity waves exist. They would be caused by such physically extreme events as the gravitational collapse of stars. Conventional physics also suggests, however, that such gravity waves would be too faint upon reaching earth to be detectable by any means available within the foreseeable future. In the 1960s however, one American scientist stuck his neck out, and built a device designed to detect gravity waves. He did this by suspending an aluminium bar in a vacuum, and then insulating it from, or controlling for, all likely interference. What he sought to do was to subtract the fluctuations in the bar due to seismic or electromagnetic factors and to control for the effects of Brownian motion and noise in the electronics. The idea was that, if these and other interfering factors were controlled, then residual changes in the length of the bar would be due to the elusive gravity waves.

In 1969, after several years' work, this scientist claimed success. Not only did he claim that he had detected gravity waves – something which, as we have suggested, seemed unlikely from the standpoint of modern physical theory – but he also reported that he had discovered them in great amounts. Unsurprisingly, this report caused a furore. Most physicists were inclined to disregard it on the grounds that it departed from theoretical predictions. Many, however, nevertheless wished to check for the existence of gravity waves for themselves – an understandable desire given the importance of the finding, if true, for the theory of physics. As a result a rash of experiments broke out in which other groups attempted to build their own gravity-wave detectors. By 1972, three years after the original report, at least thirteen experiments had been built, and the general consensus of the physical community (though the matter at this point had not been unambiguously determined) was that gravity waves did not exist at the detectable level proposed by the original experimentalist.

Before we consider the nature of the negotiations between the various protagonists, there is one interesting point that requires further elaboration. None of the 'second wave' of experiments exactly replicated the original. Indeed, except for a few cases where funding considerations required experimentalists to build compatible equipment, every detector was different from each of the others. There are a variety of reasons for this diversity. Probably the most fundamental is that none of those who sought to replicate the gravity-wave finding were convinced that the original machine had actually detected gravity waves. Most assumed that there was something wrong with that machine – that it was picking up interference of some kind and thus giving false results. Hence they had little or no incentive to build an exact copy. Furthermore (and this is really the obverse of the same argument) if it turned out that gravity waves *did* indeed exist in detectable quantities, then this would be more convincingly shown if the corroborating experiments differed in important respects. It would be much more difficult to dismiss such corroboration as further experimental error caused by the same kind of noise. And (here enter the social interests) there would be greater glory for the person who thereby *convincingly* corroborated (or for that matter, undermined) the original claims than for the person who simply attempted an unpersuasive exact copy of the original experiment.

We have mentioned that, although the community of physicists tended, with the second wave of experiments, to the view that gravity waves did not exist at the suggested strength, this conclusion was by no means universally accepted. The original experimentalist, for one, disagreed and had conducted further experiments that strengthened his commitment to the view that detectable gravity waves did, in fact, exist. In other words, the controversy continued, albeit at a reduced level.[2]

How is this episode best understood? One way is to say that the protagonists were negotiating about the meaning of a competent experiment in the field and *simultaneously* negotiating about the character of gravity radiation. Both of these were matters to be decided, and when they *were* decided then they would be decided simultaneously. If, for example, the negotiations concluded with the premise that the original experiment was not competent, then, simultaneously, it would be concluded that detectable gravity waves did not 'really' exist. The converse is equally true: a decision that the first detector was a good one would immediately imply that detectable gravity waves did exist.

The next question that arises concerns the course of the negotiations. What considerations influenced the course that they took – a course that, as we have seen, tended to the view that detectable gravity waves did not exist? Consider the network/interest theory of knowledge. We have argued that networks are constructed by detecting similarities and differences between perceptual lumps and organising these in conformity with workable and economical coherence conditions. An implication of this view is that there is no such thing as raw data – no such thing as a neutral observation language. We can thus assert with confidence that the decision about the existence or otherwise of detectable gravity waves is a cultural matter, not something determined unambiguously by nature itself. The protagonists have to decide whether to classify certain lumps (in this case traces from the gravity wave detectors) as gravity waves or as inter-ference.[3] They have to decide which of two likely networks to construct.

Now recall that all knowledge is constructed under the auspices of two guiding interests, those of natural accounting on the one hand, and social control and legitimation on the other. So far we have considered only the natural accounting side of the equation: we have suggested that if it is concluded that gravity waves do, indeed, exist, then this has serious consequences for a major part of the contemporary theory of physics. In other words, some natural accounting potential will be lost. At the same time, however, it should be noted that scientists who have committed themselves to the general theory of relativity have, as it were, invested in it. Their own fate as scientists is bound up with the fate of the theory. If the theory is declared to be false as the result of the discovery of detectable gravity waves, they will suffer, directly or indirectly. That this is the case is especially clear for those who utilise the theory successfully in other areas of physics. We are suggesting, then, that the social control implications of the theoretical stance of the physicists are also important. In our earlier examples – those of the race–intelligence and phrenology debates – it appeared that the social control implications arose primarily as a result of the social interests of external audiences. Here, however, the social interests mobilised are internal, that is, internal to the community of physicists. Many physicists risked losing out in *both* the dimensions of natural prediction and control *and* social legitimation and manipulation. Having become committed to relativity it was thus very much in their interests to show that the original gravity-wave experiment was unsatis-factory and unreliable. They were an *internal* audience with interests that were very different from those of the original experimentalists.

Two notes of caution should be inserted here. The first is that we are not accusing the theorists of unworthy motives. They became committed to a particular way of looking at the world, a particular network, and are obviously involved in it for social reasons. On the other hand, they also have every reason to suppose that their theory is workable from the standpoint of natural accounting. It is natural that they will tend to prefer the network and practices which they know to have worked in the past. Confronted by the claim that gravity waves have been detected, it is altogether reasonable for them to view this suggestion with a considerable degree of scepticism. The second is that the social commitments of the protagonists are not in all cases identical. Some may be more heavily committed to relativity than others. Obviously the original experimentalist has invested time, money and reputation in the gravity-wave detector to a very high degree. He is thus more committed to the existence of gravity waves than to the theory of relativity, and accordingly favours the former rather than the latter if a choice is to be made. Even the theorists will not have identical social interests, so some diversity in the response to the debate may be anticipated. Again, if there had been a set of remarkable readings by the gravity wave detectors that were difficult to explain in terms consistent with standard theory, then the story might have been different. However, that did not occur, so it is not surprising that interests – including commitment to particular, theoretically workable networks – led the majority of the relevant scientists to define the original readings as 'noise' rather than as 'gravity waves'. The arguments of the original experimentalist were thus inconclusive, and they were inconclusive because they failed to engage with relevant networks and interests of other physicists in a persuasive manner.

Though it is easier to see in an unusual and controversial example such as the above, the network/interest theory suggests that *all* argument and *all* knowledge is of this kind. A persuasive argument is one that engages with the actor's workable networks and interests. A 'logical' argument is one that runs along lines that the hearer knows and to which he is committed. Conversely, a 'questionable' argument is one that fails in this engagement and has nothing in common with the perceptual, social and intellectual commitments of those to whom it is addressed. To rephrase this, it can be seen that an argument or set of ideas can only have power against a background of socially-cued coherence conditions. Thus, if someone shouts 'Fire!', the words may *appear* to have the power to lead the hearers to abandon the building rather rapidly, but this is only because we have been taught (or have learned by direct experience) that fire is something that is best avoided. The call mobilises all those prior instances of the class of 'fire' learned in childhood and later life, together with the linked classes of danger, injury, heat, flames, confusion, smoke and the rest. It operates on this culturally-acquired network which allows us to define our interests with all due speed. It is important to realise that the term itself has no intrinsic power to induce any action whatsoever.

IDEALISM, LOGIC AND NATURAL RATIONALITY

This analysis has a number of implications. The first is that idealism is something that should be carefully avoided in the social sciences. For instance Weber's classic thesis on the role of ascetic Protestant ideas which we have already discussed in Chapter 11 appears, as we there noted, to allocate intrinsic psychological force to those ideas. Weber seems to be saying that the psychologically intolerable dilemma posed by the uncertainty of not knowing whether or not one is predestined to go to heaven forced Calvinists to engage in worldly activity while at the same time obliging them to avoid consuming the fruits of their labours. If this is what he is saying (and we enter the caveat 'if' since his theory is very diversely understood) then it is unacceptably idealist in explanatory mode.[4]

One does not, however, have to turn to the sociological classics to find examples of idealism in social science. It is alive and well and in many guises – interestingly often in more or less Marxist forms. The irony of this will not escape those students of Marxism who have read that standard work by Marx and Engels, *The German Ideology*, which is precisely an extended complaint about the idealism of Hegelian philosophy.[5] Yet, despite the materialism of its founders, some contemporary Marxists enthusiastically adopt idealist formulations. Thus radical students of 'media studies' are wont to ascribe conservative bias to the media by assuming that there is only one way in which broadcast materials may be interpreted, so that they virtually *force* a particular interpretation.[6] It needs to be added, however, that the analysts with supposedly privileged insight, are able to see through this otherwise coercive material. Barthes in his work on myth flirts with a similar line of reasoning:

the concept appears to me in all its appropriate nature: it comes and seeks me out in order to oblige me to acknowledge the body of intentions which have motivated it.[7]

Like the media-studies analysts, he is able to see through myth to the reality of what is going on. Indeed, French writers on ideology, discourse and language (and those influenced by them) seem prone to adopt idealist locations some way from the intentions of such nineteenth-century materialists as Marx. There is often implicit or explicit use of the writing of Bachelard with the writer of the 'epistemological obstacle' playing a pivotal role in an analysis of the way in which discourse on language is held to constrain the development of concepts.[8]

However, if ideas have no intrinsic power or value, then a second consequence follows. Not only is their reception dependent upon socially-structured cues (or coherence conditions) but, as we saw in Chapter 13, *their social significance is subject to change over time.* There is no such thing as an idea that is *inherently* bourgeois, proletarian, and so on, though there are, of course, ideas that are used in any given context by the bourgeoisie or the proletariat. The fate of knowledge is thus dependent upon social contingency. It rises and falls, or changes its significance in parallel with the social circumstances or fate of different 'carrier' groups. The network/interest theory of knowledge thus points us in the direction of the sociology of knowledge if it is our concern to understand the fate of ideas.[9] Indeed, each of the examples of controversy and conceptual change discussed in this book can, from this standpoint, be seen as studies in the sociology of knowledge and the issue is raised again in our discussion of the notion of ideology in Chapter 20.

Third, we wish to pick up a phrase that may have concerned the reader. Earlier we talked of 'logical' arguments and suggested that a logical argument is one that runs along lines that the reader knows and to which he has become committed. The question that the reader may have posed is the following: are we really saying that logic is simply a convention, something dependent upon social context?

To answer this question it is best, once again, to consider coherence conditions – those factors that structure networks and decide, as it were, what 'naturally' goes with what. The reader will recall that we distinguished two sources of coherence conditions – the psychological and the social. The psychological factors had to do with certain perceptual and inferential capacities. Thus it was argued that people are able to detect lumps in their environment and in all cases note similarities and differences between them. It was further argued that people are able to classify and simplify by attending to a limited sub-set of those similarities and differences. Again we suggested that people may be seen as inductive learning machines: if two classes have gone together in the past then, everything else being equal, it will be assumed with a high degree of confidence that they will go together again when next encountered. We briefly described Bayes's Theorem which is a particular hypothesis about the way in which learning takes place, but also noted that current inductive theories of learning are extremely primitive and underdeveloped. Nevertheless, we nailed our colours to this particular network theory/induction mast, by assuming that people generally learn (and generate networks) in this way. Thus we assumed that such 'natural rationality' is common to everyone,[10] though obviously this can only have the status of a hypothesis.

Turning specifically to the question of logic, if this is taken to be in line with natural rationality then it follows that all people are logical. If the hypothesis is right, we have no alternative but to act in terms of such natural rationality. Typically, however, the notion of 'logic' is applied to a smaller sub-set of all arguments (or people). Sometimes, and particularly in philosophy, a logical argument is held to be one that follows from true premises in accordance with a set of deductive rules.

Logicians thus consider the structure of such arguments as 'All men are mortal', 'Aristotle is a man', 'therefore Aristotle is mortal'. The suggestion is that all rational people will accept that Aristotle is a mortal, if they hold the premises to be true. This seems to be quite plausible. Indeed, it seems to be the way that people tend to work. On the other hand, logicians like to go a step further. They like to *demonstrate* that such arguments are compelling. The problem is that it proves impossible to do this unless one first assumes their compelling nature and builds this into the argument. The general difficulty with such attempts was ably revealed by Lewis Carroll at the end of the last century. He asked what would happen if a sceptic (in his case, the tortoise) said that he would not accept the conclusion that 'Aristotle is mortal' until this step had been justified. The logician (here Achilles) in answer formulates a rule

When you have 'All men are mortal' *and* 'Aristotle is a man', then conclude 'Aristotle is mortal'. 'But', says the tortoise 'you must now justify this rule. Only when you have done so will I be compelled to accept it.'

Achilles is well able to formulate a further rule, but this in turn is without justification. A further round starts, and the process is potentially endless.[11] Logic does not compel the tortoise to the conclusion in question.

The problem here is not, as we noted above, that people do not work in this way. It may well be that they do. The problem is rather that any justification of deduction presupposes *itself* – it cannot be independently justified. There is, accordingly, no independent rational reason for accepting deduction. If deductions are accepted, it is not because this is logical, but because we work that way – because of the unjustified, matter-of-fact operation of psychological coherence conditions. An empirical investigation of these poorly-understood coherence conditions is obviously important. The normative assumption that all 'reasonable' people should accept purportedly rational deductive inferences is not.

Finally, and returning to social coherence conditions, it has to be remembered that all networks are constructed under the auspices of a given set of interests. That is, networks are tools for doing a given job. They may do that job perfectly satisfactorily and 'logically', while at the same time having a set of loose ends around their margins. These loose ends are not any cause for concern under normal circumstances. We saw that many of the classes in any given network are not linked in practice as the relationship between the terms in question has no relevance from the standpoint of the actor or group concerned. Accordingly, the actors have never had the occasion to scrutinise these potential links to determine their value or their acceptability. It is obvious that such potential links offer a source for those with different interests who wish to display inconsistency within a network. To suppose, however, that this manoeuvre constitutes a fatal attack on a network is quite wrong. If those under attack are impressed by the display of inconsistency (that is, if it seems to them to offend their psychological or social coherence conditions) then the addition of subsidiary classes, or alteration of the value of links can readily reduce the inconsistency to order.

Though we do not wish to consider the matter in detail here, it will be readily seen that the tenets of deductive logic include elements of both psychological and social coherence conditions. On the one hand they relate to the former – what we have called 'natural rationality' – though they cover only a part of this by avoiding an analysis of inferential capacities. On the other hand they go beyond the natural operations of our minds by proposing a more formal series of rules that may be applied to check the consistency of a set of network links. The really important point, however, is that such formal logic is both a defeasible tool and something that cannot offer its own, independent and normative justification.

The answer to our original question 'Is logic simply a convention?' is thus clear. If by logic one means the natural workings of the mind, then the answer is 'No'. If by logic one means that which passes as an acceptable argument in a culture, or from the standpoint of a philosophical system, then the answer is 'Yes'.[12]

---

99 Since belief is a function of prior learning and interests, it follows that arguments and ideas are powerless in and of themselves. They are only persuasive if they interact with prior belief and interest in a way that appeals to the hearer.

100 Idealism is thus an unacceptable explanatory doctrine in the social sciences. Materialism, which suggests that people operate with and manipulate ideas (rather than *vice versa*) is the preferred mode.

101 The rise and fall of knowledge is thus attributable to the fate of those who believe it and to their social context, rather than to any intrinsic power or weakness of the ideas themselves. The study of knowledge in this way is usually called the sociology of knowledge.

102 What passes as a 'logical' argument is one that is in conformity with psychological and social coherence conditions. Since the latter are variable, what passes as a logical argument is also variable.

103 Deduction cannot be logically justified. If people accept deductive arguments it is simply because they work that way.

104 An argument can always be saved from a display of logical inconsistency by means of classificatory adjustment. Logic is thus a defeasible tool.

15 Scientific Socialisation and the Alignment of Networks

In preceding chapters we have considered the way in which networks, constructed as they are under the auspices of interests, inevitably differ when their guiding interests are divergent. In this chapter we tackle the alternative mentioned at the beginning of Chapter 12, that of alignment: to what extent and under what circumstances is it possible to match networks? What are the forces that tend to produce convergence rather than divergence?

Not surprisingly our answer is, at least in part, a mirror image of the causes of divergence. In Chapter 5 we argued that the latter is caused by one or all of the following: differing experience, differing interests and differing socially-structured similarity relations—that is to say, differing cultures. All of these are a function of position in social structure and the last two are entirely dependent on this. Our position in social structure makes available licensed ways of doing and seeing, interests us in certain goals and diverts us from others. Provisionally, then, it seems likely that those who occupy similar positions will tend to operate in terms of similar networks. They have been taught similar ways of doing and seeing, have acquired similar habits and become committed to similar goals.

In order to illustrate this hypothesis we consider the case of the scientific community. Following the account of scientific socialisation offered by Kuhn, upon which we have already drawn in Chapters 9, 10 and 11, we suggest that scientific training, which is typically long and rigorous, leads to a relatively high probability of practical network alignment among specialists. They share relevant socially-structured similarity relations and, given the circumstances in which they find themselves, this in turn often leads to the generation of similar professional interests.

In the second part of this chapter we consider the limits to alignment. We argue that it does not make sense to say that networks can be aligned for other than practical purposes. This is because the only test of network alignment is its workability: are all concerned able to agree about the extension and intension of terms *in practice*? Only if practice produces problems do differences in usage become manifest. Our point is that any prior agreement about extension and intension does not, by itself, guarantee that agreement will be reached under future circumstances. In order to illustrate this we turn to a Xaanthi-like example (though this time real) drawn from the history of mathematics.

SCIENTIFIC SOCIALISATION

Scientific socialisation involves a lengthy, detailed and thorough exposure to the received scientific theories, metaphors and preferred modes of manipulation and perception. If we look again at the experience of the pupil in the biology class discussed in Chapter 9 we see many of the basic features of scientific socialisation: there is an *authority*, someone (or something) who knows the accepted ways of seeing, doing and thinking; there is a *novice*, someone who is prepared to accept those received ways without fundamental question; and the *process of learning* involves practice, it involves manipulation and physical exploration in order to link the network proffered by the teacher to perceptual lumps available in a chosen part of the environment.

Though Kuhn's model of scientific socialisation is more fully developed than this example,[1] and there are obvious substantive differences between the experience of the fourteen-year-old pupil and the undergraduate or graduate who is learning about a branch of science with the aim of becoming a professional, the example of the biology lesson nonetheless stands for much scientific learning.

First let us consider the role of the scientific teacher or textbook. We have indicated that these may be seen as sources of authority and for that reason, we treat them as identical in the present context. They both offer cues about the proper ways of seeing, doing and thinking. They are, in other words, prejudiced guides to nature. They do not offer a dispassionate display of the evidence together with rival theoretical interpretations. They do not, for instance, offer the phlogiston theory of combustion as an alternative to the oxygen theory. If the former appears at all, it is almost certainly confined to an historical preface that exemplifies the progress that science has made in casting aside prejudice in favour of the truth. Rather, a version of the truth—the oxygen theory—is presented as the correct way of making sense of the appropriate lumps in nature.

This is, of course, exactly what we would expect from the standpoint of the network theory of knowledge. The material world cannot be approached via a neutral observation language. The lumps of nature are classified in theoretically relevant ways in order to constitute data. A dispassionate approach to the phenomenon of combustion is not to be expected. Rather, commitment to one or another theory together with its associated observations is the order of the day. Theory and observation are thus presented as a package, a package which is displayed as having internal consistency guaranteed by the weight of authority. We see here, then, something that may be characterised as the transmission of a culture. A network is being transmitted lock, stock and barrel. The apprentice scientist is not being taught to put prejudice to one side. He is most certainly not being taught to question received wisdom. He is rather being turned into a scientist precisely by acquiring that wisdom or prejudice, call it what you will.

The next thing to note is that a science text typically presents a theory together with exemplary applications of that theory. Here, like the fourth form biology teacher, it suggests how the preferred theoretical network may appropriately be linked to nature. Kuhn discusses these applications in the following terms:

> Given the slightest reason for doing so, the man who reads a science text can easily take the applications to be evidence for the theory, the reasons why it ought to be believed. But science students accept these theories on the authority of teacher and text, not because of evidence. What alternatives have they, or what competence? The applications given in texts are not there as evidence, but because learning them is part of learning the paradigm at the base of current practice.[2]

Once again, Kuhn stresses the role of authority. But what

concerns us here is the role of practice, of application. As we saw in our earlier and more general discussion of the acquisition of networks, it is not possible to learn the proper use of terms if these 'freewheel in mid-air', unattached to applications or instances of use. Rather, the proper extension of a term must be learned before it can be appropriately used. As a child learned, by guided trial and error, to distinguish between trucks and cars and learned what physical lumps may be treated as 'the same' and therefore properly classified as trucks, so the apprentice scientist learns to see events as instances of the operation of physical laws or classes. In this way the child and the scientist both come to be competent language-users. Situations that were previously seen as disparate become classified as similar. Similarity relations (to use Kuhn's expression) are thus acquired.

Consider, now, in a little more detail, what Kuhn says about learning. In what follows he is describing how a competent scientist is able to rework laws or law sketches such that they are applicable to instances not previously encountered:

> A phenomenon familiar to . . . students of science . . . provides a clue. The[se] . . . regularly report that they have read through a chapter in their text, understood it perfectly, but nonetheless had difficulty solving a number of the problems at the chapter's end. Ordinarily, also, these difficulties dissolve in the same way. The student discovers, with or without the assistance of his instructor, a way to see his problem as *like* a problem he has already encountered. Having seen the resemblance, grasped the analogy between two or more distinct problems, he can inter-relate symbols and attach them to nature in the ways that have proved effective before . . . . The resultant ability to see a variety of situations as like each other, as subjects for $f = ma$ or some other symbolic generalisation, is, I think, the main thing a student acquires by doing exemplary problems, whether with a pencil and paper or in a well-designed laboratory.[3]

If Kuhn's characterisation of scientific learning is correct, then it differs little in principle from other kinds of learning. It involves authority, drill and the practical application of terms or explanatory schemes to a wide range of instances that, thereafter, are habitually treated as the same. In addition, since specialist

scientists arguably undergo a broadly similar pedagogical experience, first at school and then at university, to a fair extent they
share such specialist culture. Thus, although there are differences
between different kinds of specialists, within each area a culture is
shared for practical purposes, at least some of the time. It is this
shared culture that allows the research scientist to proceed
without argument about the 'basics', for the basics have long ago
been settled and built into the content and form of what is
transmitted in the course of scientific pedagogy. The basics, then,
form the habits of scientific perception and reasoning. According
to Kuhn it is only on rare occasions when puzzles arise which
seem to defy solution in terms of the received scientific wisdom,
that the basics are called into question and the cultural frame-
work is subjected to scrutiny.[4]

The suggestion, then, is that scientific socialisation is organised
in such a way as to generate a relatively high chance of practical
consensus – a high probability that the networks of practitioners
will be aligned for practical purposes. It may, perhaps, be the case
that such consensus is less general than suggested by Kuhn. We
have already seen some cases of controversy and there are many
more. Nevertheless, his point is fundamentally well-made. The
biographies and hence the experience and social cues of scientists
are standardised for many professional matters within each
specialist community. Those who do not fit in, who fail to learn
the received network, who fail to acquire the intellectual perceptual and practical habits and routines are dropped by the
wayside. They fail their exams and leave school or are diverted
into other walks of life. In the course of their training the students
often, in addition, acquire the habit of dividing their scientific
from their social commitments. If this division can be effectively
perpetuated into their professional lives it is then possible to put
potentially divisive extra-scientific commitments to one side in the
practical day-to-day task of working as a pure or applied scientist
(though as we have seen this is neither universal, nor necessary for
the pursuit of matter-of-fact empirical knowledge).

In addition to its rigour, the training is long, usually involving
at least six years at university level. This obviously requires the
investment of much time and effort, and often of money too. We
may say, then, that the typical present day professional scientist
has invested in his or her science. He or she has become
committed to it, or more precisely to the expertise that has been so

expensively acquired. We encountered the notion of commitment to a way of practising science in the last chapter when we talked of the way that most physicists rejected the claim that gravity waves were detectable because they had become committed to, and found useful, the basic physical theory of relativity. There we noted that this inclined them to reject deviant claims. Here we wish simply to note that insofar as they have bought into a similar scientific culture and perceive its potential utility, the interests of scientists will be aligned and they will act in common to preserve the integrity of their presumptively shared cultural resources and procedures.

Our argument, then, is that specialities in science, like certain other organisations, are structured in such a way that the likelihood of the alignment of networks is maximised. All the conditions that we indicated at the beginning of this chapter are fulfilled to a fair degree: relevant experience, relevant habits and relevant socially-structured similarity relations are all substantially shared, and these in turn tend to generate similar aims and courses of action in any given situation. Hence interests are also likely to overlap substantially. Science is thus an institution that tends, when everything else is equal, to generate practical consensus within its branches – though it is frequently the case that everything else is not equal.

THE LIMITS TO ALIGNMENT

Even, however, in those cases where there is apparently complete agreement, this is no guarantee that such consensus will be sustained under new circumstances. A point similar to this arose in the course of our discussion of Xaanthi's taxonomy, when confronted with an anomalous animal – the whale – whose proper classification depended on an active decision made by the Martian. This was because there was no guidance within the actual scheme of classification itself about how it should be applied to warm-blooded aquatic animals. In the past, warm-blooded animals had been classified as mammals and aquatic animals as fish. Now, in the face of anomaly, a decision was required, and clearly different actors might reasonably have made that decision in different ways.

Let us consider an actual historical example that illustrates this point. This concerns Euler's theorem of polyhedra.[5] If one examines a number of simple polyhedra – let us say cubes, tetrahedra and prisms – inspection reveals that the number of vertices plus the number of faces, less the number of edges, is equal to two. This may be conveniently written in the following form:

$$V + F - E = 2$$

It can be shown that this theorem is true for such cases as those mentioned just above by means of a series of common sense moves.[6] On this basis, historically, Euler's theorem of polyhedra was established, and all appeared well. However, in the course of time a number of possible anomalies arose which tended to fall into two general classes. First, there were those proofs which, while seemingly in conformity with the prescribed methods, nevertheless produced anomalous results.[7] Second, there were apparently anomalous polyhedra, those for which the formula

$$V + F - E = 2$$

did not apply. Figure 15.1 depicts two such possible anomalies ($V + F - E = 3$ for the first and 4 for the second). Leaving aside the question of anomalies in the proof procedures and results, what can be said about the anomalous polyhedra? Broadly speaking there were three kinds of responses. First, mathematicians might accept that the anomalies presented by such polyhedra were genuine and hold that it was necessary to modify the theorem. Second, they might alternatively insist that they did not constitute anomalies because they were not 'really' polyhedra. And to support this line of reasoning they might redefine what they meant by a polyhedron in a post-hoc manner. That is, they might insist that these anomalies had never *really* been polyhedra.

 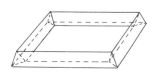

FIGURE 15.1   *Anomalous polyhedra*

It was just that this had not previously been made explicit. Finally, they might simply note that the definition of the term had not been sufficiently clear in the past, so that it was genuinely uncertain whether such forms should be counted as anomalies or not.

Historically, each of these options was adopted at one time or another by one group or another. What we want to note is that, confronted with an anomaly, both the extension and intension of the term 'polyhedron' become a subject for negotiation. The discovery of an anomaly raises the question of extension: is it or is it not to be counted as a polyhedron? At the same time, of course, the intension of the term – what the instances properly have in common – becomes questionable.

Here then, in a real-life example very like that of Xaanthi and the whale, we see the problems that inevitably arise for a system of classification when anomalies arise. The intension and extension of network terms offer no guide to action. The intension of terms may, of course, be redefined, but this is the result of an active – and ultimately conventional – decision and does not result from the simple explication of something that everybody 'really' knew all along. It is not surprising that, under these circumstances, people make different decisions about how to revise the extension and intension of classes. Nor is it surprising that controversy sometimes erupts in circumstances in which there was prior practical agreement, including what were apparently secure areas of the natural sciences.

It is worth noting again that this conception of knowledge adheres closely to materialist premises. What we are saying, in effect, is that knowledge itself offers no guide to action whatsoever. *Decisions* about how to extend knowledge have to be made on other grounds. What grounds? Well, here we cannot avoid pointing once more in the direction of interests. Where interests are shared, then it should be relatively easy to arrive at an agreement about the proper way of extending networks to handle anomaly. We illustrate such a case in the first part of Chapter 16. Where, as in many branches of the social sciences, they are not shared, diversity and controversy will more probably result.

The point of this chapter, then, is that network alignment is a function of social circumstances, including especially shared biography, shared social experience and shared position (or interests). Networks do not enforce their own uniform extension or application. Alignment can, accordingly, only be practically achieved in appropriate social circumstances. For this reason it only ever makes sense to talk of agreement or alignment for practical purposes, even in those cases where alignment appears to be complete. Thus, even in science, which is organised in such a way as to maximise the likelihood of consensus, this is a fragile achievement that is dependent upon social contingency.

---

105 Practical network alignment is most likely where experience, social cues and interests are shared by all concerned.

106 Science is an example of an institution which is designed to align relevant experience, social cues and interests, and hence to maximise the chance of network alignment.

107 Scientific socialisation is a lengthy, rigorous, authooritative and practical process. It teaches students the proper ways of seeing, interpreting and understanding natural phenomena.

108 Despite such shared socialisation, network alignment can only ever be achieved for practical purposes. This is because, in the face of anomalous empirical instances, the network itself offers no guide as to how it should be revised. This is, of course, a matter of choice. A decision has to be made.

109 Continuing network alignment thus rests upon a continuing shared view about what constitutes the best decision, and hence on continuing shared interests.

16 Normal Science and the Operation of Interests

At the end of the last chapter we were left with the conclusion that there is nothing at all robust about knowledge. It does not determine its own applications. It does not have the power to impose itself upon agents. *If* it is accepted and *if* it is extended in agreed ways, then this must be because actors have achieved a practical agreement about the utility of that knowledge in a particular extension. The example of Euler's theorem of polyhedra suggested that conflicting interests will lead rapidly to conflicting networks in the face of anomaly or novelty.

In this chapter we describe a particular piece of network extension, again drawn from the natural sciences. Our aim in this example is to make two major points. First, despite what we have described as the fragility of knowledge, it is nevertheless important to understand that practical agreement is often possible, if not only the mental maps and habits of the agents are shared for practical purposes, but also, if the field of interests within which they are operating is convergent. Our case, drawn from the history of X-ray crystallography, makes this point well. Second, this example also shows what most scientists spend most of their lives actually doing. Our examples have included some spectacular cases of disagreement and we will return to the question of major conceptual shifts in the next chapter. Such revolutionary episodes reflect, however, only one aspect of the social processes of science. It is therefore appropriate to describe an empirical case in which network extension was consensually achieved.

X-ray crystallography is a technique developed just before the First World War, which permits the determination of the three-dimensional molecular structure of substances susceptible to crystallisation.[1] A beam of X-rays is shone through the crystal that is to be studied, and a small part of that beam is diffracted in a pattern whose form is a function of the arrangement of the atoms in the crystal (see Figure 16.1). The crystallographer therefore has a kind of 'picture' of the structure in which he or she is interested. However, it is not possible to move directly from the X-ray diffraction pattern to the crystal structure, as any given diffraction pattern can in principle be produced by an indefinite number of crystal structures. Rather it is necessary to *guess* a plausible structure and then test this to see if it generates the observed diffraction pattern – or at least, one similar to it, in which case adjustments can be used to arrive at the correct structure.

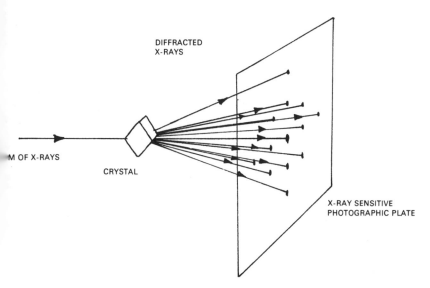

FIGURE 16.1   *X-ray diffraction by crystal*

The method of trial and error – try a structure, see if it works; if not, try again – is perfectly suitable for simple crystalline structures. For instance, the number of plausible arrangements of sodium and chlorine atoms capable of producing crystalline salt is very limited. However, in the case of more complex molecules, the permutations become very large and trial and error ceases to be a sensible way of proceeding. Certain physicists, for instance W. L. Bragg, proved to have great skill in guessing probable structures, but with extremely complex molecules – for instance globular proteins which have molecular weights of many thousands – even such spectacular skills come unstuck. How, then, might the complicated diffraction patterns be 'read'? How might such complex structures be determined? One brilliant crystallographer – J. D. Bernal – capitalised on an idea previously used in other crystallographic work. He suggested that if it were possible to compare the diffraction patterns of very similar molecules, then it would be possible to 'subtract' one pattern from the other and come up with a diffraction pattern of the *difference* between the two crystal structures. Since the resultant pattern would be relatively simple, it might be easier to interpret and a map of the differences in crystal structure would thus be built up. Such a map would be a very important clue in an attempt to determine the structure of the rest of the molecule. It would greatly limit the plausible possibilities and would permit progress by means of intelligent guesswork and successive approximation.

Bernal proposed two possible methods for creating pairs of molecules that differed only slightly. One involved making use of the fact that some proteins adopt two crystalline configurations depending on the amount of water of crystallisation present. The other involved making compounds of protein and heavy metals. In this way different but similar heavy-metal-protein compounds might be compared with each other and with the unaltered protein. It was the latter avenue that led to success, but it was only twenty-five years later, after an immense amount of skilled work, that this was achieved with the solution by J. C. Kendrew and M. F. Perutz, of the structure of the proteins haemoglobin and myoglobin, for which they were each subsequently awarded the Nobel Prize.

Even a short account of this scientific development suggests that the work done was by no means humdrum. Despite the fact that the scientists concerned knew exactly what they were trying to achieve, they did not know how they were going to achieve it in detail. The technical difficulties standing in the way of such crystallographers as Bragg, Bernal, Kendrew and Perutz were immense. The gap between each empirical instance and the network of theory was very considerable. The development of methods for bridging this gap – for extending the network – took up the efforts of a group of brilliant physicists and chemists for a whole generation.

Several things need to be said about such work. The first is that it is similar in many ways to the training undergone by scientists. In that training, which we described in the last chapter, scientists are taught to link empirical instances to general and explicitly theoretical explanatory schemes. Let us rephrase this in terms of the network theory of knowledge. What they are doing is simultaneously manipulating the relatively theoretical and relatively empirical parts of the appropriate network. The theory is, of course, extended by means of the various mathematical tools that are the stock-in-trade of the physicist. It is extended and altered until it takes a form that is more easily applicable to the recalcitrant empirical instances. At the same time, however, the relatively empirical parts of the network are also subject to manipulation. Nature is, as it were, 'put through the hoop' until data that can be reasonably connected with the appropriate parts of theory have been constructed. Though this network theory re-description of scientific work may seem somewhat abstract, in fact it precisely describes the work undertaken by the Braggs, Bernal and the rest. Much of their work involved the manipulation of nature to produce readable diffraction patterns. This, for instance, involved much chemical experimentation in order to generate the necessary protein-heavy atom compounds. At the same time, however, mathematical tools – for instance, the notion of 'reciprocal space' and 'Fourier transforms' – were attached to the original diffraction equations in a manner that rendered these somewhat more applicable to complex diffraction data.

Our first point, then, is that this kind of scientific work, which in many ways mirrors scientific training, is highly innovative, indeed creative, but in no way involves breaking any rules. It might, perhaps, be best described as 'creative conformity'. It is this sort of science that Kuhn has in mind when he writes of 'normal science' or the process of 'articulation':

> Few people who are not actually practitioners of a mature science realize . . . how fascinating such work can prove in the execution. And (this point) need(s) to be understood. Mopping-up operations are what engage most scientists throughout their careers. They constitute what I am here calling normal science. Closely examined . . . that enterprise seems an attempt to force nature into the preformed and relatively inflexible box that the paradigm supplies.[2]

Our second point concerns the question of network alignment:

how do X-ray crystallographers and, for that matter, other practitioners of normal science, manage to come to a practical agreement about the proper extension and intension of terms under novel circumstances? We have seen that the idealist notion that the terms somehow impose their own application is unacceptable. The materialist alternative is the only answer. Normal science solutions, which depend upon the workable and practical agreement of all concerned, are only possible because the relevant actors have, through experiencing similar socialisation, acquired similar habits of thought and ways of seeing and in addition, are also subject to a similar field of interests.

This point can be made more forcefully if we briefly look again at X-ray crystallography. There were, of course, occasional disagreements in the area, but these never involved the crystallographers in internal debate as to whether or not the technique had been properly extended or applied. Thus, when Perutz and Kendrew finally published their structure determinations of haemoglobin and myoglobin, these solutions were greeted with acclaim. There was no controversy about whether or not they had properly extended the method. Their use thereof was immediately seen as altogether workable. Why was there such general acclaim? The only answer available to us, as we have already suggested, is that these crystallographers operated in terms of both a common culture and a common field of interests. Empirically, in this case, we have to note that it is actually rather difficult to practise crystallography. The crystallographers had undergone a rigorous and lengthy training. They had, for practical purposes, developed common standards and habits for judging problems and solutions and deciding what was to count as a workable solution. In addition to a set of presumptively shared mental habits, they also operated within a substantially shared field of interests. This common conception of interest arose from the fact that they had all unreservedly 'invested in' crystallography and sought to use it to determine as many and as complex structures as might prove possible.

Their efforts were channelled, in particular, by an informal agreement about what constituted the most interesting and important problems remaining to be solved. Such an agreement (often found in specialist areas of science) of course contributes to and helps to structure the field of interests. It defines how the goal of natural prediction and control may be best articulated, while at the same time having implications for social control. The person who solves an 'interesting' problem will receive recognition and social rewards of one kind or another – in this case the Nobel Prize! Thus, the publication of a solution for the structure of myoglobin (a very 'interesting' case) would, so long as it conformed to the standards of technical acceptability, immediately achieve considerable acclaim. The successful scientist would not only have advanced the field of X-ray crystallography but at the same time his or her own standing in that field. And this, of course, is what actually happened. There was no difficulty about the practical alignment of networks under such circumstances. A success for Perutz and Kendrew instantly became a success not only for them, but for the entire field. The method was correspondingly revealed in its increased power, and all crystallographers benefited in some measure from this reflected glory.

We wish to conclude with a note of caution. Though our crystallographic example reveals that a practical alignment of networks can be achieved over a long period of time under the appropriate circumstances, there is no necessity that such a state of affairs will continue. The next crystallographic result to be produced might be seen as an anomaly by other crystallographers; there might be questions about its workability. The interests of practitioners might have ceased to be substantially uniform, their networks might have altered in relevant ways, perhaps as a result of changes elsewhere in science. In other words, one is never warranted in assuming that an area of normal science will continue in that mode just because it has so existed up until the present time. Indeed, we return to the consideration of disruptive anomaly in the next chapter.

---

110 Practical alignment of networks occurs in certain areas of science – those areas that Kuhn calls 'normal science' – which fulfil the conditions described in proposition 105.

111 Normal science activity is in many ways similar to scientific socialisation. It involves a consensual attempt to bridge the gap between relatively theoretical and empirical parts of the appropriate network by manipulating both theory and data to achieve a workable match.

112 The fact of a past tradition of normal science does not guarantee that this will continue. Each new result may, in principle, be judged anomalous and lead to crisis or fragmentation.

17 Anomalies and Scientific Revolutions

We concluded the last chapter with a caution: the fact that networks have been previously aligned in workable solutions is no guarantee at all that this happy state of affairs will necessarily continue into the indefinite future. A new instance which challenges the existing wisdom and fragments the community of scientists may, in principle, arise at any time. In this chapter, in pulling together some of the themes that have been touched upon earlier, we consider the various possibilities open to any group in the face of anomaly. Again we approach this topic by means of examples drawn from the natural sciences, but most of what we have to say is perfectly general.

MISFITS AND ANOMALIES

Our starting-point is the proposition: the experience of anomaly is widespread. That this is the case can be seen if we remember that any given network inevitably handles only a small part of the available information. Similarities and differences might have been constructed in quite different ways. There is much in nature that is beyond the inevitably limited grasp of any given network. Anomalies and unexplained happenings are rife. To speak metaphorically, there are always things going on at the periphery of one's vision that one cannot make out properly. It is a characteristic of human cognitive activity that this will be the case. Much will escape scrutiny, or simply be inexplicable.

So long as the inexplicable is of little importance it is undisruptive. Sometimes, however, instances that do not quite fit pose a more direct challenge to the established networks. We have described several cases in which such anomalies were brought into prominence as a result of the interests or activities of one group or another. For instance, the gravity-wave anomaly appears to have been generated by the unusual activity of a particular individual. The arguments about the size of the frontal sinuses were generated by a clash of divergent political and social interests. These two instances both led to public controversy. Often, however, misfits are generated and then routinely disposed of in the course of experimental or theoretical work, by those who have no particular interest in their perpetuation.

Consider, as an instance of the latter, a routine incident from a piece of contemporary normal science. We are in a biochemical laboratory, a laboratory which specialises in a technique for measuring the rate at which cells take up chemicals from their environment.[1] A series of experiments has been undertaken to determine whether a particular chemical compound called DIVEMA, has led to an increase in this rate of uptake. The experimentalists, who have had previous experience with DIVEMA-like molecules have little expectation that there will be any such increase. At a meeting to consider the outcome of the experiments, the data in Figure 17.1 are presented. To read this figure look first at the result marked 'control' on the bottom line. This represents the rate at which substances were taken up in the absence of DIVEMA. Most of the other results are quite close to that of the control. However, two results (S9 and S14, both at 10 μgm) are distinctly *low*. In other words, it looks as if, at very low concentrations, DIVEMAs S9 and S14 may actually *inhibit* the uptake of measured substances. The question is: what should be made of this result?

CONCENTRATION	CODE NUMBERS OF DIFFERENT DIVEMAS			
	S9	S12	S14	S10
10 μgm/ml	1.66 ± 0.05	2.4 ± 0.04	1.72 ± 0.26	
50 μgm/ml	2.56 ± 0.28	2.00 ± 0.2	2.19 ± 0.004	2.01 ± 0.13
100 μgm/ml	2.54 ± (2)	2.4 ± (2)		
CONTROL	2.34 ± 0.2			

FIGURE 17.1   *Rate of uptake of substrate as influenced by DIVEMAs of several kinds, at three different concentrations*

In principle there are at least three possible interpretations: the results might be genuine, in which case the experimentalists will have to change their views on the biological effects of DIVEMAs; the results might be explained by saying that the experimental method is altogether unreliable, and would be best abandoned; or they might be explained by saying that these *particular* results (though not the method as a whole) are unreliable and therefore best ignored. To put this in slightly different language, we may say that the scientists are presented with a problem: a misfit that, if taken seriously, will generate an anomaly. It will force them to alter either the experimental or the theoretical aspects of their networks.

Now let us consider their interests. They are heavily committed to the method in question, for they have spent a number of years developing it. We may predict, then, that they will not choose to treat the method as fundamentally unreliable. Though they are not as heavily committed to their theoretical expectations that DIVEMA will have little or no effect on uptake by cells, they still quite strongly anticipate this result. Our prediction, then, is that they will prefer not to admit that the results represent chemical reality. This leaves them with the third option: to discount these particular results, though not the method as a whole. Our argument, then, leads us to the view that they will ignore this misfit. They will choose not to treat it as an anomaly even though, from another point of view, it seems to be a suitable candidate for such treatment.

In practice this is in fact what happened. The group looked at the results as a whole, and concluded that, overall, DIVEMA had no stimulatory effect. In doing so they talked about the way in which results were 'within experimental error'; they looked at apparently anomalous results, and discounted them by referring to 'the experimental conditions'; they claimed, for instance, that the substrate taken up was from 'a strange batch', that the experimental cells were also 'strange', and that the total number of experiments was too small to produce truly significant results.

It may be that the reader's first reaction is to say that this is a case of shoddy or unprofessional science. This reaction, however, is inappropriate. The scientists had good reasons to suppose that the experimental system was reliable. It had produced workable results in the past. Again, they had good reasons for their belief that DIVEMAs would not stimulate uptake, and they were, in any case, perfectly right to suggest that the results were ambiguous.[2] In general we might also note that it is a routine experience, both within and outside science, that things often go wrong. This is sometimes called Murphy's Law: 'If things *can* go wrong, then they *will*'. If, every time that things go wrong the results have to be taken with total seriousness, the networks of knowledge in terms of which we operate would rapidly degenerate. So each time that things go wrong, a decision has to be made: is this the result of a genuine anomaly, or is it simply a result of the operation of Murphy's Law? Most of the time, like the biochemists, we are protective of our networks, and assume that the latter is the case. And most of the time it transpires that our decisions are perfectly workable.[3]

The case of the biochemists is typical of much of what goes on in science on a day-to-day basis. There is much evidence that troublesome misfits are routinely denied the status of anomalies. Indeed, we might say that this is the first line of network defence.[4] Reports, for instance, that sea-serpents or flying saucers have been sighted are denied by experts. And such exotic findings constitute the tip of an iceberg whose concealed sections are represented by common and unreported events like those described in our biochemical example above.

ANOMALIES AND REVOLUTIONS

It sometimes happens, however, that misfits are recognised and become the object of considerable attention. Under such circumstances a number of possible outcomes are possible, some of which are described by Kuhn for the case of natural science. First, the anomaly may be 'normalised'. After further study and manipulation of either or both of the more theoretical and more empirical parts of the network, these may be reconciled. Thus further empirical investigation may lead to the realisation that, in fact, the anomaly is readily explicable in terms of available theory or method. Alternatively, rather more major, but still reformist theoretical revision may assimilate the troublesome anomaly. More typically, however, these two processes occur alongside one another. Our Xaanthi example helps to make this point, as does the case of Euler's theorem of polyhedra. However, instances are easily found in the history of science. As a similar example, consider briefly the case of the discovery of the planet Uranus. Sir William Herschel, using a telescope greatly superior to those of his predecessors, observed that one of the bodies examined appeared to have the form of a disc rather than being a point source of light like most stars. Further observation revealed that this disc had motion relative to the stars and Herschel concluded that he had discovered a comet. After further observation, however, Lexell calculated the probable orbit of the body, and decided that it was planetary in nature. As a result, Uranus became a new planet and a comet was deleted from the astronomical network. In addition, various stars were removed from the latter, as a number of observers had, in the previous century, seen what was now taken to be Uranus but had, at the time, been interpreted as stars.[5]

If anomaly denial and network shuffling are common responses to misfits, another possible outcome is that of radical network change. Kuhn calls such transformations 'scientific revolutions', and we conclude this chapter by considering such episodes by means of a further empirical example, that of the changes that took place in chemical theory and practice in the last part of the eighteenth century. Though the whole story of this 'chemical revolution' is complex, it revolves in large part around changes in the theory of combustion.[6] It was generally believed before 1777 that burning bodies give off an elementary substance called phlogiston. This phlogiston theory of combustion, which had been the subject of intense development by chemists, unified, organised and explained a wide variety of chemical and biological observations. For instance: it explained why certain substances are easily burned – they are rich in phlogiston. It explained why combustion which takes place in a confined space causes a reduction in gas volume – the phlogiston which is given off by the burning body spoils the 'elasticity' of the air. It explained why a candle burning in a confined space goes out in the course of time – the air becomes saturated with phlogiston. It explained why a mouse or other creature breathing in a confined space eventually expires – the air again becomes saturated with phlogiston. It explained why metals have more in common than their ores – metals are a combination of calx and phlogiston (and thus have phlogiston in common) whereas ores are formed by different kinds of calx which have nothing in common. All in all, then, the phlogiston theory offered a parsimonious explanatory scheme which covered a wide range of phenomena. As a result of the chemical revolution, however, this conceptual edifice was re-placed by one that was very different: the oxygen theory of combustion. Many of the above phenomena were redescribed and explained differently as a result of this change. Some – for instance, the qualitative similarities between many metals – were no longer susceptible to easy explanation at all. On the other hand, other phenomena which had been distinctly troublesome from the standpoint of phlogiston theory became readily explicable.

Let us now, therefore, consider the situation in chemistry in the early 1770s, and concentrate in particular upon those phenomena which contemporary chemists took to be troublesome – that is to say, upon the potential anomalies. Broadly speaking, troubles had developed in two areas, those of the chemistry of gases and of quantitative analysis. The former had had a long and venerable history. Starting with the development of the air-pump, scientists had come to take the view that air was an active ingredient in chemical reactions, rather than a passive, all-enveloping fluid. In 1756 Joseph Black determined for the first time that there was more than one kind of gas, when he isolated what he called 'fixed air' (which we would now call carbon dioxide). Using the phlogiston theory a number of chemists, including Joseph Priestley who was to play a major if reluctant role in the chemical revolution, began to distinguish experimentally an increasing number of gases. Priestley was a fine and innovative experimentalist and discovered four new 'airs' in the period 1767– 73. He also discovered that while the processes of combustion, putrefaction and respiration used up about one fifth by volume of common air, the purity of the latter was restored by the action of plants. In 1774, in the course of his pneumatic experiments, he obtained a colourless gas by heating red oxide of mercury. In his attempts to determine the nature of this gas, he established that it had the effect of causing a lighted candle to burn with unusual vigour. In satisfactory conformity with phlogiston theory, he thus identified it as 'dephlogisticated air'. He had isolated the gas that we now identify as oxygen.

Thus far the progress of the theory of phlogiston and its guiding role in chemical investigation appears unproblematic. However, the proliferation of gases discovered after the work of Joseph Black (Priestley himself discovered ten in all) proved increasingly difficult to interpret in terms of this theory. It was not that each new gas was entirely unassimilable to the theory. It was rather that the complexity of the latter seemed to grow at least as fast, if not faster, than the empirical facts it was supposed to cover. We need here to remind ourselves that one of the criteria for the workability of knowledge is that it should account for, predict, and permit control of the natural world in a reasonably economical manner. A theory that requires revision each time a new natural phenomenon is discovered – in other words a theory that runs into a series of accounted anomalies – tends to lead to doubts and questions among its adherents. We have seen that anomalies do not inevitably lead to radical change – Priestley himself remained an unconverted phlogiston theorist until the end of his days. However, it is enough to note that chemists in the early 1770s felt some concern about the ability of this theory to handle and account for the newly discovered plethora of gases.

This was not, however, the only area of chemical unease. Another had grown out of the introduction into chemistry of the balance, and the increasing concern of some chemists with quantitative considerations. Thus, by use of the balance in combination with some of the techniques of pneumatic chemistry, it had become clear that the roasting of metals and their consequent conversion into ores led to an *increase* in weight – and, as some chemists came to believe, an increase in matter as well. One investigator who was particularly concerned with this gain in weight was Antoine Laurent Lavoisier, a brilliant French chemist who was subsequently to lose his head in the French Revolution as a result of his tax-farming activities under the *ancien regime*. In 1772 Lavoisier deposited a sealed letter with the Secretary of the French Academy of Sciences in which he noted that when sulphur and phosphorus were burned they increased in weight. He hypothesised that this occurred because they absorbed 'air'. Notice that this is a hypothesis which, if not inconsistent, nevertheless scarcely seems to be consistent with the theory of phlogiston. The latter would have interpreted such combustion primarily in terms of the expulsion of phlogiston.

Lavoisier, like a number of other quantitative chemists, therefore clearly had his doubts about phlogiston theory. Such doubts, however, did not lead him to abandon it, at least publicly. And, we should note, there was no hard and fast reason for him to do so. Untidy it might be, but as in the case of the confusion of gases, phlogiston theory was quite capable of accounting for the apparent increase in weight that occurred when certain substances burned. It might, for example, be the case that phlogiston had a negative weight. Its departure from a burning substance would thus tend to increase the weight of the latter. Or again, it might be replaced in the burning matter by another, heavier, substance. The possibilities were endless. There were many available hypotheses, though to many they seemed elaborate and insufficiently predictive.

Lavoisier heard of Priestley's work of 1772 on red oxide of mercury and proceeded to replicate it. Unlike Priestley, however, he was uncertain that the gas should be identified as dephlogisticated air, and undertook additional experiments in order further to determine its characteristics. He found, for instance, that in combustion and the roasting of metals, only a part of the volume of 'common air' was lost. This led him to the idea that 'common air' must be composed of two major components one of which was absorbed in the course of combustion. This he called 'oxygen' (the 'acid-maker'). The other was 'non-vital air', 'azote', or, as we now say, nitrogen. In 1777, in a memoir to the French Academy, he argued against the phlogiston theory by suggesting that combustion was caused not by the expulsion of phlogiston, but rather by the combination of oxygen with the burning substance. The initial stages of the chemical revolution were complete. An alternative theory had been proposed, one that seemed to many, though not to all, to explain the qualitative data on combustion more satisfactorily. It was, of course, incompatible in most respects with phlogiston theory.

This example suggests several points. The first is one that we touched upon in Chapter 8 and to which we return in Chapter 22. It may appear, at first glance, that the oxygen theory is superior to its displaced rival, the theory of phlogiston. Though there is a sense in which it *must* be preferable (or why would it have replaced the latter?) the precise nature of this superiority is not very obvious. We started our account with a partial description of the explanatory scope of the theory of phlogiston. We noted that, although some of the phenomena in question were equally well interpreted in terms of oxygen theory, this was by no means always the case. The *qualitative* explanatory scope of the new network was limited in the extreme. Thus, it was not until much later that new explanations for the quality of materials became available. The new network was good at certain things. It handled quantitative data well. It showed promise with respect to the chemistry of gases. These advances had, however, to be balanced against the losses already mentioned.

In what sense then, if at all, is oxygen theory better than that of phlogiston? Our answer can be little more than a paraphrase of the preceding paragraph. It was better and more workable in relation to certain phenomena – those which contemporary chemists had chosen to treat as troublesome anomalies. It was not, let us remind ourselves, closer to the truth in the sense that it corresponded more accurately to reality – we have already considered the drawbacks of correspondence theory and chosen instead, the alternative pragmatic conception of knowledge. We have to say, then, that *phlogiston theory was better because it seemed to the majority of contemporary chemists to be a better tool for handling the problems with which they were primarily concerned.* Given their mental habits and the circumstances in which they found themselves, it was predominantly in their interests to opt for the promise of oxygen theory rather than to stay with the well known but accountably unsatisfactory theory of phlogiston.

Note the way in which interests enter the picture. No scientist was *forced* to change by the knowledge itself. That much is clear, because such individuals as Priestley were not converted. If scientists chose to adopt oxygen theory this was because of their assessment of the relative utility of this new tool compared with the old, given their particular interests. If scientists disagreed about the profitability of the theory, this must, in principle, be explained with reference to differences in experience, socialisation, situation and mental habits. In the present context we do not have the data or the theoretical sophistication to press this suggestion home. But one thing is clear: the conservative Priestley should not be pilloried for irrational resistance to received truth. Such Whig interpretations of the history of science which understand such changes as the simple casting out of error, and the consequent move to a closer approximation to the truth must be rejected. Such an approach, though it has its uses, will help us little if we want to understand either the relationship of our knowledge to that of our predecessors, or the social and intellectual dynamics which led from their beliefs to our own.

The second point concerns the question of continuity. Revolutionary though this episode was, it does not represent a complete break in the networks of chemistry or a total retooling. There was, for instance, a substantial body of observational material that was affected relatively little by the theoretical reorganisation. Many of the observations on gases, on what we would now call oxidation and on the preparation of metals, were largely unchanged. Indeed, the crucial quantitative measurements were to form a central feature of the observational end of the new network. Large parts of the empirical part of the chemical network thus survived the change. In fact, they formed the very basis upon which the new theoretical network was built. Once the phlogiston chemists chose to treat certain observations generated within their network as troublesome to it, we may say (with some rhetorical exaggeration) that the theory of phlogiston contained within itself the seeds of its own destruction! More accurately, if less picturesquely, we should note, rather, that chemists used the weaknesses of the theory of phlogiston to explore the shape of the anomaly, and to build this into a reconstructed theoretical network, a different kind of chemical tool.[7]

In this chapter we have considered the move from misfit, to anomaly, to reaction to that anomaly. We have chosen cases from the natural sciences, but there seems little doubt that these processes are quite general. Non-scientific networks undoubtedly encounter the same kinds of troubles, and people have available essentially the same kinds of options.

---

113 Any network will generate misfits, that is, instances that are not easily interpretable in terms of obvious network extension. This follows from the fact that a network necessarily involves loss of information.

114 Whether such misfits are accorded significance and noticed as anomalies depends upon a decision by the actors concerned, which is in turn a function of their conceptual habits and social interests.

115 Once a misfit has been accorded the status of an anomaly, there are further decisions that have to be made about how the anomaly will be handled. A range of options is available, though it should be understood that these overlap, or shade into one another.

116 Where actors are strongly committed to their networks, there is a wide armoury of legitimations and excuses available which permits them to discount the apparent anomaly and preserve the network unaltered. This is an extremely common strategy.

117 Sometimes, however, the anomaly is accorded significance. In this case a further set of possibilities is
opened up. The anomaly may finally be reconciled
with the network through the manipulation or revision of either or both the theoretical and empirical ends of the network.

118 Another possible outcome is radical network
change. In science this is sometimes called a
'scientific revolution', though there are always elements of continuity however radical the change
(see proposition 53).

119 There is no easy or overall sense in which the new
network may be said to be superior to that which
preceded it. The best we can say is that it served the
interests of the relevant actors more satisfactorily.

120 The outcome of the interaction between potential
anomaly and network, like standard network extension, is thus a function of social interests and
conceptual habits.

Part IV

Social Science and
Network Theory

In previous chapters we have outlined the network theory of knowledge, and in particular its application to natural science. We now consider its implications for social science. Generally speaking network theory is permissive with respect to social science. It tells us little, for example, about the kinds of models that might best be utilised in exploring social science problems. This is because, as we noted in Chapter 8, it is essentially descriptive rather than prescriptive. It only becomes prescriptive when a theory under scrutiny breaches what it takes to be a realistic theory of knowledge. We have already seen at least one case of this: since it is a materialist theory which suggests that people direct ideas rather than ideas directing people (Chapter 14) alternative idealist conceptions of the role of knowledge are seen as unrealistic. In the chapters that follow we consider a number of other prescriptive consequences for social science practice.

We start by looking at those theories of knowledge which distinguish between good and bad knowledge in a way that is fundamental to their explanatory strategy. It is important to be clear about what is being intended here. We are not suggesting that it is impossible or inappropriate for social-science investigators to make judgements of truth and falsity in their roles as citizens. Naturally we all do this. Neither are we suggesting that no judgements are appropriate in a professional social science context – we are, after all, pursuing what we take to be certain prescriptive implications of the network theory and the latter follow naturally from the adoption of a particular account of the way in which knowledge is generated. Rather, we are suggesting that, as a result of having adopted network theory, those alternative accounts for the generation of knowledge which assume good knowledge is to be explained in a manner that differs from bad knowledge, should be rejected as unrealistic.

Naturally this prescription depends upon a commitment to network theory. Ultimately it cannot be *demonstrated* that alternative prescriptive accounts are definitively wrong. Indeed one of the virtues of the network theory is that it predicts such demonstration to be impossible.

Nevertheless it is worth detailing the reasons for refusing to make the customary explanatory distinctions between good and bad, true and false, and modern and primitive. The first, which we have been arguing in previous chapters, concerns the workability of network theory. Our view is that it really does account for what is at present known about the growth of knowledge. But second, and this is important for the social science prescriptions that follow, it does so in an economical manner by finding general principles that explain the growth of all knowledge, whether good or bad, in the same way. Parsimony is, of course, a matter of taste. Despite the various difficulties that we have suggested stand in the way of such a programme, there is nothing *per se* impossible about providing different types of explanations for 'objectively' true and false knowledge. On the other hand, we believe that there is value in pushing general and parsimonious explanatory principles as far as they will go and it is the implications of this preference that we explore in the chapters that follow.

Our approach is, then, broadly consistent with what David Bloor has called the 'strong programme' of the sociology of knowledge.[1] The strong programme has, he suggests, four tenets.

(1) It is *causal*, concerning itself with the factors that generate knowledge.
(2) It is *impartial*, that is, it assumes that both truth and falsity (or other such pairs of opposites) require explanation.
(3) It is *symmetrical*, assuming, as we have been suggesting, that the same kinds of factors explain both true and false knowledge.
(4) It is *reflexive*; since it aims at generality it explains its own derivation in terms of the same kinds of factors.

We start with questions of impartiality and symmetry by looking at three areas of social science where there has been a persistent tendency to distinguish between the true and the false and then to explain these in different ways. The first such area is that of primitive thought. Here the 'manifest' inadequacy of native belief is often held to require an explanation different in kind to that accorded to our own scientific, and hence rationally explicable, knowledge. The second area is common sense. Again, this is often distinguished from science, and is held to be explained by different kinds of factors. The third such area is that of ideology. Here the argument is a little more complicated. Abandoning our predominantly empirical approach, we suggest that the assymetrical and the symmetrical have often co-existed in the analysis of ideology, and we attempt to tease these apart in the work of Marx and Mannheim. We also note that as the impartial and the symmetrical gain ground, so the concept of ideology has a tendency to become general and lose its normative function.

The network theory has strongly relativistic overtones that find their expression not only in the requirements of impartiality and symmetry, but also in that of reflexivity. In Chapter 21 we discuss the so called 'problem' of relativism and argue, against most present day views, that there is nothing self-contradictory in adopting a form of methodological relativism. Indeed such a stance is necessary if general and parsimonious explanations for the generation of knowledge are to be mounted. Various arguments against relativism – and notably the view that it is self-defeating – are considered and shown to be incorrect.

Next we turn to the question of *verstehen*. *Verstehende* sociologists have in general displayed a deep interest in understanding beliefs and actions in their own terms, and have often argued that it is inappropriate to import judgements of truth and falsity from other social contexts. There is thus an obvious similarity between the condition of impartiality and the practice of *verstehende* sociology. However, the commitment to impartiality is often coupled with the view that neither causal nor comparative analysis of alien belief-systems is appropriate. We consider this position and argue that network theory reveals both these options to be available to the social scientist, so long as realistic conceptions of 'cause' and 'comparison' are entertained. The widespread tendency of *verstehende* sociologists to reject these options rests, we suggest, upon a rigid but unrealistic conception of natural science.

What, then, is different about social science if it is not the fact that the study of actors' meanings requires some entirely different and special approach? If, in other words, there is no basic conceptual distinction between the natural and social sciences? The answer to this question is easily seen in the context of network theory: the field of interests that lies behind and directs social science knowledge is much more obviously diverse than that which operates within certain branches of natural science. Furthermore this field of interests relates much more to a global concern with social legitimation than is typically the case in natural science. We explore these differences and their consequence – the fact that there is little or no consensus in social science. Our suggestion is, then, that social science is distinctive not because it is conceptually different *per se* from natural science, but because the social conditions of its production are very different.

Finally, we turn to another vexed question – that of the relationship between social science and philosophy. Our argument is that for too long social science has been unduly influenced by the particular preoccupations of philosophy. We suggest that social scientists should stop doing 'misbegotten epistemology' and concentrate, instead, upon social science issues. Chapter 24 thus constitutes a kind of declaration of social science independence.

---

121 If network theory is realistic, then both those beliefs that are thought to be true and those taken to be false should be explained by the same *kinds* of factors. We should, therefore, be 'impartial' with respect to truth and falsity and 'symmetrical' in explanatory approach.

18 The Social Structure of 'Primitive' Ideas: the Azande Poison Oracle

INTRODUCTION

Primitives, the old argument runs, are unlike you and me. Here in the West we are more advanced. Our economic development has run apace for three centuries. Our science and technology are superior, incomparably superior to those of the Kalahari bushmen. We have greater control over natural forces. The question is, why?

In the nineteenth century many took this state of affairs for granted, and ascribed Western superiority to basic physiological and evolutionary differences: we were simply more developed than our semi-simian cousins in Africa. Others, though noting the differences, ascribed them not to mental torpor on the part of the natives, but to different mental habits. Lévy Bruhl, for instance, argued in *La Mentalité Primitive* that we have to understand the natives in their own terms: it is no good, he said, trying to impose our own habits of thought. If we do so we will simply fail to understand what makes the primitive tick:

> The Eskimo manner of thinking . . . gives the impression of being very superficial, because they are not accustomed to follow to any extent, what we call a definite line of reasoning attached to a particular object. In other words, their thought does not raise itself to abstraction or to logical formulation. It sticks to observed images and to situations which follow laws that are understandable only with difficulty.[1]

Instead of logic, the native has recourse to magic:

Primitive mentality, like ours, worries about what causes events. But it does not search for them in the same way. It lives in a world where innumerable occult powers, always present, are always acting or ready to act . . . every fact, no matter how particular, is taken immediately as a manifestation of one or several of those powers.[2]

It is not surprising, in this view, that native thought should often seem to disobey the rules of logic and inference, for it is mystical and, indeed, prelogical.

Lévy Bruhl's writing has been developed by subsequent authors in two rather different directions. On the one hand there was the stress on the differences between them and us. Their magic was unlike our logic. Much social anthropology up to the present day has indeed been written in this idiom.[3] On the other hand, anthropologists, particularly those who have contributed to the literature by means of major ethnographic studies, have rather tended to stress the second part of Lévy Bruhl's thesis: that cultures must be understood in their own terms and seen, as it were, as a total package.[4] One such anthropologist, E. E. Evans Pritchard, wrote a classic study of the mode of operation of oracles among the Azande,[5] a tribe in the southern Sudan. In the next few pages we describe the mode of operation of one Azande oracle, the *benge* poison oracle, before we consider its logical status.

AZANDE RATIONALITY

It is first necessary to understand that the Azande attribute nothing to chance. For them routine misfortune can always be ascribed to the operation of witchcraft or other malign influence. Thus, if a granary falls on an Azande causing him injury, it is important to discover *why* this occurred. It is not that the Azande fail to recognise that such a collapse has a physical origin – for instance, the undermining activities of termites. It is rather that they ask additional questions: given that the granary was ready to collapse, why did it collapse when it did and on the particular injured party? For them the answer will probably be witchcraft. Thus, the Azande ask more specific questions and isolate more specific causes than we would typically do under the same circumstances. Whereas we would simply attribute the collapse at that time and place to chance, or to bad luck, the Azande immediately inquire into the origins of possible witchcraft. They make this inquiry by means of oracles. Oracles are the key means available to the Azande to uncover what is going on in the otherwise concealed world of witchcraft. Since witchcraft is ubiquitous, and no action of any importance can be planned without taking its possible operation into account, oracles play a central role in Azande society.

The most important of these is the *benge* poison oracle. A consultation with this oracle is a complex and elaborate matter. It requires a supply of *benge,* a poison that has been carefully prepared in an appropriate ritual manner from the roots of a creeper that is available only in the Congo rain-forest, many dangerous miles from Zandeland. Expensive and hazardous expeditions are occasionally made to collect the root, and to reduce it to the powder which is actually used during the consultations. In addition to the powder, a supply of chickens is also required. These, though much more easily acquired than the poison, represent a considerable outlay as, in the course of the seance, many are used and some of these will be killed.

The person who wishes to consult the oracle repairs, with an operator, to a secluded place outside the village where they will not be disturbed. The operator, having ensured that he is in a state of ritual purity (which involves prior abstinence from certain kinds of meat and from sexual intercourse) takes a pinch of paste which has been prepared from the poisonous powder, forces it down the chicken's bill and addresses himself to the poison in the chicken.

> Oh *benge* [he may say] If it is witchcraft that has caused the questioner's child to fall ill, then show that this is the case by killing the chicken.

He shakes the chicken to and fro in order to cause it to swallow the poison, and continues to address the poison in such a manner for several minutes, though always returning to the basic question. Finally, the chicken either dies, or it survives. It is in this way that the oracle returns its verdict. In this example the death of the chicken would indicate that witchcraft was, indeed, the cause of the illness of the child. However, the Azande are very thorough and check that the oracle is working properly by asking the same question the other way round. In this case the questioner would take another chicken, prise its bill open, pour poison down its throat and say

> *Benge*, if there is truly witchcraft at work here, then save the chicken, do not kill it.

Only if the oracle gives the same response the second time around, is it deemed to have given a valid answer. Verdicts that are inconsistent are disregarded. A valid answer is, however, taken as authoritative. The Azande does not doubt or question his oracle in this eventuality. He acts in accordance with its guidance. It is in this way, then, that the Azande discover what is going on in the otherwise concealed world of witchcraft, that they determine the causes of past misfortunes, and in terms of which they plan their future course of action.

One's immediate reaction is, perhaps, to dismiss the poison oracle as an illogical way of conducting affairs. How, one might ask, can it possibly make sense to consult an oracle which gives 'answers' that presumably depend upon such factors as the strength of the poison, the size of the dose administered and the constitution of the chicken, rather than knowledge on the part of the poison of the (presumably non-existent) doings of witches? Such a dismissal depends, however, upon a correspondence theory of truth. It assumes that witchcraft beliefs and all the paraphernalia of oracle consultation do not accord to reality. Rather are the results of the oracle better explained by true knowledge of the effects of certain chemically-definable poisons upon such living organisms as chickens. If, instead of jumping straight to a correspondence theory which involves applying our own beliefs to an evaluation of Azande practice, we instead adopt the alternative pragmatic theory of knowledge recommended in network theory, the apparent incongruity of belief in the poison oracle is nowhere near as obvious. We have to ask, then, whether the oracle is workable from the standpoint of the Azande. *From their point of view* is it irrational for them to hold it?

One approach to this is to ask: what do the Azande do when their oracle is inconsistent? That is, what do they do when it gives non-commital results — when, for instance, the poison kills two chickens in a row, and thus gives no answer? Or again, what do they do if the predictions of the oracle are subsequently disproved? If, in other words, the oracle is failing *in their own terms*, how do they respond to this? Should they not, quite frankly, say to themselves that the oracle has failed and cast around for a new and more satisfactory way of regulating their lives?

Evans Pritchard suggests that in actual practice they do not do so. They are strongly committed to their oracles and the failure of the latter by no means discomfits the Azande. Rather, they have available an elaborate set of hypotheses to explain why the oracle has failed to function on the occasion in question. Thus they may say that the wrong variety of poison was used – there are other similar creepers in the forest which can only be distinguished from the genuine article by experts. They may say that the necessary taboos, either for the preparation of the poison or for the conduct of the seance, have not been properly followed. This will cause the oracle to malfunction. They may say that the owners of the forest from which the poison-substance was taken are angry. They may say that the poison is too old, that it has been used too much, or that it is 'foolish' and too strong. Finally, they may ascribe the failure of the oracle to witchcraft, sorcery or the anger of ghosts. Each of these causes of malfunction induces its own characteristic mode of failure. 'Foolish' poison kills all the chickens indiscriminately. Old or excessively-used poison saves all the chickens. The chickens die slowly in the event of intervention by sorcery and so on.

What we have here, then is a series of misfits – incidents which do not fit with the basic theories and beliefs about the oracle – which are explained away by means of what we might call excuses. To use the terminology that we established in the last chapter, we might say that these are misfits that are not granted the status of anomalies. Evans Pritchard writes that:

> Azande admit failures and seek to explain them away by one of the secondary elaborations of belief suitable for such situations. Since, as a rule, experience is socially defined . . . the revelations of the poison oracle accord easily with experience.[6]

This may seem unsatisfactory. A system of beliefs is being saved from overthrow by a set of seemingly arbitrary secondary elaborations. However, if it *is* unsatisfactory, then it is unsatisfactory in precisely the same way as the biochemical beliefs that were discussed in Chapter 17, for the two situations are analogous. In each case a practical set of beliefs, a network, is used to establish a workable mastery of the natural world. In each case that network encounters misfits. In each case those misfits are not allowed to challenge the networks, that is, they are denied the status of anomalies. In each case this denial is done by means of a repertoire of excuses, secondary elaborations – call them what you will – which do not form an immediate part of the network that generated the misfit in the first place. To repeat, if the procedures adopted by the Azande to preserve their beliefs are unsatisfactory, then so, too, are at least certain parts of modern science.

In the light of the network theory of knowledge, then, the Azande beliefs no longer look quite so odd. The theory argues that we classify and discriminate perceptual lumps in a way that workably serves our interests. It notes, further, that this involves an inevitable loss of information, that there will be loose ends, misfits, that will require some kind of explanation. One way of handling misfits, as we saw in the last section, is to grant them the status of anomalies and to reorganise the more theoretical aspects of the relevant networks. But there is no necessity for such a course to be followed. It will be adopted only in those cases where, for one reason or another, it serves the social interests of at least some of those who are involved. The procedures preferred by the biochemists and the Azande are thus a function of their lack of interest in challenging the misfit-producing beliefs. The biochemists have invested in their method to the point where they would be unwilling to doubt its adequacy. So it is, too, with the Azande. The poison oracle is an institution central to their society: it is immensely authoritative; it is a cornerstone upon which rest many other institutions. The Azande have become thoroughly committed to it. They have no interest in treating the misfits that it generates as anomalies. They have no particular interest in replacing it with something else. Accordingly, like the method used by the biochemists, in the practical circumstances at hand it rests as an unchallenged authority, classifying, discriminating and telling them how best to look at the relevant aspects of their social and natural worlds.

Azande theory is not, therefore, 'prelogical' in the sense intended by Lévy Bruhl. The same rules of evidence and reasoning apply to the Azande as to us. If the poison oracle, for instance, fails to work, the Azande *notice* that this is the case. They justify continued belief in the oracle by ascribing failure to other, intervening causes. Their mode of reasoning is perfectly 'logical'. Or, to be more precise, it appears that their psychological coherence conditions are like ours. Their modes of reasoning do not depart from anything that would be called reasonable in our culture. It is rather the content of their beliefs, their social coherence conditions, that seem so odd. This, however, is less surprising, for it is self-evident that different cultures believe different things about nature.

We can summarise the argument so far, by reinterpreting Lévy Bruhl's distinction between logic and magic. Logic, or at any rate the capacity to classify, distinguish and notice incompatibility or misfit, is something common to both science and magic. Differences are located in the premises, networks, or beliefs in which the actors have invested. Of course, Lévy Bruhl is right in one important respect. Unless we understand native networks – that is, the social coherence conditions of a culture – we will not understand how they reason. All will be a mystery to us.[7]

DIFFERENCES BETWEEN SCIENCE AND THE PRIMITIVE

The natives, then, appear to be reasonable. They indulge in all the same mental antics that can be found in any other area of social life, including science. They become committed to their networks in much the same way as anyone else. They preserve those networks by means of the same kind of manoeuvres. The differences between science and the primitive cannot be sustained with reference to inherent mental powers, nor to psychologically generated coherence conditions. Can they be sustained in any way *other* than by saying that they are simply different in content? Our answer to this is 'yes', but in conformity with the network theory of knowledge and the requirements of impartiality and symmetry, we have to locate differences not within the structure of the knowledge itself, but rather in the social contexts which generate belief. In other words, we must look at the context of interests within which science and primitive beliefs are created.

The first point is that it may well be the case that scientific beliefs are more prone to change as a result of several features of the social structure within which science is lodged. First, as we noted in Chapter 16, scientific interests are organised in such a way that there is a premium on normal science innovation. Scientists are rewarded to the extent to which they extend networks to novel phenomena. Within a scientific network, therefore, change is taking place, extension is occurring and metaphors are being transferred. By contrast, so far as one is able to tell from the admittedly static representation of Zande culture offered by Evans Pritchard, such extension does not take place with respect to the poison oracle. It handles the everyday run of planning and misfortune. Its practitioners do not have any incentive to go and find potentially explicable novel phenomena which it might explain. There is, then, no interest in extending its range.[8]

Second, (and in a sense more interestingly) the social dynamics of science possess the tendency to generate misfits that, under certain circumstances, subsequently become anomalies. We have seen that this misfit-to-anomaly progression need not necessarily occur. Many misfits are nipped in the bud and dismissed by means of 'secondary elaboration'. Under certain circumstances, as we saw in the case of the 'chemical revolution', they are, however, highlighted, accorded importance, and thereby lead to network transformation of a more or less radical nature. The scientist like Lavoisier who successfully initiates such a network transformation is accorded high status. Thus, though the risks are high, the rewards are also great and it may be in the interests of the scientists concerned to attempt conceptual reform under certain circumstances. By contrast, Evans Pritchard's depiction of the Azande suggests that there is no particular reason why anyone should want to risk their neck and try to make a name for themselves by setting up some rival to the poison oracle. Given the legal and political implications of the oracle (to which we return later) this course of action might indeed be hazardous. Interests here, then, would tend to lead to the dismissal of misfits, rather than their elaboration into fully-established anomalies.

But behind such considerations there is a more profound set of factors at work. Zande society is substantially undifferentiated. Though actors to some extent occupy different statuses, the society is relatively simple. People in it understand most of what there is to know about it. Their society is not like ours where any individual only knows a small part of what goes on. Zande society is relatively undifferentiated whereas ours rests upon a complex division of labour. Even within science there is such differentiation. There are chemists and physicists, biochemists and biophysicists, X-ray crystallographers and people who study neutron diffraction. The difference in complexity between Zande society and our own has at least three important implications for the social coherence conditions of their networks.

First, our society breeds specialists. Most of us do not have to know how to make clothes, undertake horticulture, build houses or catch fish. For that matter, our scientists do not require a general command of physics, chemistry, biology and the rest. Our doctors, even our general practitioners, do not have to be able to diagnose and treat all our diseases. It is enough for them to know where to send the patient with the ominous symptom. By contrast, Zande society does not breed many different kinds of specialists. Though some may be better than others at certain tasks (and a few posts are reserved for specialists), the relative lack of division of labour means that there is a corresponding lack of specialisation. There is no such thing as a paediatrician in Zandeland. Correspondingly, knowledge is less compartmentalised and is, inevitably, less esoteric in undifferentiated societies.[9] Overall, it is *more* detailed, esoteric and compartmentalised in differentiated societies. We enter the caveat 'overall' because the extent to which there is knowledge about any *particular* phenomenon obviously depends crucially on the array of interests in a given society. It is reputed, for instance, that Eskimos know a great deal about snow.

A second feature of differentiated societies which is substantially absent in undifferentiated societies is that they characteristically generate a very wide range of different interests. We must beware, of course, of depicting primitive societies as happy, uncomplicated Edens where all live happily together. This is simply not the case. Nevertheless, given their relative simplicity, they cannot generate the massive variety of differing interests found in differentiated societies. This complex of interlocking interests has an important consequence: it almost inevitably generates social change.[10] Groups pursue their interests and make demands upon other groups. Those other groups react to these demands in a manner that, so far as possible, serves their interests. New action, new beliefs, new interests and new institutions are constantly being born, flowering and declining, as groups find them useful or not, or as the latter themselves rise and fall.

If this is true in general it is, of course, also true for science. Internal innovation or successful puzzle-solving affects the way in which scientists assess their interests. With the discovery of the structure of DNA, for instance, certain able scientists are reputed to have cast around and asked the question: what will be the next problem whose solution will bring a Nobel Prize to the lucky solver? Though this example dramatises and perhaps personalises the issue, the point is nevertheless general: change begets change in a social structure such as science where there is a premium on change. Externally, of course, as social conditions change, scientists and technologists find that they are granted resources to a greater or lesser degree. They find that they are asked to solve problems that are of interest to powerful groups. Overall, then, the interaction of interests tends to generate change, both in those interests themselves and correspondingly in the esoteric knowledge available within the society. In sum we might say that the interdependence of actors and institutions makes it highly probable that networks will be less conservatively handled in the long run in differentiated societies than in their undifferentiated neighbours.

There is a final difference between the two types of society that should also be mentioned. In a differentiated society it is possible, at least in principle, to dissociate investigation of the natural world from global social control implications. Major social control implications are not, for instance, immediately obvious in the case of X-ray crystallography. Naturally, this process is by no means complete. External social interests in legitimation often direct the growth of knowledge and, as we have seen, no knowledge is without some social control implications. Nevertheless, despite these caveats it is often possible, in a differentiated society to extend or reform esoteric knowledge without becoming involved in major social control problems. By embracing the theory of plate tectonics in geology one does not thereby call into question the basic methods of social control in the United States. The same option is not typically available in an undifferentiated society. There, a major challenge to natural knowledge is, at one and the same time, likely to be a challenge to the religious and political order, for these are all sustained in mutually supporting or at least mutually interrelated, structure. Knowledge about the world is at one and the same time knowledge about society and its proper mode of functioning. A challenge to Zande witchcraft beliefs is simultaneously a challenge to the legal system and the political structure. Our point then is that it is much easier to innovate in a society where one's innovations have no obvious and immediate effects elsewhere – where no major consequences for social control or legitimation appear to follow.

Our knowledge about primitive societies is patchy. They are almost certainly less static, homogeneous or consensual than such anthropologists as Evans Pritchard tended to suggest. Nevertheless, our argument in this chapter rests upon a simple difference in degree of complexity between 'primitive' and 'modern' societies and this difference most certainly exists. Our position is as follows: savages process information in much the same way as anyone else. Psychological coherence conditions are shared by all human beings. The networks that they create are thus eminently workable. They constitute a practically-adequate guide to interaction with the world, given the interests by which they are directed. That there are differences between primitive and scientific knowledge is indisputable. These differences should, however, be explained in ways that do not breach the requirements of impartiality and symmetry. They should be explained, in other words, in terms of the same *kinds* of factors. The network theory suggests what the latter will be. Differences will be caused by the different social locations within which knowledge is generated, and the different purposes for which it is used. They will, in other words, be a function of social interests. Differentiation leads to the possibility of highly esoteric scientific knowledge, it raises the chances that scientists will adopt a nonconservative stance in relation to their knowledge because it rewards certain kinds of change, it fosters divergent and changing fields of interests and it increases the likelihood that scientific knowledge will be dissociated from a major interest in global social control.

---

122 Primitive beliefs are as rationally based as our own. Primitives, like us, construct networks that adequately serve their practical interests. The psychological coherence conditions that underlie their networks are identical to ours. Accordingly we

should explain their beliefs in the same way that we explain ours – impartially and symmetrically.

123 Like scientists, primitives defend their networks by refusing to turn misfits into anomalies.

124 Differences between scientific and primitive networks result from differences between the social contexts in which they are produced. Science is produced in social context that encourages certain kinds of change.

125 Social differentiation tends to encourage network change. It does this for three reasons:

(a) it may favour the active generation of esoteric knowledge
(b) it may foster a relatively non-protective attitude towards established belief
(c) it tends to provide opportunities for the generation of knowledge with few social control implications.

19 The Social Structure of Common Sense

In the last chapter we applied the requirements of impartiality and symmetry to the case of primitive knowledge and suggested that differences in social interests and their structure quite adequately explain the evident differences in content between primitive and scientific belief systems. Here we adopt the same kind of strategy with respect to common sense: we suggest that the latter is in no way methodologically different from 'rational' or 'scientific' belief systems, despite the fact that such a contrast is often made. Once again such differences as there are in content are explicable in terms of the interests that direct them. We start with a couple of examples of common sense reasoning.

Children are sometimes presented with tests that purport to measure their educational progress. If their answers to these tests correspond to the expectations of the tester, then the children are held to be competent in certain respects. If they do not, then this is held to reflect upon their inferior puzzle-solving capacity. Let us consider this in more detail.[1]

Children are presented with three pictures: those of an elephant, a bird and a dog. They are asked to match one of these pictures with the word 'fly'. The tester expects that the competent child will choose the bird, yet many actually choose the elephant. When they are asked why, the children tend to respond that the elephant is actually 'Dumbo', the Walt Disney cartoon character which flies by flapping its ears. Or they are presented with a picture of a castle with a drawbridge, moat and turrets, and asked to determine which three letters, C, G, or D, matches the picture. Many choose D (for Disneyland) despite the fact that the tester expects that they will choose C for castle. Or again, they are presented with three pictures: a little girl, a plate of cookies and a dog, and asked to match them with the word 'bake'. Many indicate the plate of cookies, the correct response, but others mark the little girl *and* the cookies, or the little girl alone. When they are asked why, they are reported as saying that little girls do the baking and as interpreting the picture of the cookies as buttons or potatoes.

What can we learn from such occurrences? Initially, we are impressed by the fact that although the children get the answers wrong from the standpoint of the tester, they nevertheless have good reasons for their non-standard responses. It may be, perhaps, that a picture of an elephant does not lead *us* to think of Dumbo straight away but, given the experience of an American child, the latter response is perfectly comprehensible. Leaving aside the testing implications of these findings, what is really being uncovered by the test responses and the reasons given by the children for their answers is the network of classes in terms of which they structure their experience. That they choose to emphasise somewhat different similarities and dissimilarities should not surprise us. The experience and interests of children are different from those of adults.

What we *can* establish by looking at these and similar data, are that the cognitive practices of children are exactly like those of adults and are appropriately described in terms of network theory. Children, faced with perceptual lumps, operate, like us, by noting certain similarities and ignoring others. They choose, in the case we mentioned at the beginning of this section, to notice differences between elephants and dogs. They interpret a line-drawing as a little girl and ignore other possible connections. They interpret another line-drawing variously as a plate of cookies, potatoes or buttons, classifying it in different ways, but none the less classifying it and acting on the basis of that classification. And it is not only the similarities and differences that are constructed. Inferences are made about the connections between classes. Some children, for instance, are reported to assume that baking goes along with little girls and, conversely, that it has nothing whatsoever to do with buttons.

Overall, then, these children are operating with networks in the same way as adults. It is only the *content* of these networks that is in any way different. Otherwise the situation is identical. Children use their networks to perceive and act in practically workable ways. They are able to theorise explicitly about the connections between classes and they are, of course, able to extend classes to deal with instances that are novel. They act, therefore, like scientists. At the level of cognitive operation there is no difference.

Common sense is like science – or perhaps it would be better to say that science is best seen as the application of common sense to esoteric phenomena that are not ordinarily of interest.

Let us take another example. This comes from a study of the action of residents of a halfway house.[2] A halfway house is an institution established by the penal authorities to allow prisoners to build up contact with the outside world before their final release from custody. Inmates who have served most of their sentence are supposed to live responsibly in the house while seeking and holding a job outside. They are supposed to pay a rent to the authorities out of their wages and to obey certain house rules: they are not, for instance, supposed to bring drugs into the house. Given the semi-penal nature of the institution it is not surprising that inmates develop their own set of rules about how to act towards the authorities and each other. These inmate rules are predicated on the assumption that co-operation with staff is best avoided. If, for instance, another member of the house has broken the house rules, it is against the inmates' 'code' to convey this fact to the authorities.

Now consider the following. A resident is wandering through the hall of the house asking loudly 'Where can I find that meeting where I can get an overnight pass?',[3] within the hearing of residents and staff alike. He is trying to find a meeting which forms part of the programme of the halfway house. However, anyone who attends such meetings is in danger of being seen as someone who is seeking favour with the authorities, and is consequently being disloyal to other inmates. Accordingly, the ethnographer, Wieder, understood that what this resident was really saying was:

> I'm not going to that meeting just because I am interested in participating in the program of the halfway house. I'm going to that meeting just because I would like to collect the reward of an overnight pass and for no other reason. I'm not a kiss-ass. Everyone who is in hearing distance should understand that I'm not kissing up to staff. My behavior really is in conformity with the code, though without hearing (this reference to an overnight pass), you might think otherwise.[4]

The resident's problem is that his behaviour is interpretable in terms of two classifications in the inmate network. It may be seen as a case of disloyalty, of seeking favour. Those who go to events organised by staff are liable to find that their behaviour is interpreted in this way. Alternatively it may be seen as acceptable, code-following behaviour, because residents are allowed to pursue their own interests, even if this means attending meetings organised by staff from time to time. This, of course, is exactly like any other problematic case of classification – for instance, does the word 'bake' associate with a picture of a little girl, or a picture showing objects on a plate? Residents, like children, operate with networks which emphasise certain similarities and differences and ignore others. In ambiguous cases – where the proper extension of the network is at question – residents will try to ensure that the classification which best serves their interests is sustained, and this is what the inmate in question is doing.

In all conceptual respects, then, these examples of common sense reasoning exhibit the same properties as scientific reasoning. The fluidity of concept application is identical in a halfway house to a biochemistry laboratory or a community of mathematicians. People operate with classificatory networks which rest upon a selection of similarities and differences, and ignore others. They see, act and theorise in terms of these networks. Since networks do not impose their own extension, there may be doubt about the best way to interpret events that are easily open to interpretation in more than one way. In such cases people may enter into negotiations to try to maximise the likelihood that the extension will be in a way that workably serves their interests. Our conclusion, then, is that the network theory of knowledge is appropriately applied indifferently to all forms of knowledge, whether ancient or modern, scientific or common sense, high status or low. It is simply a statement about the universal ways in which human beings create workable generalisations about their circumstances,[5] and thus exemplifies the principles of impartiality and symmetry with respect to all belief systems.

Once this position is adopted, such differences as there may be between science and other forms of knowledge must be understood as being generated by the same *types* of causes. Specifically, these causes must be understood as residing in the social structure of the interests that lie behind these forms of knowledge rather than the differences between 'everyday' and 'scientific' methods. Science, as we have seen, has certain structural attributes that tend to cause it to generate knowledge of the empirical world that is esoteric, provisionally consensual, dissociated from global interests in social legitimation and control, and subject to change.

Though these distinguish it in a pragmatic matter from many aspects of common sense knowledge, it is even less possible to generalise about the content of the latter than it is of the former. Common sense is not a single body of knowledge. It is as pervasive and varied as social structure itself. Though one may with great profit study routine and everyday reasoning in all sorts of contexts, one would anticipate no general findings with respect to the *content* of common sense knowledge.

What, then, is happening when the scientific is divided from the 'merely' commonsensical? We suggested an answer to this question in Chapter 8. When partial and asymmetrical analysis is proposed then there is often a global interest not only in *description*, but also in *prescription*. Those authors who create such 'criteria of demarcation' are trying to prescribe rules of intellectual hygiene for those whose interests are far different from their own. Sometimes they are quite explicit about this aim, as is, for instance, Popper in his early writing.[6] There is, perhaps, little harm in such open prescription. One is, after all, at liberty to take it or leave it as one wishes. When the prescriptions become concealed behind a legitimating layer of naturalistic rationalisation then the situation becomes more serious. The later writing of Popper and his followers falls into this category.[7] So, too, does that of Gaston Bachelard, the French historian and philosopher of science mentioned in Chapter 14, whose work is particularly interesting in the present context because it is precisely and explicitly an attack on common sense as this relates to science. It is Bachelard's hypothesis that a number of conceptual and observational habits have to be broken before objective knowledge can be arrived at. At least some of these 'epistemological obstacles' are ingrained deeply in common sense. It is, for instance, vital to overcome 'first experience' which impedes – indeed, altogether prevents – the formation of an appropriate critical spirit. Thus, he writes:

> First experience, or to be more exact, the initial observation is always a first obstacle to scientific culture. This initial observation presents a wealth of images; it is picturesque, concrete, natural and easy. It has only to be described and marvelled at. Then one believes that one has understood. We begin our inquiry by characterising this obstacle and showing that there is a rupture rather than a continuity between observation and experimentation.[8]

Other obstacles mentioned include hasty and facile generalisations[9] and the metaphorical forms that these adopt.[10] Thus we are told that:

> the scientific mind must constantly struggle against images, analogies and metaphors.[11]

Bachelard's view, then, is that science can only develop in direct *opposition* to common sense, and his advice is explicitly directed at those who are entrusted with the education of children.

However, if the tenets of impartiality and symmetry are adhered to and the network theory of knowledge is accepted as realistic, then Bachelard's interpretation of the significance of eighteenth-century scientific change must be roundly rejected. But so too must his understanding of common sense. The latter is conceptually or methodologically identical to scientific reasoning. It is 'picturesque, concrete, natural and easy' only from a certain standpoint, that of one who has become committed to a set of interests that differs from those of the person whose knowledge is being so criticised. It is natural that one often finds the knowledge of other social groups inadequate but as we have argued both here and in the last chapter, there is no good reason for supposing that this results from 'primitive' cognitive habits.

---

126 Like scientists, children and lay-adults operate in terms of networks. Though the *content* of these networks differs, overall they exhibit the same properties – the selection of similarity, difference, association and the rest. There is, in short, no 'epistemological break' between common sense and science. Impartial and symmetrical analysis of the two is appropriate.

127 Common sense networks dictate their extension no more than do scientific networks. Events are susceptible to classification in more than one way, and where interests are divergent, negotiations about the 'proper' extension of a term may occur as actors seek applications that best accord with their own interests.

---

20 The Social Structure of Ideology

We concluded the last chapter by noting that there is a difference between the prescriptive concerns of many philosophers and the more descriptive and explanatory concerns that underlie the network theory of knowledge. Unfortunately a concern with global prescription that breaches the requirements of impartiality, symmetry, causality and indeed reflexivity is built deeply into many areas of social science. Thus there are many attempts to explain the generation of true knowledge in ways that are different in kind from that which is false. One such area is the analysis of what is called ideology. In fact, however, work on ideology also contains much that is consistent with the requirements of impartiality and symmetry, and is posed in terms of an idiom of social interest that sits comfortably with the network theory. Accordingly, it is important to tease the impartial and the symmetrical from the partial and the asymmetrical and examine the consequences for a theory of knowledge of doing without the notion of ideology at all. We start with the writing of Marx in which, as has often been noted, the concept of ideology achieves its first approximately modern statement.[1]

MARX AND IDEOLOGY

As is well known, Marx offered a detailed theory of the class-nature of capitalist society. This takes the form of a materialist *theory of interests*. Capitalism and its crises cannot be understood until it is seen that two great classes – the bourgeoisie and the proletariat – are locked together in a contradictory unity. The bourgeoisie, defined by its ownership of the means of production, is forced by the nature of its position to extract surplus value from the working-class. Conversely, the working-class which is defined by its lack of ownership of the means of production, is obliged to sell its labour-power at a rate defined in the labour market. With this labour-power (and other means of production) the capitalist produces goods whose exchange value is greater than the exchange value of its component parts – a difference that is explained by the fact that the amount paid for labour-power is smaller than the value of the work done. It follows, then, on this theory of surplus value, that the economic interests of the two great classes are diametrically opposed. It also follows that capitalism contains within itself certain contradictions – between capital and labour on the one hand and between the class relations and productive capacity on the other. The latter arises because various aspects of the class organisation of production – for instance the macro-economic failure to find demand for the goods produced – impede the development of technically efficient production.

If Marx starts, analytically, with an interest model, he quickly moves to an explanation of the consciousness of people in society. His argument, though complicated in detail, is quite simple in outline. By and large people in capitalist societies do not appreciate the true class-nature of their society. They adhere, instead, to a variety of beliefs, many of which have the ideological consequence of concealing the truth about class relations, class contradictions, and their true material interests. The idea that such 'ideology' is false is built deep into Marx's writings.[2] Its falsity is not, however, arbitrary. It is very much a function of social structure and of practice.[3] Neither is it, as the authors sometimes seem to suggest in their more enthusiastic moments of polemic, entirely dream-like in its fantasy. This is because it relates to and helps to *constitute* the appearance of society, that is, it contributes to the maintenance of class society by defining and ordering the relations of production in a way that conceals their contradictory and class-defined nature. The worker may carry on, for instance, in part because he or she is convinced of the rectitude of the system, while the owner of capital genuinely believes that fair profits are being made rather than exploitative surplus value extracted.

Ideology is thus practical in nature, not simply distorted. The conception of practicable and workable, but this time presumptively true, social knowledge appears in the course of discussion of revolutionary practice. Here the argument is that when the material conditions of production sufficiently advance then the conditions will develop in which a revolutionary class, and hence a revolutionary (non-ideological), consciousness can emerge.[4] Everything depends, however, on *practice* which emphatically involves interaction and labour in the real material world, not upon abstract conceptual critiques.

If ideology is distortion engendered by class-practice, then it is also an *interested* distortion: it serves the interests of the bourgeoisie rather than the proletariat, for it is the former that exploits the latter, not *vice versa*. In *The German Ideology* Marx and Engels make a number of suggestions about how ideology operates to serve these interests: it depicts bourgeois interests as being identical to those of the entire society: it represents itself as rational and universally valid[5] – a line of argument that is developed by Marx at some length in *Capital* where he talks of the interested and socially contexted nature of classical economic analysis which solved some, but only some, of the problems of interest to Marx. Other tricks include mystifying ideology and detaching it from its orgins.[6] These stratagems should not, however, be taken to mean that ideology is a deliberate and premeditated lie. Though occasional aspects of ideology may have been artificially and knowingly created to deceive, it is, as it were, much more ingrained, much more related to practice, than this would suggest: the capitalist is simply incapable of penetrating appearances in order to understand the essence of the society that has created him.[7]

Marx makes considerable play of this distinction between what is on the surface and inessential, and what lies below the surface and is important:

> . . . in respect to the phenomenal form 'value and price of labour', or 'wages', as contrasted with the essential relation manifested therein, *viz.*, the value and price of labour-power, the same difference holds that holds in respect to all phenomena and their hidden substratum. The former appear directly and spontaneously as current modes of thought; the latter must first be discovered by science. Classical Political Economy nearly touches the true relation of things, without, however, consciously formulating it. This it cannot so long as it sticks in its bourgeois skin.[8]

This language is somewhat reminiscent of that of Lévy Bruhl which we discussed at the start of Chapter 18. Here we have 'phenomenal forms' which appear 'directly and spontaneously'. There there were 'observed images'. Here we have 'essential relations' and there we had 'abstraction (and) logical formu- lation'. Even more is it reminiscent of Bachelard's distinction between 'initial observation' and 'scientific culture'. Of course Marx is not to be blamed for sounding like either Lévy Bruhl or Bachelard – he wrote *Capital* long before either of them set pen to paper. Neither should the language that he uses conceal the importance of his critique of political economy. Furthermore he offers the outline of a viable theory as to why classical political economy could not become 'scientific' – to have done so would have been to reveal the essentially contradictory and ultimately the antagonistic nature of capitalist society. Nevertheless the scientistic and evaluative language should warn us that something is not quite right. Specifically it should suggest that Marx is having recourse to a correspondence theory of knowledge and using this to erect a distinction between science (which gets to the essence) and ideology (which preoccupies itself with appearances).

Marx's interest theory of knowledge with its pragmatism thus co-exists uneasily with a correspondence theory of truth. The unease arises from the fact that interests are *directly* used to explain bourgeois knowledge: the bourgeois and his ideologist will adopt a practicable version of what serves their interests. Imputed interests thus do a direct explanatory job with respect to bourgeois beliefs.[9] Objective interests are *not*, however, directly used to explain the (similarly) ideological knowledge of the proletariat. This is because the structural interests of the latter are held to be at variance with that ideology – indeed that ideology has the prime function of masking those interests. So far, as the generation of knowledge is concerned, these 'objective' interests of the proletariat have little role to play until the latter realise their nature, that is, until they become a class for themselves. In the meanwhile a different kind of interest – a practical concern to manage appearances – is of more importance.

In the last analysis, then, the prescriptive features of Marx's theory of knowledge – his concern with global social control – tend to reduce its general analytical power. In what is, admit- tedly, a much more sophisticated and interesting version, we are pulled back in the direction of the 'asymmetrical' explanatory stance that underlies all correspondence theories of the generation of knowledge. Bourgeois knowledge is false, and interested. Revolutionary proletarian knowledge is true, and interested. The reasons given for the true/false distinction, apart from a scientistic rhetoric, have to do with the claim that the bourgeoisie cannot face the essence because to do so is not in its interest, whereas the proletariat, for precisely the same reason, can. The political and normative reasons for wishing to make such a distinction are obvious, but analytically they are not. The 'essence' has been very elusive, even to the proletariat. The concept of objective working-class interests does little if any explanatory work in understanding why it is that the proletariat behaves in the way that it does. Analytically such an imputation is redundant if the aim is to create an impartial, symmetrical and causal theory of the existential generation of knowledge, rather than the pursuit of a global interest in social control.

Yet Marx was far too great a thinker to let prescription blind him to the importance of general analysis. There are two theories of knowledge in his writing. The prescriptive co-exists with a much more interesting one about the generation of all knowledge (whether science or ideology). This stresses their common origins in the practice of classes as they pursue and articulate their goals in a social structure. It also offers decisive insights about the methods available to social groups as they attempt to manipulate one another. For political reasons, however, the prescriptive theory of ideology has often come to the fore with theories about the failure of the working-class to produce revolutionary knowledge – theories that are posed, for instance, in terms such as 'false consciousness'. There has, however, been another stream of inquiry committed to the tenets of impartiality and symmetry, that has played down prescriptive asymmetries in order to advance the task of a general understanding of the existential determinants of belief. The task has not been easy – few authors have completely succeeded in disentangling the partial from the impartial in the interests of generality. With this thought in mind we turn to the writing of Mannheim.

MANNHEIM AND THE SOCIOLOGY OF KNOWLEDGE

Karl Mannheim is often held to have 'generalised' Marx's insight about the interested and distorted nature of ideology. The basis of such a generalisation is, as Mannheim observed,[10] that once *one* system of thought is revealed as being structured by the social context in which it occurs, there is little to stand in the way of turning this insight around and applying it to *all* systems of thought. Mannheim's work in the sociology of knowledge is largely concerned with the exploration of this theme.

Here again the notion of social interest is crucial. Individuals and groups are seen as developing and deploying systems of belief under the auspices of interests. Individuals generate 'particular ideologies' which more or less deliberately disguise reality. These disguises are perpetrated because true recognition of reality would not be in the interests of the individual concerned. More fundamental, however, are 'total ideologies' – the structure or composition of the 'mind' of an age or a social group.[11] Total ideology refers to something more like a *Weltanschauung*, and its analysis involves questioning the total world outlook and relating it in appropriate ways to social structural determinants, and in particular to the interests of 'carrier' groups which may or may not be social classes in the sense defined by Marx.

Mannheim puts forward a number of ways of understanding this relationship. Thus in his essay on conservative thought[12] he talks of the 'basic intentions' of carrier groups, and the way in which these are articulated into styles of thought in the course of struggles and conflicts. He refers, for instance, to the conservative (German) reaction to (French) enlightenment thought. The latter, which was 'carried' by the bourgeoisie, involved the development of rationalism to as full an extent as possible: it stressed the importance and ubiquity of general laws and causes, opposed qualitative and analogical thought and assumed truth to have a universal validity. It found its expression in a number of intellectual areas, but especially in bourgeois economics where, very obviously, and in a manner pungently analysed by Marx, it served the interests of the owners of capital. Mannheim argues, however, that this style of thought (like any other) suppressed certain aspects of reality – in particular it failed to articulate the experience of social classes that were outside or played little part in the extension of capitalism – in Germany, the peasantry, the *petit bourgeoisie* and the nobility. At the point when a social reaction against the bourgeoisie became possible (essentially with the end of the Napoleonic era in Europe) an intellectual counter-movement to rationalistic 'natural law' style arose. This involved

the articulation of a romantic holistic and conservative conception of politics and the state which served the interests of non-
bourgeois groups in a variety of ways. With this conservative
political thought was born a 'conservative' style of thought that
articulated those features of experience suppressed by rational
'natural-law' thought, and in particular the concrete, the qualitative, the holistic and the historically specific.

Ideologies are thus, for Mannheim, tools that articulate, reflect
and advance the interests of carrier groups. They are, however,
more than this for they fail (as in Marx's writing) to accord with
the reality of social life. Consider, for instance, the distinction
between ideologies and utopias:

> The concept 'ideology' reflects the . . . discovery . . . that
> ruling groups can in their thinking become so intensively
> interest-bound to a situation that they are simply no longer able
> to see certain facts which would undermine their sense of
> domination. There is implicit in the word 'ideology' the insight
> that in certain situations the collective unconscious of certain
> groups obscures the real condition of society both to itself and
> to others and thereby stabilises it.[13]

Utopian thinking is the mirror of this. It is thinking that sees only
those aspects of reality that tend to undermine it and is 'not at all
concerned with what really exists'.[14] Between ideologies on the
one hand and utopias on the other, there are ideas that
correspond to the reality of social life and that are 'situationally
congruous'.[15] These, however, are relatively rare, for it is
Mannheim's view that:

> only a state of mind that has been sociologically fully clarified
> operates with situationally congruous ideas and motives.[16]

What does it mean to be 'sociologically fully clarified'? The
controversial answer to this question again involves a conception
of social interest: if the great classes of society are so strongly
bound by interest that their conception of reality is distorted, then
it must be those groups – particularly intellectuals – that have the
possibility of removing themselves to some extent from class
interests that stand the greatest chance of minimising distortion.
These will be groups that have understood that all social

knowledge is situationally determined, their own included. They will, accordingly, have understood that knowledge is dynamic, not static. They will have given up any simple intention of denouncing views with which they disagree (for not to do so would involve making their own views which are also situationally determined appear absolute). On the other hand they will avoid the temptations of relativism which, in Mannheim's view, is a theory of knowledge that fails to take account of the fact that belief is socially determined. Instead they will adopt a 'relationist' position – one which stresses the links between knowledge and social structure and attempts an analysis of the different socially contexted truths available. By transcending and assimilating those particular points of view in the light of a knowledge of their social derivation this relational view offers an optimum account of reality.[17] This will be one that is unfragmented, provisionally valid (that is, situationally congruous) but given that social structure changes over time, also dynamic.

As with Marx, there are therefore two strands to Mannheim's analysis of ideology in uneasy co-existence – the partial and prescriptive on the one hand, and the impartial and the descriptive on the other. Indeed, it would not be unfair to claim that much of his work, and in particular that described above with respect to the role of the relational sociologist of knowledge, is precisely Mannheim's attempt to specify the relationship between them. He starts impartially and symmetrically by noting that all knowledge is situationally determined. As we have seen, the concept of social interest plays an important part in making the link between belief and social context. He then generalises and comes to terms with the suggestion that *all* knowledge is socially relative.[18] Having so generalised, however, asymmetry re-enters with prescription. This is because the sociologist is now able to determine the 'congruity' of a given system of ideas. Non-evaluation thus leads back to judgement and prescription, albeit of a sociologically informed, revisable and contexted form.

What is *added* to the analysis by such a judgement? Analytically it is very difficult to see any positive answer to this question. This is because Mannheim uses a notion of political practice. He assumes that ideologies are developed by groups to serve their interests in the course of political struggles. Though he has much less to say about practice than has Marx, he is at his naturalistic best when talking of such struggles. These analyses offer an impartial and symmetrical account for the causes of belief, one that does the kind of job that is required in a general sociology of knowledge. Suddenly, however, judgements of congruity and incongruity are introduced. These are not based upon the perceptions of those under study about the adequacy of their beliefs. Rather they rest upon the sociologist's (relationally) superior understanding of reality. A pragmatic theory of knowledge is supplemented by one that has the same function as a correspondence theory of knowledge – even though Mannheim goes to great lengths to argue against the notion that *any* social knowledge could permanently correspond to social reality. Thus a normative element appears, but one that contributes nothing to the analysis because the fate of an ideology is dependent not upon the degree of its supposed congruity with reality but rather upon a symmetrical concern with the interests and fate of the 'carrier' group itself.

Why this evaluative element? For Mannheim the answer is political. The role of the sociologist of knowledge is not simply to study the rise and fall of ideologies. It is, in addition, to provide a counterweight to one of the consequences of the discovery that all knowledge is socially contexted. This is the fact that the universal debunking of ideologies leads to loss of certainty,[19] and in turn to a scepticism and relativism that has a caustic and destructive effect upon the body politic. For relationism – a judgement of congruity and incongruity based upon the best available synthesis of world views – will permit the development of a form of political science that will understand the whole of society, not merely different parts, and accordingly permit the pursuit of a scientific politics.[20]

One can understand why Mannheim, writing in the 1930s, should have thought that this was a desirable goal, just as one can understand why Marx, writing in Victorian England, should have regarded the overthrow of capitalism as a desirable necessity. However, such global concerns with social control risk introducing asymmetrical analyses of belief – analyses that reduce the generality of explanation by explaining the good and the bad in different ways. If the aim of social science is a general and parsimonious explanation, then such special pleading – inconsistent as it is with the network theory of knowledge – must be carefully avoided. In fact, Mannheim, like Marx, offers a symmetrical theory of knowledge. The partial judgements of

216 *Social Science and Network Theory*

incongruity are, in large measure, tacked on for political reasons in a manner that does not undermine (though it does obscure) the symmetry of his analysis. Perhaps this is one of the reasons why those writers who remain primarily committed to an interest in social control and legitimation find his writing on ideology inadequate. Thus a recent author, writing of Mannheim, notes:

> . . . every point of view has an ideological character. It is therefore very difficult to envisage what is really specific to the concept of ideology. When the concept is universalized in such a way that it may cover all parties in all epochs, it ends up with very little meaning and loses its critical capability.[21]

This diagnosis is quite correct. The only difference we have with its author, Larrain, is that we do not see this trend as anything to complain about. The real questions for those who are committed to impartial and symmetrical forms of analysis are not how best to breathe political life back into the concept of ideology, but rather whether it is possible or analytically appropriate to retain the term at all.

BARNES AND IDEOLOGICAL DETERMINATION

The answer to the first of these questions is a qualified 'yes'. One writer – Barry Barnes – has recently argued that a notion of 'ideological determination' if not 'ideology' can be retained in a manner that is consistent with the tenets of symmetry and impartiality, while at the same time retaining some of its traditionally pejorative connotations. He makes this argument by relating ideological determination to one of the great interests that lie behind the generation of knowledge – that of rationalis- ation and persuasion:

> Knowledge grows under the impulse of two great interests, an overt interest in prediction, manipulation and control, and a covert interest in rationalisation and persuasion. Our defi- nition of ideological determination has essentially identified it as the mode of operation of this second great interest.[22]

Knowledge is thus a tool or resource that may do two kinds of tasks – tasks that in most empirical cases it probably combines at least to some degree.[23] An interest in rationalisation and persuasion is usually, however, concealed because if it is overt it will almost certainly fail. This can be easily seen from several of the examples that we discussed in earlier chapters. Thus we followed Harwood in suggesting that much knowledge about the relationship between race and intelligence is best understood as being in part directed by political interests. Why do not political protagonists merely state that they are for or against racial equality? Why do they latch on to the statement of hereditarians and environmentalists with such gusto? The answer is that the provision of an apparently factual case adds credibility and rhetorical weight to the political position concerned. This knowledge, then, is directed and utilised by a *concealed* political interest. Were the latter to declare itself and say 'We are using this knowledge to influence your political views' its credibility as rhetoric would be undermined. This is, of course, precisely one of the tactics used by critics – if, as Mannheim noted, knowledge can be shown to be related to the interests of a social group it becomes devalued.

Yet even if knowledge is ideologically determined it does not necessarily follow that it is false. Though it may lose credibility, it may also, suggests Barnes, turn out to be workable in terms of an overt interest in prediction and control. The case of phrenology (discussed in Chapter 13) illustrates this well. Knowledge about frontal sinuses was advanced as a result of the debate, despite its ideological determination. It is for this reason that Barnes prefers to avoid the term 'ideology' and talk instead of 'ideological determination'. In this way his position is consistent with the principles of impartiality and symmetry, for he does not distinguish between good and bad knowledge and then seek to explain these in terms of different types of causes. Rather he depicts all knowledge as being directed by the two great interests mentioned above. It is true that he regards prediction and control as a legitimate interest and covert rationalisation as illegitimate. This, however, does not vitiate the symmetry of the explanation for two reasons. First, people themselves operate in terms of such a distinction; they, too, look upon rationalisation as illegitimate and allocate lower credibility to its products than they do to those of overt prediction and control. Second, nothing is being said

either about the truth of the knowledge that is ideologically
determined or about the rationality of those who have developed
it. These are seen as working rationally to advance an interest in
legitimation both with respect to the *content* of their knowledge
and to the fact that they try to conceal that interest. Unlike Marx
or Mannheim, then, Barnes does not use reality as a litmus paper
to discriminate knowledge into two classes. His explanation is
symmetrical and in full accord with the network theory of
knowledge. It is materialistic: knowledge is seen as a tool and is
thus analysed as a resource which people use and develop in the
pursuit of the interests that we have discussed.

Barnes' account of the imputation of interests warrants closer
attention. Unlike, say, Marx, he does not have a pre-given macro-
social theory about their nature and distribution. Also, given the
pragmatism of his theory of knowledge, he rejects the suggestion
that there can be anything about the intrinsic features of a body of
knowledge that will reveal the interests that produced it. The job
of connecting knowledge to interest is thus complex[24] but the
most promising present way of making the connection is to use
verstehen. We may place ourselves, he says, imaginatively in the
position of the person expressing beliefs and assess the plausibility
of any rationalising account advanced for holding those beliefs.
This possibility, he suggests, is particularly available to us where
such an account is presented as being implied by some well-
institutionalised and routinised body of knowledge, as is often
found in the natural sciences. To take an absurd example which
nevertheless illustrates the general principle, anyone who claimed
that 2 plus 2 equals 5 and went on to argue that this was implied
by current arithmetical knowledge could (most probably) be
demonstrated to be deviating from normal arithmetical practice.
It could then be presumed that they were operating on the basis of
interests that diverged in some concealed way from those lying
behind the institution of modern arithmetic. Barnes' method of
imputation is thus low-level, empirical, indeed experimental,
albeit, as he himself notes, beset by a variety of technical problems
that are particularly daunting if there is no background of
institutionalised normal practice against which to measure the
belief in question.

We have no doubt that *verstehen* is, indeed, an appropriate
technique for the imputation of interest. Indeed, it can be both
rigorous and scientific and any suggestion that it is untestable,

wishy-washy or unwarrantably subjective should be resisted.[25] Our doubts relate rather to the status allocated to 'normal practice' in Barnes' account. It is obvious that there are institutionalised practices and beliefs; many examples have been discussed in earlier chapters. It is also obvious that they must be directed by interests of one kind or another. What is less obvious, however, is that they can be used as a background *against which* to measure concealed social interests. This is because even normal scientific practice embodies concealed interests in social legitimation of one kind or another. The biochemists that we discussed in Chapter 17 had a legitimating interest in maintaining the viability of their method in the face of results that could be read as suggesting its unreliability. They accordingly produced rationalisations for discarding large quantities of data and publishing only certain 'findings'. Furthermore, this process of selection was not reported in the finished paper that was sent to the journals. There was an element of concealment here. This was not badly motivated. Nor was it unusual. Thus, our comments should not be read as a complaint about their decisions. It is widely reported in the sociology of science literature that there is a disjunction between the public and private faces of science. Indeed, when the private face is described, the reaction is often one of disillusionment. Lay persons report that if science is like that, then it must be shoddy and professionals note that *their* part of science does not display such a concern with career, professional advancement and cutting corners. In other words, it appears that when 'what really goes on' in science is described, it loses credibility in exactly the way described by Barnes when concealed interests in social legitimation are revealed as standing behind a body of knowledge.

The idea that there are 'local', 'professional' or 'cognitive' interests is one that is found in much recent work in the sociology of science. Andrew Pickering, for instance, in a study of modern high energy physics, writes that:

> One can speak of the group or groups having expertise relevant to the articulation of some exemplar as having an 'investment' in that expertise, and, as a corollary, as having an 'interest' in the deployment of their expertise in the articulation of the exemplar. An 'interest', then, is a particular constructive cognitive orientation towards a field of discourse.[26]

Indeed there is, by now, quite a body of work precisely concerned with exploring the economic metaphor that lies behind such notions as scientific 'investment'.[27] Surely, then, a further move has to be made here. It is not, as Barnes argues, that some fields of inquiry including parts of differentiated natural science may become 'almost entirely dissociated from functions of legitimation and persuasion'.[28] It is rather that an interest in legitimation and persuasion may, in some cases, line up with an interest in prediction and control. There is then no tension between these interests because the social interests of those concerned in legitimating and persuading coincide with, are bound up with, indeed are constituted by an interest in the effective capacity to predict and control.

If this is the case, then all knowledge is ideologically determined in the sense defined by Barnes and it is indeed the case that the term loses its specificity. The latter can, perhaps, be restored if a distinction is made between knowledge produced under the auspices of a *local* interest in persuasion and legitimation, and that produced by a *global* interest therein. Indeed, looking at the examples cited by Barnes, it does seem to be this distinction that he has in mind, and this would certainly make sense of the empirical cases we have mentioned in earlier chapters. Thus a *local* interest in social legitimation and persuasion would account for the case of the biochemists. Their knowledge does not, at least on the face of it, reflect an interest in social control and rationalisation that extends beyond their own position in a local social structure. It can be characterised as an attempt to manage their way through a small part of that social structure – an attempt that involves addressing knowledge claims at a highly differentiated and probably small audience. A *global* interest would be exemplified by, say, the case of phrenology. In this case knowledge was being used to do 'social work' – to persuade audiences on a grand scale that this or that version of social structure is preferable. And, insofar as that knowledge functions in relation to the vital interests of much wider audiences, the revelation that there is a concealed interest in broader social rationalisation is accordingly more harmful to the standing of that knowledge and its capacity to operate on or advance those interests.

This, then, is an option that can be followed if it is desired to preserve the notion of ideological determination. Our view, however, is that the game is scarcely worth the candle. An impartial and symmetrical theory – one that notes that an interest in prediction and control *invariably* co-exists with an interest in social control, persuasion and legitimation – seems quite adequate if the aim is the more parsimonious explanation of the growth of knowledge. It is this theory – a theory drawn indeed, from Barnes' own writing – that has informed our understanding of what it is that lies behind and directs the growth of knowledge. Imputations of ideological determination contribute little to this understanding.[29] Indeed, they tend to conceal its straightforward impartiality.[30]

---

128 Marx offers a theory of ideology that rests in part upon a correspondence theory of knowledge, but also contains a strong pragmatic element.

129 The correspondence theory relates to certain basic and purportedly real class-interests. The pragmatic element assumes that knowledge is a function of practice in a social structure.

130 In so far as Marx explains the beliefs of groups in his theory of ideology, the explanation rests on the latter pragmatic theory and is accordingly in conformity with the tenets of impartiality and symmetry.

131 Mannheim's theory is similar to that of Marx, having elements of both a correspondence and a pragmatic theory of knowledge. The latter predominates. However, the distinction between ideology and 'situationally congruous' knowledge rests upon a modified correspondence theory of knowledge and thus breaches the tenets of impartiality and symmetry. Attributions of 'ideology' tend to become devoid of meaning in the pragmatic theory.

132 Barnes' theory – that of knowledge as a tool directed by two great interests, one an overt interest in prediction and control and the other a concealed interest in social legitimation – does not breach the tenets of impartiality and symmetry and is pragmatic in nature.

133 However, all knowledge is directed in part by a concealed interest in social control, though this may coincide with an overt interest in prediction and control. Thus, to argue (as does Barnes) that certain knowledge – that directed by at least the former interest – is ideologically determined is unsatisfactory.

134 To sustain an attribution of ideological determination it would be necessary to distinguish between *local* and *global* concerns with social control, and identify ideological determination with the latter.

135 There seems to be little reason for making this distinction. It would, accordingly, be best to assume that terms such as 'ideology' and 'ideological determination' have no place in a symmetrical theory of knowledge.

21 The 'Problem' of Relativism

In the last three chapters we have hammered home the implications of one message in three different contexts. The message is that theories of social science action or knowledge that distinguish between 'good' or 'right' on the one hand and 'bad' or 'wrong' on the other, and which then proceed to explain these in different ways, are incompatible with the network theory of knowledge. The latter suggests that *all* knowledge is generated as a result of the same types of factors. It accordingly adopts the principles of impartiality, symmetry, causality and reflexivity in an attempt to formulate the most general possible theory for the causes of knowledge. Such an approach to analysis has, however, strong relativistic implications. Relativism is a doctrine which says that what passes as true or rational knowledge is always a function of the circumstances in which it is produced. It goes on to say that there can, accordingly, be no final or context-free criteria to show that one belief system is preferable to another – that all such criteria are themselves context-dependent.[1]

Most philosophers find relativism an unacceptable doctrine and many have tried hard to show that it is fundamentally flawed. They would, for instance, find the way in which we have used the terms 'belief' and 'knowledge' interchangeably to be evidence of our confusion. This is because they tend to distinguish between 'mere belief' – what people happen to hold to be true – and 'knowledge' which can be justified in what they take to be a context- or relatively context-free manner. The relativism of the network theory of knowledge undermines this distinction. If the theory is correct, then all knowledge is a function of circumstances – an emergent consequence of the interaction of the natural world and social cues. In this chapter we attend briefly to the philosophical arguments against relativism and by suggesting their inadequacy, further bolster our case for impartial and symmetrical analysis.

The arguments advanced against relativism fall into three major groups.[2] First, it is argued that belief systems do indeed have something in common – they share a basic rationality. But if this is the case then it becomes possible to judge between beliefs by considering how far they embody that rationality. In particular, it becomes possible to measure how far social or psychological distortion has undermined the operation of that rationality. In this view of knowledge, then, that which is rational requires no further explanation for in the absence of undermining forces rational beliefs will naturally arise. The social sciences (and in particular psychology and sociology) have a role in explaining belief only in so far as it is irrational. A psychology or sociology of error but not of truth is possible.[3]

What is this common core of rationality? Different writers locate it in different places. Some argue that certain logical operations (for instance negation and contradiction) are necessarily to be found in all languages: that if this were not the case we would not be able to recognise other languages as languages at all. It is simultaneously easy and difficult to see what is intended here. On the one hand, it is easy to see that there may, indeed, be logical operations in common to all languages (though we should also remind ourselves that *our* understanding of what we have in common is, if the relativist view is adopted, both provisional and revisable). On the other hand, it is difficult to see what consequences this has for the relativistic network theory of knowledge. If all languages share it, then this provides no basis for distinguishing, in an evaluative way, between them. They simply use it in different ways.[4] Those who want to discriminate between our rational talk and the irrational practices of others obviously cannot use what all languages have in common to make that distinction.

Another possible source of shared rationality lies in the fact that everyone lives in the same natural world. Thus, it is argued that all languages must share certain empirical referents and it is this common pool of shared empirical categories that permits the communication which in turn makes comparative evaluation of belief systems possible. However, in the light of network theory this argument carries little weight. There is, as we argued at length in the first part of this text, no natural and self-evident way of classifying phenomena in the natural world. All classification is a function of the interaction between 'lumps' in the environmental and social cues. As we showed for the case of Euler's theorem of polyhedra, even amongst those who sincerely believe that they are in complete agreement about the uses of terms, the possibility for future disagreement is always present. Neither is it possible to use natural science as a benchmark for what is to be known about the natural world, for this too rests upon a shifting classificatory basis. Arguments against relativism that rest (in however attenuated a form) upon the possibility of a neutral observation language have to be rejected.

The second type of argument against relativism suggests that it is self-refuting and runs like this: if, as the relativist argues, there is no way of demonstrating the superiority of one system of knowledge over another, then there is, of course, no way of demonstrating the superiority of relativism over non-relativistic theories of knowledge. But relativism claims non-relativistic theories of knowledge to be completely wrong. Relativism is thus internally inconsistent, indeed self-defeating.

In reply, the relativist notes that the first part of this claim is correct. It cannot, indeed, demonstrate its absolute superiority. No knowledge can, as we have seen, force itself upon anyone in the abstract, nor oblige him or her to act in any given way. Relativism is, of course, no exception to this rule.[5] This does not, however, mean that it is self-defeating. The relativist's admission that he cannot compel conformity with his relativism is simply a realistic description of the nature of knowledge. Indeed, the word 'admission' in the above sentence is conceding too much. It is no 'admission' to depict the status of knowledge accurately and workably for practical purposes, and, of course, the conclusion that relativism is self-defeating does not follow from this 'admission' in any case. There is nothing self-defeating about the claim that knowledge cannot compel a conclusion. This is simply a depiction of how things appear to be – a depiction consistent with network theory and the principle of symmetry this time applied reflexively. It is the other 'absolutist' theories which fail to understand the pragmatic nature of knowledge. They falsely claim their capacity to demonstrate absolute superiority. The relativist knows that no such demonstration is possible, though he also knows that in a given social context people may find his (or any other argument) persuasive. There is nothing self-defeating about this.

A third type of argument arises from what is seen as the lack of standards of relativism – the idea that it advocates, either directly or by implication, the view that one way of looking at things is as good as any other and, correspondingly, that it undermines quality, rigour and the pursuit of truth by proper means, in favour of undisciplined and uncorroborated self-expression. Or, alternatively, that since belief is a function of social or psychological causes, this opens the way for 'mob-rule' – the social dictation of what passes as truth – rather than attention to the facts.

The basic point to be made about the claimed lack of standards fostered by relativism is that network theory is not a *prescriptive* theory at all. It does not tell people to have no standards. Rather it *describes* what appear to be certain basic features of knowledge. One of these features is that the standards which people adopt appear to be context-dependent, not general. What they take to be an adequate explanation thus depends upon their problems, interests, training and their social location in general. It is easily observed, in other words, that the standards of argument vary between contexts. This kind of descriptive relativism does not, therefore, advocate anarchy or hedonism. It says, on the contrary, that there are standards, but that these are local and thus variable between contexts.

The same goes for the claim that relativism advocates 'mob rule' even if only implicitly. Again, the argument is that there are *local* standards – that nature and convention *together* structure networks. Accordingly, the 'mob rule' view is not only an illegitimate argument against relativism from consequences. It also misunderstands the nature of knowledge and network theory by supposing that the effect of social or psychological influence on knowledge will necessarily be to undermine an acceptable description of the natural world.

We therefore suggest that none of the arguments advanced with such energy against relativism – those from translatability, self-refutation, 'mob rule' or hedonism – should be taken as showing the incoherence or impossibility of a symmetrical and hence relativistic analysis of the social world. Perhaps the most interesting of these arguments is that from self-refutation. This is because it *presupposes* that which it sets out to demonstrate, namely the incompatibility between the social determination of knowledge on the one hand, and its rationality on the other. This presupposition suggests that there is an 'incommensurability' between the positions of the relativist on the one hand and the rationalist on the other; in other words, that rationalist arguments do not really engage with relativism. Correspondingly, however, it is also the case that relativism cannot demonstrate that rationalism is wrong. It cannot be exhaustively demonstrated that knowledge is not teleologically drawn to rational or empirical truth, that some kinds of knowledge are not closer to the truth than others.[6] This in turn suggests, finally, that the choice between the two is metaphysical. If one is predisposed to make absolute judgements about the superiority of one's own beliefs, then one will be predisposed to rationalism. If, on the other hand, one is prepared to concede that one's views cannot be ultimately validated and accordingly is willing to accept a certain level of cognitive uncertainty, then one may be prepared to entertain a version of relativism. The advantage of so doing, as we have sought to show throughout this book, is that symmetrical analysis of the 'true' and the 'false' becomes possible, with a corresponding possibility of explanatory parsimony.

It comes as no surprise to discover that many philosophers display a professional interest in broad social control and legitimation rather than, or as well as, an interest in natural accounting, prediction and control. To put it simply, if prescription were removed, it is not immediately apparent what role epistemologists would have left to play. It is further unsurprising, however, that such writers display a tendency to conceal their interest in legitimation behind accounts that present themselves as naturalistic. The progress of Popperian philosophy of science displays this well. What starts as an undisguised piece of philosophical moralising in *The Logic of Scientific Discovery*[7] is gradually concealed behind an apparatus of naturalistic description that includes such platonic touchstones as the 'third world'.[8] Nowhere is this naturalistic base more fully developed than in the writings of Imre Lakatos, whose moral judgements are dressed up in an elaborate terminology of 'progressive' and 'degenerating' problem-shifts.[9] Interestingly, Lakatos finds himself in a bind. The naturalistic basis of his moralising displays a dangerous tendency to undermine the latter altogether. Gone are the clear injunctions about scientific procedure that originally flowed so easily from the pen of Popper. In their place complex historical judgements about programmes of research are required — judgements that may only be possible long after the event and with the benefit of hindsight. The element of moralising is still there – it is, in Lakatos's view, vital to distinguish the 'progressive' from that which is 'degenerating'. But its *application* is much obscured and more difficult – both of these consequences result from the fact that Lakatos has felt compelled to take the history of science seriously in order to show that the 'best' science actually advances in the prescribed way. There are obvious parallels between this and the fate of the concept of ideology – a concept that retains its normative component only with difficulty when it is applied in the context of a serious concern with the impartial study of the existential determinants of all forms of belief.

Why are philosophers so concerned to moralise? Why are they so willing to demarcate in terms of intellectual criteria? And why do they so roundly reject the relativism of the network theory? We have already hinted at an answer. Their professional interests lead them to do so and the reason is this: if the network theory of knowledge is realistic, then such differences as there are between belief-systems must be located not in rules of intellectual hygiene but rather in the social location of the believers. Obviously, strictly conceptual rules cannot discriminate between different systems of knowledge if the real difference is located in social interests. If this is indeed the case, then it is to social science that we shall have to turn to understand such differences as there may be. It is small wonder, then, that so much philosophy preaches the autonomy of good knowledge from common sense and social interests. Once that autonomy is lost it will be difficult to define a prescriptive role for epistemology – a condition which must come perilously close to having no role at all.[10]

---

136 The network theory has relativistic implications because it notes that the success of argument and conceptions of what constitutes the truth can only be understood if the local circumstances of the production of knowledge are considered. There are, in other words, no general criteria for determining the truth or superiority of any network.

137 Arguments against relativism from translation are not persuasive. Those that are based on claims about the universal nature of certain logical operations either fail to discriminate between languages or depend upon particular contextual judgements of the nature of these operations. Those that work from a version, however disguised, of the concept of a neutral observation language are inconsistent with the conception of observation found in network theory.

138 The network theory is not relativistically self-defeating because it does not make final claims about its own correspondence with reality.

139 The network theory does not suggest that knowledge is distorted by the operation of psychological or social influences. It notes, instead, that such influences direct the way in which empirically adequate networks are constructed.

140 Network theory, in its relativism, does not deny or undermine intellectual standards. It simply notes that standards are locally generated.

141 Nevertheless, 'rationalism' and relativism are incommensurable. Just as rationalism does not show that relativism is essentially flawed, so relativism cannot demonstrate that rationalism is wrong.

22 The Problem of *Verstehen*

In the last four chapters we have argued that explanation of the social should be impartial and symmetrical – that an approach should be adopted which explains the 'good' and the 'bad' in the same way. Advocacy of non-prescriptive and relativistic approaches to social analysis has, however, always been common in so called '*verstehende* sociology' – that part of the discipline that takes people's meanings seriously. We touched upon the reason for this in our discussion of Lévy Bruhl's work: taking people's meanings seriously can be interpreted as trying to display the internal rationality of their actions and beliefs, no matter how strange these may appear to be at first sight.

It will be obvious that such a '*verstehende*' approach cannot be far distant from the symmetrical network theory mode of explanation that we have advocated. In this chapter we address the relationship between the two and, using network theory, reconsider some of the standard problems of *verstehende* sociology. In particular, in what follows, we consider the importance of people's meanings for explanation in social science, the way in which these meanings are learned and finally, whether there is anything about '*verstehen*' and meanings that divides social-science explanation irrevocably from that of the natural sciences.

We choose to broach these issues by attacking on a narrow front, and looking at an influential little book by Peter Winch called *The Idea of a Social Science*.[1] This book is a manifesto for a certain kind of *verstehende* sociology. It sets itself apart from those social scientists – Durkheim is the most prominent classic example – who hold that meanings and beliefs are of minimal importance or a positive distraction to scientific social science.[2] But it also takes issue with writers such as Max Weber who tried, in some sense, to bridge the distinction between natural and social science by arguing that social analysis could and should be adequate at the levels of both meaning and cause.[3] Causes, according to Winch, are illegitimate explanatory tools in social science. The virtue, then, of taking issue with Winch's version of social science is that it allows us to situate ourselves with respect to a large body of literature concerning the scientificity of social science and the special problems attached to meaning.

We start by outlining three aspects of Winch's thesis,[4] a thesis that is based on the essentially Wittgensteinian insight that:

> A man's social relations with his fellows are permeated with his ideas about reality. Indeed, 'permeated' is hardly a strong enough word: social relations are expressions of ideas about reality.[5]

If this is so then, says Winch, the social sciences involve *conceptual analysis*: to understand a society we have to understand its concepts, the way in which they relate together and the way in which they are deployed. In other words, the social sciences are much more closely related to philosophy than they are to natural science, for like philosophy they are concerned with the analysis of *what it makes sense to say* in a given society. It is this kind of conceptual analysis that constitutes *verstehen*, which accordingly has little or nothing to do with individual empathy.[6]

Secondly, it follows that there is a difference in kind between social action and mechanical behaviour. This can be expressed in a number of ways. One way is to note that social action is rule-following in a way that is quite different from the law-following behaviour of physical systems. Causal explanations postulate some kind of mechanical relationship: if a billiard ball is given a certain initial velocity, then by taking into account loss of energy as it, for instance, rebounds from the cushions of the billiard table, it can be predicted that the ball will come to rest at such and such a spot. The ball has no choice in the matter. It cannot breach the laws of mechanics. Social action is not, however, of this sort. Though we often talk of social rules these do not stand in a mechanically causal relationship to subsequent action. There is a gap between the expression of a social rule and the action that it governs. This can be seen in a number of ways. There is, for instance, the possibility of a mistake. The person concerned may break the rule and walk on the grass. There is, as it were, an

element of *choice* that does not exist for the billiard ball.
Furthermore, social rules or reasons have an indisputably *moral*
element. They are used to justify action, make it intelligible, to
supply an acceptable motive. Thus the jealousy and revenge of a
wronged spouse do not automatically lead to murder. They do,
however, provide a possible explanation if this takes place, one
that makes sense even if it does not elicit approval. Accordingly,
the job of the social scientist is to seek out the accepted standards
of behaviour – social norms and rules and the repertoire of
justifications, motives or interpretative resources to which the
members of a society have recourse. Action is explained – though
not mechanically – when it can be linked to this moral repertoire.
It can be further investigated by means of additional conceptual
analysis in which different justifications can be compared in terms
of coherence and plausibility. Social explanation has, in sum,
nothing to do with the attribution of mechanical causes that is
typical of the natural sciences.

His third major point concerns the impossibility of comparative social analysis. He mounts this argument by noting that both
the natural and the social sciences depend upon generalisations,
that is, the capacity to connect like with like. However, while the
natural scientist has only his or her own rules for determining
what is 'like' what, the social scientist must also take into account
the views of the people he or she is studying: the notion of a
'wronged spouse' is something that is culturally specific, as is
(perhaps more obviously for people in Western culture) the
Karam belief that the '*kobtiy*' is not a '*yakt*'. But the social
scientist then encounters an impossible dilemma if comparative
analysis is to be attempted. On the one hand there must be
agreement *within the social science community* about what may
legitimately be seen as 'like' what. On the other hand, what goes
with what is determined by the cultures under study themselves
within their own context of rules and classifications. The danger is
obvious – unlike will be compared with unlike if any comparative
analysis is attempted, since cultures classify differently.

LEARNING ABOUT SOCIAL STRUCTURE

As we have seen, network theory treats human beings as inductive
learning-machines. People are seen as selecting among the many

similarities and differences in their environments on the basis of social cues. In this way networks of classes are established, and objects are treated as 'the same' or 'different'. It will also be recalled that not all those classes have direct empirical referents – that is, not all can be *directly* related to physical 'lumps' in the environment, even though they are all so tied in some way and there are no entirely abstract terms.

An analogous approach is possible for social learning – for the act of *verstehen*. Indeed, though we did not highlight this, some of our earlier examples included the acquisition of social lore. 'Granddad' is not a natural kind any more than are 'cassowaries' or '*kobtiy*'. Certain lumps in the environment are so catalogued and others are not. The child learns inductively what may be treated as 'granddad' and what should not. It learns to attend to certain similarities and differences rather than others.

Now consider the process of building up these classifications. They are, in the first instance, attached to 'lumps' in the environment, but already they form a kind of network. The child cannot use the term 'granddad' in a competent manner without at the same time knowing how to distinguish between 'granddad', 'grandma' and 'other people'. The process of ostension, in other words, involves links not only between class and perceptual environment, but also between different classes. As we have seen for the case of natural kinds, the links between classes develop certain qualities. 'Granddad' is, for instance, seen as going with 'grandma', 'granddad' is seen as the source of 'presents' and so on.

Not all social terms are, however, directly related to obvious 'lumps' in the environment. Just as with natural kinds, empty classes may be generated or (to put this in a slightly different way) theoretical objects may be created. Let us take an example. One of us has a son who is two and a half at the time of writing. He has just been learning about Christmas. That is to say, he has been building upon and extending a set of classes that he was previously able to use with some degree of competence. He knew, for example, the names of a wide variety of animals and was able to identify people and babies both in real life and from pictures. He was then presented with an Advent calendar – one of those nativity scenes with animals and people gathered round the baby Jesus – and pronounced it to be a 'zoo'. Given his prior experience of people and animals this was not an unreasonable induction. It was, however, wrong. Explanations therefore followed which drew his attention to the culturally approved reading of the scene (see Figure 22.1). Other experiences related to Christmas followed – the singing of carols, the decorating of a fir tree, visits to charitable Father Christmases and finally, on Christmas day itself, presents from Father Christmas and the traditional roast turkey.

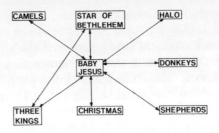

FIGURE 22.1 *Approved reading of an Advent calendar*

What has been learned from all this? The answer is, a social institution in the most obvious sociological sense has been acquired. He has learned that a group of events, objects and actions (see Figure 22.2) may be fitted together by relating them to the class of Christmas. This is at one and the same time an interpretative stance and a guide for action. Already he sings. Perhaps next year he will competently make presents for his parents and expectantly hang a stocking up by the chimney.

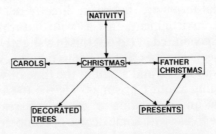

FIGURE 22.2 *The network of Christmas*

We have already noted that much social learning is abstract – the case of Christmas fits this well. We also need to note that the acquisition of systems of social classification, again like natural classifications, is always practical. The child has certain interests and these guide it in its acquisition of knowledge. Poor Christian children, those of very pious parents, or Moslems, will, obviously enough, develop a theory of Christmas that differs from the affluent and largely secular Western version described here. The knowledge acquired about Christmas is what is needed to manage one's way through that festival in a workable manner. In addition, however, another point needs to be made. As with natural knowledge, we cannot ever know that our social knowledge coincides with that of other people. To put it more formally, even with complete agreement about the extension of a social term at a given time there may still be subsequent disagreements with respect to either intension or extension.[7]

VERSTEHEN

We can now return to the question of meaning and *verstehen* in social analysis. The first thing to say is that the description we have just provided of the child's Christmas constitutes nothing other than an example of *verstehen* – of 'conceptual analysis'. We have, indeed, exemplified Winch's suggestion that ideas and social relations are closely related. The description of the child's network is an attempt to see the world from within a culture that attributes a certain meaning to the term and which organises its actions accordingly. But this, in and of itself, does not demonstrate that the Durkheimian notion, that meanings should be avoided, is wrong. Just because one *can* do *verstehen* does not mean that one *ought* to. Perhaps it would be best to ignore the meanings of all concerned, and concentrate on similarities and differences other than those of interest to the people involved.

Despite the protestations of *verstehende* sociologists, there is nothing inherently absurd about such a suggestion. One can imagine, perhaps, a study of the energy economy of what we otherwise think of as social gatherings. Or, perhaps less far-fetched, there is the possibility of understanding how brains react and adapt to stimuli of various kinds. What *is*, however, the case is that such enterprises would hardly be social sciences as we understand them. They would not attend to phenomena that were socially constituted by the people concerned. Or, to put it another way, they would tell us nothing of 'Christmas', or of the social or historical factors that have led it to take its present form. Nor, indeed, could they tell us about the symbolic importance of 'festivals'. This is because 'Christmas' is a classification that comes from the people themselves and the notion of 'festival' depends in turn upon a workable understanding of categories such as Christmas. Again, as a matter of fact, it is the case that social scientists and historians have wished to explain *social* events – that is, events that achieve their status *by virtue of the classificatory acts of those concerned*. Thus, as we noted in Chapter 8, even Durkheim in his exemplary study of suicide, makes use of social meanings. The notion of 'suicide' itself is social and, as he himself was aware, attributions of suicide by officials are a function of their culture. Again, his types of suicide make sense as explanations in part at least because they accord to our common-sense notion that (to take the case of egoistic suicide) people will be more prone to take their own lives if they are unhappy, more likely to be unhappy if they are lonely and (if this is not a tautology) more likely to be lonely if they are insufficiently integrated into society.[8] In this case then, it is not only the phenomenon to be explained that comes from the culture, but also the explanation itself.

If social science in its present form appears to be closely related to the networks of the cultures that it studies, then should it not follow Winch's advice and abandon its pretensions to scientificity, comparative analysis and causality? Should it not, rather, see itself as a conceptual exercise akin if not identical to epistemology?

We want to answer these questions by considering what it is that is going on when a social scientist enters a culture in the course of his or her investigation. To make it easier to see what happens, imagine this to be a rather distant culture – one alien to the investigator. In fact, the social scientist is in much the same position as any other beginner – for instance the $2\frac{1}{2}$-year-old just mentioned. He or she gradually acquires a working knowledge of that culture – one that allows passage through the daily round of conversation, documents, rituals and all the rest. To this extent, as we have indicated, Winch is right. Determining the difference between '*kobtiy*' and '*yakt*', and the mythical relationship between the former and the classificatory cross-cousins is obviously important if one enters Karam society,[9] just as knowing the code and how to use it is vital if one wants to interact in an American half-way house.[10] However, the social investigator is not quite like those who are round about, for his or her *interests* differ somewhat from those of the majority of members of the culture. We do not know how many anthropologists there were among the Karam, nor how many sociologists were present in the half-way house, but it is a safe bet that in both cases they were in a small minority. The interests of the social investigator thus diverge from those of the natives, and accordingly, what counts as a workable knowledge of that culture also differs. For what does the social scientist have to do? At its most general the answer is that he or she has to *translate* aspects of that culture, literally or metaphorically, and represent these as *examples* or *instances* of some phenomenon of interest to (say) the community of anthropologists. For Wieder, in his half-way house, this utterance is an example of the essential reflexivity of discourse. For Bulmer, the animal taxonomy of the Karam is an example of a belief-system which symbolically reflects dominant social tensions and concerns. For Marx the lengthening of the working-day is a case of increasing surplus value. For Weber the development of a particular bureaucracy is an example of the developing rationalisation of economic activity, and so on. To put it another way, theoretical or metaphorical description is always involved. Objects of interest are translated into another, illuminating context.

At this point the sceptical Winchian will want to blow the whistle and argue that, in treating one symbol-system as if, in certain respects, it were like another, we have in fact broken the injunction against comparing unlike with unlike, that we are riding roughshod over important distinctions. Our reply to this is to say that it may indeed be the case that we are ignoring important distinctions, but then we ask the question: important to whom? For here we should remind ourselves of one of the most basic assumptions of the network theory – all systems of classification emphasise a small sub-set of the possible similarities or differences to be found in the world, and social knowledge does not differ in this respect from natural knowledge. It is not necessarily a problem if the Karam notice differences where the anthropologist detects similarities. The anthropologist is guided by a different set of interests. Neither is there any particular need to worry about the fact that the anthropologist is losing information in the course of his or her simplificatory classifications: this too, is a feature of all knowledge. This, then, is the crux of the difficulty with Winch's argument about the impossibility of comparative social science. *All* comparisons involve the matching of objects that are ultimately unlike. If Winch's objections to comparative analysis were sustained they would apply just as much to natural science, indeed to common sense. Conversely, since comparisons of what are ultimately unlike with unlike are universal, there is no particular reason to treat social science as if it were particularly impotent in that respect.

It is interesting to note that Winch's commitment to cultural idiosyncrasy wavers at times. Thus, he permits the utilisation of analysts' concepts so long as these are preceded by an understanding of the concepts of the native culture:

> liquidity preference is a technical concept of economics: it is not generally used by businessmen in the conduct of their affairs but by the economist who wishes to explain the nature and consequences of certain kinds of business behaviour. But it is logically tied to concepts which do enter into business activity.[11]

Here, of course, the technically faulty assumption is made that business culture is homogeneous – that one firm may legitimately be compared with another. No such assumption could be sustained by the purist. Their differences are manifest, and it is improper to ignore them. In practice, however, economists routinely (and rightly) do so. Yet there is no difference in principle between this case (which has Winch's blessing) and the examples we have previously discussed. In practice unlike is routinely compared with unlike, and treated as if it were the same. Whether any given comparison is legitimate is a function of its workability, not of a metaphysical preference for stressing dissimilarity.[12]

REASONS AND CAUSES

In the previous section we have argued that Winch is right to suggest that meanings are central to social life and accordingly that *verstehen* – the act of acquiring competent use of the networks of the culture under study – is an important aspect of social science investigation. At the same time, however, we dissented from the conclusion that comparative social analysis was illegitimate: for practical purposes comparison may, indeed, be highly appropriate, even though in the last instance it is, like all knowledge, a flawed simplification.

What now of Winch's third proposition – the suggestion that there is a basic difference in quality between causes and reasons and that, accordingly, social science explanation should engage with and be built up in terms of reasons? His argument leads him to reject Weber's view that the explanation of social events should be adequate at both the levels of reason and cause. There is no point, says Winch, in looking for statistics to bolster an explanation posed in terms of meanings. Instead, what is required is further conceptual analysis.

Let us start by reminding ourselves that in network theory the relationships between the classes are variable with respect to strength. Some are very firm: we confidently assert that mammals are warm-blooded, a link between two classes that for us has the probability of unity. Others, however, are less secure. We mention this because one of the reasons given by Winch for finding social life to be different from its natural counterpart has to do with the fact that physical laws are mechanically and necessarily followed, whereas with social laws there is always a choice – people may *choose* to break the rules. In fact, by itself, this is a quite inadequate reason for distinguishing between 'reasons' and 'causes' for there are many probabilistic links in natural networks.[13] There is, therefore, no reason why we should not treat social rule-following and breaking in exactly the same way as its natural counterpart. Indeed, that is what routinely occurs: if we are unable to predict the way in which important individuals or institutions will act we generate further network links in an attempt to improve our predictions. We talk, for instance, of the 'interests' of the people concerned or the fact that they were under the influence of factors of which we were ignorant. In and of itself, then, the strength of a relationship between two classes, whether these be a motive and an action, or a physical impetus and a consequence, is no evidence for the distinction that Winch wants to assert between explanations posed in terms of reasons and those deployed in an idiom of cause.

In fact this division is seen, additionally, as qualitative in nature. Social science is concerned, he suggests with *what it makes sense to say or do* in a given society. Rules and reasons are locally generated; they are not universal. As we have indicated, there is much with which we can disagree in this thesis. Standards of conduct and argument are, indeed, culturally located. This does not, however, mean that those local standards are sufficient to explain everything of concern to the social analyst. It is, in fact, most unlikely that they would, for once again it has to be noted that the interests of the latter almost certainly diverge from those of the former. The analyst poses different questions and comes up with correspondingly different answers, albeit answers that relate, in one way or another, to the categories of the natives.

Consider, for instance, the difference between the interests of the phrenologists in early nineteenth-century Edinburgh and those of the late twentieth-century historian of science.[14] The phrenologists wished, perhaps, to advance their doctrines and to score points off their opponents. Accordingly they developed their studies in particular ways – they argued, for instance, about the structure and size of the frontal sinuses and in general about whether or not there was a brain–skull parallelism. The historian is not, by contrast, interested in the sinuses *per se* at all. The concern is, rather, in showing that there is indeed a connection between such apparently esoteric debates on the one hand and broader social interests on the other, and this object is pursued by gathering certain kinds of data. Some of it is obviously 'meaningful' – attacks by phrenologists upon their opponents, for instance. Some of it is less directly so – evidence concerning the social location of proponents and opponents of phrenology for example. These pieces of evidence are, however, all deployed in a new context – they are designed to tell a story that differs from and may not have been available to the contemporary protagonists.

There has, then, been a shift away from the actors' own accounts and motives though a version of these forms a part of the evidence of the historian. The shift involves the theory that *social interests* lie behind the deployment of the phrenological and anti-phrenological arguments and that the development of the debate cannot be properly understood unless it is realised that these esoteric arguments are doing 'social work' of one kind or another. Loosely, then, it is being proposed that social interests *caused* the debate to take place.

What is intended by the term 'cause' here? This has little to do with constant conjunction. The existence of a dissatisfied and increasingly important bourgeoisie does not invariably correlate with the adoption of phrenological beliefs. As far as we know, it only happened on this one occasion. The analyst can rather be treated as saying something a great deal more circumspect. What he is really saying is that if one is interested in the phrenology debates, then it is also *interesting* to note that in this context social factors operated to lead a bourgeoisie to adopt phrenological beliefs because, for a variety of reasons, these were unacceptable to the elites that they wished to displace. Correspondingly, had this social interest not been operating, everything else being equal there would have been no school of phrenology and no controversy.

Causes are, therefore, interesting because they explain interesting, unusual or otherwise noticeable events. But they are explanatory because they offer a satisfying metaphorical re-description. Posed in network theory terms, then, causes may be seen as interestingly or relevantly explicit narrative re-descriptions. They are, as it were, the links in the plausible story that is always involved in metaphorical re-description, links that achieve their plausibility from their position in another domain.[15]

It will by now be clear that causes in the sense just defined may be identical to reasons – think of the relationship between the assassination of the Archduke Ferdinand and the onset of the First World War. They may be related to, but not the same as, reasons – think of the phrenology example just cited. Or they may, indeed, be entirely divorced from reasons, as in many natural-science explanations. It will also be clear that reasons may or may not be causes. Thus, the reasons given by phrenologists for believing that the frontal sinuses are normally small in size do not coincide with (though they relate to) the causes of this belief as attributed by the historian. There is thus no particular reason for the social scientist (or historian) to make a fetish of the meanings of the natives. There is certainly no reason why he or she should divide reasons from causes in the manner recommended by Winch. The only requirement placed upon the analyst is that the translations inevitably involved in converting native to social-science categories should be workable for practical purposes. The social science re-description should defensibly relate to the categories of the natives. There is certainly no reason why native systems of reasoning should not form part of a 'causal story' assembled by the social scientist – why a translated version of the reasons imputed to natives should not be treated as part of an efficacious chain.

It is, in fact, quite difficult to avoid the conclusion that parts of Winch's text are little more than an attack on theorising in social science. The gist of his prescription is to resist, or at least to restrict, the kind of explanatory re-description that we have been discussing. Admittedly, he somewhat hedges his bets. We have already quoted him as saying that analysts' concepts are acceptable if they are 'logically tied' to those of the natives. But this, to judge by the examples he gives – from economics and psychoanalysis[16] – is a fairly restrictive requirement. Interestingly, however, it is also vacuous from the standpoint of network theory: categories are logically related not by virtue of any properties that inhere in them, but rather because they are *treated* as logically related within a given culture. What counts as a logical relationship is thus a function of social negotiation and the interests of the negotiating parties. What counts, therefore, as a proper 'translation' of native concepts (to use the looser term that we prefer) is variable. And, as the ethnomethodologists have endlessly demonstrated, what were previously taken as acceptable translations may, if there is an interest so to do, be represented as inadequate. Winch's formulation thus only achieves definite prescriptive sense within an idealist conception of knowledge, but within this conception he proposes crippling restrictions on the kind of theorising open to the social scientist. All in all, it is quite remarkable that philosophical *fiat* should be taken as rendering illegitimate so much interesting and worthwhile work in social science.

CONCLUSION

Verstehen thus forms a valuable – indeed essential – part of social analysis. So too do comparative and causal analysis. The latter are perfectly compatible with the former. Perhaps the feeling that they are not is in part informed by an unrealistically rigid conception of what it is to be scientific: that science can only study observable phenomena, that cause implies something rigid and that scientific comparative analysis implies perfect similarity between the objects to be compared. If these conceptions of science are prevalent then they are mistaken. The network theory though formal in one sense, shows science to be a more fluid enterprise than is suggested by the standard stereotypes. It is high time that it was used to inform and defuse some of the standard debates of social science. 'Meanings' do not distinguish social from natural science in any fundamental manner. All that has to be noted is that social science has certain technical problems of data collection – just as, for example, do those who study solar neutrino flux[17] – but that its conceptual structure is essentially the same as that of natural science. Accordingly, social science need not only be impartial and symmetrical. It can, in addition, be causal in explanatory form.

---

142 Members of a culture learn about social kinds in the same way as they acquire knowledge of natural kinds. Social institutions are acquired in this way, practically, from the interaction of 'lumps' in the environment and social cues.

143 The act of *verstehen* involves the acquisition of a social network in this way.

144 If it wishes to explain categories constituted in social networks, social science must to some extent use *verstehen*.

145 However, the interests of social scientists differ from those of the members of the culture they are studying. Accordingly, what counts as an adequate account of a culture is a function in part of those interests, and that account or translation may properly differ from the native's own version.

146 In comparative analysis the social scientist treats as 'the same' parts of different cultures that, in principle, differ from one another. However, in doing so, he or she differs not at all from the natural scientist who also compares unlike with unlike. Accordingly, there is nothing wrong with comparative social science that is not wrong with comparative natural science. The problem in both cases is a practical one: is the comparison workable?

147 The fact that links in networks of social explanation are weak is no reason for abandoning a language of causality. There are many weak links in networks of natural explanation.

148 Since the interests of the social scientist differ from those of the people that he or she is studying, so too will their networks. Networks of the former, in seeking to account for actions of the latter may include some links or 'causal stories' which correspond to reasons available to the latter, and some which do not. There is no reason for the analyst to limit him or herself to those links available in native culture. Indeed, (see 149) it is most unlikely that a satisfactory social-science explanation could do so.

149 Adequate 'causal stories' are those that explain or account for an interesting, unusual or otherwise noticeable event. They are explanatory because they re-describe the event in question by locating it in a different network.

150 The requirement sometimes imposed by social scientists that analysts' explanations must be logically tied to those of the natives ignores the fact that what counts as a logical tie is negotiable and a function of interests.

23 Science and Social Science

We have argued that the social sciences cannot be distinguished from the natural sciences in terms of their explanatory structure. They are both properly causal in idiom, just as they avoid the temptation to explain the 'good' and the 'bad' in different idioms. Yet there are few who would disagree that the social sciences look different from the natural sciences. Their credibility is lower, their status less secure and their disputes more public. In this chapter we offer a tentative explanation for these differences that is consistent with the network theory. Not surprisingly it is an explanation in terms of social interests and their distribution. First, however, we want to offer an example of different social science approaches to what is apparently the same phenomenon.

In recent years, particularly in the United States, there has been an upsurge of interest in the sociology of sport. As in other areas in sociology, the explanations and understandings of sport are divergent. For the sake of illustration we will limit ourselves to three views of sport which fall roughly into the Marxist, Durkheimian and Weberian traditions of sociological theory.[1]

From the Marxist perspective, sport is considered to be a part of the superstructure of society, that is, it belongs to the realm of ideas and values: sport is a part of society's culture. In turn, the superstructure is influenced by the relations of production. In other words, sport reflects the political and, more particularly, the economic relations of society. Thus, sport within the capitalist mode of production will be exploitative. It will reflect not only the class organisation of society, but it will in addition serve the interests of the ruling class. Hoch criticises professional sport in America as essentially an opiate which serves to preserve the capitalist system:

(sport) robs people of their power to make decisions and their creativity, and sets them in search of opiates in consumption and entertainment.[2]

Sport, then, from this perspective, is diversionary and is a barrier to the raising of revolutionary consciousness. However, in capitalist societies sport is not only a narcotic. It also becomes a commodity to be consumed. Speaking of the development of Western urban–industrial society, Riordan writes:

> In the course of these changes, many sports become commercialised and adapted for mass consumption and diversion, dominated by the profit motive and emasculated by the needs of a 'sports industry'.[3]

The commercialisation of sport is witnessed by exorbitant admission prices to sporting events, the sale of clothing emblazoned with the logos of favourite teams or the names of sports personalities, by the product endorsements of sports stars and so on. It is not, however, only the consumer/spectator who is being exploited but also the playing participants. Now it may be difficult to imagine exactly how professional sportsmen who are paid enormous amounts of money might be said to be exploited, but the Marxist sociologist would argue that the players are treated, like any industrial workers, as a commodity whose labour is bought and sold. Indeed, even the players themselves are bought and sold on the transfer market and they have little control over their careers. Thus they are dehumanised and alienated from their true selves.[4] Writers in the Marxist tradition such as Hoch view sport as 'a mirror, a socialising agent and an opiate of the society it serves', and in order to change the exploitative nature of sport nothing less than a radical change in the economic structure of society is necessary.[5]

The Durkheimian-style approach to sport resembles the Marxist in one key feature and that is with respect to the *religious* nature of sport.[6] In describing sport in capitalist society as an opiate, implicit reference is made to Marx's infamous description of religion as the opiate of the masses. Durkheim's view of religion, however, is that far from being an opiate, it is *functional.* That is, religion, or some other substitute, is necessary for the survival of society. Durkheim recognised that orthodox forms of religion were in decline and that the integrative functions of religion (that is, the sense of solidarity with, or belonging to, a community) would also reduce in importance. Writers in the Durkheimian tradition (for instance, Robert N. Bellah, Phillip E. Hammond, Shils and Young) have suggested that the requirements for integration would be met in modern industrial society by 'civil religion'. Civil religion amounts to the 'sanctification' of the nation-state. In other words, objects, people, and events associated with secular aspects of life are granted an elevated sacred or religious status. So, for example, in the United States the Constitution and the Bill of Rights parallel the holy books of the Bible. Similarly, US history has spawned heroes or saints for whom great monuments were erected (for example, George Washington, Abraham Lincoln). Such saints are not only immortalised in stone, but also have designated feast days or holidays set aside in their honour.[7] Other holidays commemorate great events such as the nativity of the nation (Independence Day). Likewise, the American flag is a sacred object and there exist strict rules of flag-etiquette which specify that the Stars and Stripes should not be flown at night or in inclement weather, that it should be folded in a certain way, and that a flag that touches the ground and is therefore defiled should be destroyed (but only by fire).

This notion of civil religion can easily be extended to sports. (Indeed, sport and civil religion are very closely tied in the US. Sporting events are frequently preceded by the national anthem and major football games often feature patriotic pre-game shows.) Sports are followed with something akin to religious devotion. Edwards apparently concurs with this sports/religion parallel and suggests 'If there is a universal popular religion in America, it is to be found within the institution of sport'.[8]

The 'collective effervescence' characteristic of religious services is also witnessed at the cathedral-size sporting stadia of the western world. At 'important' games (be they soccer, American football, rugby, basketball, baseball or cricket) 50 000 or more devotees cheer, incant, sing their anthems and brandish symbols of their loyalty in a display of emotional and social solidarity. Perhaps it is not merely coincidental that the trophies for which these teams compete (particularly in European soccer) resemble oversized chalices.

Sport is thus strongly marked by non-utilitarian loyalties and commitments, by much ritualised or ceremonial behaviour, by expressive symbolism, and by ideological creeds justified in terms of 'ultimate' values or ultimate conceptions of the good life.[9]

Further religious imagery (this time American) is seen in the various 'Halls of Fame' into which baseball, football and hockey 'greats' are inducted. These are indeed hallowed halls and induction into them represents the seal of canonisation.

Our third example of approaches to the sociology of sport lies within the Weberian tradition. One of the main themes in Weber's sociology is the idea that society and its institutions evolve in such a way that they become progressively more rational. That is, social change is essentially a movement toward greater bureaucratisation and a concomitant increase in specialisation, efficiency and calculability.

The Weberian approach to the topic of sport is best represented by Guttmann.[10] Guttmann argues that the evolution of sport has been marked by increasing quantification and role-specialisation. Citing historical data, Guttmann argues that in the ancient Greek Olympic games the quantification that we associate with the modern Olympics was non-existent. Although the Greeks were capable of measuring the distances that various objects such as javelins were thrown, no measurements were actually taken. Similarly, the heights or the lengths of different forms of athletic leaps were not computed. It was sufficient that the winning individual athlete had thrown further, jumped higher, or run faster than his competitors. All measurements, then, were relative. Since no 'absolute' measurements were taken, no measurements were recorded and hence there were no records to break.

Modern sports have moved away from this qualitative mode of athletic assessment and rely on more quantitative criteria. The evaluation of sporting prowess is now a matter of measurements which lend themselves to statistical manipulation. Performance has been re-defined in terms of the objective quantifiable criteria of 'how fast?', 'how many goals for or against?', 'how many yards gained?', 'how many strike-outs?', 'how many "career runs"?' and other measurable facts expressed as rates and averages. Entire books are devoted to such enumerations and the truly avid sports fan is, in turn, apparently obliged to commit to memory vast amounts of sporting records and associated trivia.

The notion of the all-round sportsman or sportswoman has become somewhat of an anachronism. Not only do athletes tend to specialise in a particular sport, but they also tend to specialise in one aspect of that sport. There is a growing division of labour. For example, in soccer there are forwards, strikers, mid-field players, defenders and so on, and in baseball there are specialists in pitching or outfielding. However, growing specialisation in sport is nowhere as evident as it is in American football in which team players will enter or leave the field of play many times depending upon offensive or defensive contingencies. Specialists in throwing the ball or specialists in catching long forward passes are employed only for those parts of the game that demand their specialist tasks. In a sixty-minute game an expert in kicking the ball may appear on the field for a total of less than five minutes. American football too, is a highly formalised activity in other respects, and success has less to do with individual players' spontaneity than to regimented planning and set plays. From this Weberian perspective, the growing quantification in sport is a specific example of the more general trend in modern society. Sports do not, however, *reflect* growing specialisation and rationality. They are part and parcel of these.

In Chapter 18 we referred to Lévy Bruhl who suggests that the distinction between magic and logic are located in the premises, networks and beliefs in which actors have invested. Much the same could be said of the differences between explanatory modes in the social sciences. The differences between the three views of the sociology of sport reflect a deep lack of consensus with regard to premises, networks and beliefs. Why should this be? The first thing to note is that, typically at least, the social world is 'closer to home' than the natural world. Of course, we have views about the natural world, and sometimes – as in the biological nature of male/female cognitive differences, the dangers attached to the peaceful uses of atomic power and the acceptability of the theory of evolution by natural selection – these views turn out to be controversial. By and large, however, attitudes to the natural world are less highly-charged and more readily form an un-controversial background to daily life than do their social counterparts.

Why is this? There is, as we have argued throughout, no strictly conceptual or methodological reason for such a difference. Indeed, we have cited a number of cases where there has been acute controversy within the natural sciences and anyone who keeps an eye on the scientific press will know that this is extremely common. Therefore it is not that there is inevitably consensus in natural science and controversy in social science. Neither can it be that natural science lacks directing interests in social legitimation. We argued in Chapter 20 that a concealed interest in social rationalisation and control is ubiquitous, even in the natural sciences. The answer must lie, rather, in the distinction that we made there between a *global* and a *local* interest in social legitimation. Or, to put it slightly differently, it must lie in the nature of the audiences at whom the knowledge is directed or by whom it is used. Quite a large part of natural science practice is directed by an interest in social legitimation that has direct consequences for or refers to only a small and highly differentiated audience. Such audiences often have ways of concluding the disputes that do arise within a limited period of time. To rephrase this, often in cases of controversy one of the protagonists will quite quickly succeed in legitimating his or her position and will, accordingly, have engaged in successful (though local) social control.[11]

In the social sciences the situation is frequently quite different. Global interests in social legitimation operate or, to put this in terms of audiences, much social science knowledge is directed, whether intentionally or not, at large non-specialist audiences in a manner that either serves or is designed to manipulate their interests. Furthermore, these social-science audiences are not simply larger. They also lack the social means to conclude disputes that are available to restricted and differentiated natural science audiences. To put this differently, it is quite rare that controversy will be quickly and decisively concluded because the protagonists will lack the means for engaging in successful social control. The audiences and their interests will be too heterogeneous to allow a single social-science view to develop. Accordingly, it is the failure to develop differentiated and esoteric social-science fields that explains the endemic state of controversy that is to be found in so much social science. As a result, much social-science knowledge plugs directly or indirectly into global concerns with social control and manipulation – concerns that are typically though not necessarily at variance with an interest in prediction and control. So it is that we have our Marxist, Durkheimian and Weberian sociologists of sport. So it is that we have such a diverse range of explanation of all socially-contentious subjects from imperialism and economic performance to the analysis of drug-taking. So it is that we have different metaphors or models of society.

Might a unified social science nevertheless be possible? Is it something to which we might aspire? There are two ways in which this question can be approached. One of these – the hope that philosophy might provide a bridging 'metatheory' to judge the quality of different social-science theories and link those that pass this test together – seems to us, however superficially attractive, to be fundamentally misguided. We deal with this in the next chapter. The other, sociologically informed, way of considering the question is to ask what kind of society it would be that would reduce the heterogeneity of social-science audiences and ensure that the interests directing social-science research were all aligned. Unfortunately there seems to be only one kind of society that would fit the bill – a totalitarian one. Here the conditions for a unified social science would be most closely approximated. And, it is perhaps worth adding, the need for a unified social science would be greatest in such a society, for it would be the handmaiden of a ruling group seeking to control and co-ordinate the actions of an entire population in every respect. We can be sure that sociology in particular would come into its own under such circumstances. Instead of being a low status ornament to the academic life – as in the liberal democracies – it would be the central discipline in a concerted programme of social control. And it is, of course, the case that as a discipline it is taken a good deal more seriously in those countries, such as the Soviet Union and in Eastern Europe, where serious attempts have been made to plan entire social structures centrally.[12]

The prospects for a thoroughgoing totalitarian society are, we trust, dim and accordingly the prospects for a unified social science are also distant. This has at least three major implications for the conduct of social-science investigation in the foreseeable future. The first is that it will remain fragmented and ridden with conflict. The Marxists will offer one (or more likely, more than one) analysis of, say, sport, while the functionalists will offer another, or others. They will argue and these arguments, being a function of different interests, will not be open to resolution in a manner acceptable to both sides. Considered in the abstract, then, there is little point in arguing with those who take a very different view of the social world, though this is not to say that these arguments cannot produce less-direct advantages.

The second conclusion follows directly from the first. It is that grand synthesising schemes that aim to relate particular social science points of view together in some additive way are doomed to failure. The social scientist who offers a synthetic scheme to cure the present fragmentation of these disciplines must thus be treated with the greatest suspicion.[13] This does not mean that those who borrow bits and pieces of rival theories and proceed to construct something new from those borrowings should be scorned. Such an activity, directed by a particular interest in understanding a particular phenomenon in a given way is entirely legitimate and constitutes one of the indirect advantages of discussion with those with whom one has little in common. Rather, suspicion has to be directed at those whose work is directed by a desire to synthesise a 'unified social science'. The social conditions for such an enterprise do not exist and however worthy such an ecumenical enterprise may appear at first sight, it is, in fact, ill-founded.[14]

This fact can be seen once it is recognised that such general theory rests, albeit often in a somewhat confused manner, upon a correspondence theory of knowledge. Knowledge is seen as reflecting reality, so the more 'partial' bits and pieces of knowledge that can be collected from here and there and patched together, the better. The pragmatic network/interest theory of knowledge that has been argued in this text, stresses, as we have noted, that knowledge selects from and simplifies nature. Much is lost, but given the particular interests that direct the knowledge, this does not matter. The idea that it would, in some way, be possible to fit all these 'perspectives' together is obviously untenable.

This leads to the third conclusion that may be drawn from the fragmented state of the interests that lie behind the social sciences. It is that a plausible, if not in some absolute sense the best, way to proceed is to identify a particular specific interest in prediction and control in relation to a particular subject-matter (or a set of related subject matters), adopt or adapt a set of intellectual tools that appear to be appropriate to the subject-matter from the standpoint of the interest, and push those tools (that is, networks) as hard as they will go. We are suggesting, therefore, that social scientists mimic, insofar as this is possible, the research activity of natural scientists who do not spend their time worrying about questions of global social control or how to unify their work with that of all other scientists, but rather aim to solve much more restricted and localised problems. Certainly scientists worry about how their work relates to that of specific others working in the same or closely-related fields. Again, they borrow from other fields where this appears desirable. But, as a species they do this not because they wish to unify all of, say, biology or advance a vision of society, but because the problems that arise have practical implications for their research programmes. We are suggesting, then, that social scientists should commit themselves to the specific objectives of particular research programmes. We are suggesting that they attempt to identify soluble puzzles. And we are suggesting that, so far as possible, they, like Kuhn's 'normal scientists', solve those puzzles by means of metaphorical extension, borrowing from adjacent networks, and the rest.

It will be objected that this advice ignores the fact that the social sciences differ from the natural sciences in manners which we have described above and that, accordingly, it makes little sense to suggest that social scientists should 'puzzle-solve' in the Kuhnian manner. It is, as we have noted, the case that there are no more-or-less unified paradigms in social science that command the respect of all relevant practitioners, and that what counts as a 'finding' in one branch of, say, sociology may be ignored or treated as controversial, in another. The social scientist cannot expect his or her work to receive the general recognition that is accorded an outstanding contribution to an area of normal natural science. But this aside, there is no reason why a sense of puzzle-solving and advance should not be achieved within particular and more limited communities of practitioners. 'Progress', albeit progress for a limited number of people only, can be achieved if prac-titioners eschew the temptation to pursue global concerns about social control and the desire to spend too much of their time in ultimately fruitless negotiations with those with whom they have little in common, but rather develop their own particular puzzle-solving tradition.[15]

In some ways this conclusion may be rather disappointing. It is saddening to recognise that in the social sciences, context is extremely limited, success very local and 'truth' very shortlived. But failure to recognise that, as social scientists, we would operate better 'locally' than 'universally', 'professionally' rather than as general agents of social control, will tend to lead to schemes that are doomed to even local failure with respect to prediction and control.

---

151 In the social sciences there are typically divergent views and understandings of phenomena of interest.

152 This often arises because the analyses offered are directed at large non-specialist audiences, have major implications for social control and are subject to analysis from the standpoint of a variety of different interests.

153 A unified social science would be facilitated in a society where all sponsoring interests were aligned – that is to say, a totalitarian society.

154 Ecumenical attempts to unify social science by fitting together its components as in a jigsaw are likely to fail in the absence of an alignment of interests because they rest upon a correspondence theory of knowledge.

155 A plausible way of working in social science is to select resources that have bearing on a limited range of puzzles and attempt to solve those puzzles while substantially ignoring alternative practices unless these can, in turn, be treated as resources.

156 Successes will only be local, but they will at least be successes.

157 This approach is not 'irrational'. It rather notes that rationality or adequacy is something that can only be determined locally.

---

24 Self-confidence and the Redundancy of Philosophy

In this text we have sought to be matter-of-fact, empirical, and down-to-earth. In talking about the nature of knowledge, the way in which it is acquired and how it is liable to change under the direction of social interests, we have used many examples. In considering the relationship between 'science' and 'non-science' we have again used illustration. Our argument about the relationship between the two has been that such differences as there may be are best seen as a function of the operation of social interests, rather than as residing in a special scientific method.

It is inevitable, and indeed proper, that although we have been primarily concerned with a descriptive and matter-of-fact account of knowledge, we have at times, particularly in the last part of the book, made judgements about what kind of practice, scientific or social scientific, is desirable or (and this often amounts to the same thing) possible. The prescriptive implications of our account are clearest where alternatives simply seem to be inconsistent with the facts as we seen them. Let us enumerate some of these:

1) The network/interest theory approach forcibly suggests that agents have to be seen as active sense-making beings. They must be seen as *doing* things with their knowledge, fashioning it and extending it in accordance with their interests. They are not like puppets, and are most certainly not to be understood as 'cultural dopes'. If the network/interest theory is correct then it follows that certain types of social theory – notably those that suppose that ideas can dominate or control people and those that assume that people are pre-programmed, role-playing zombies – are wrong. A surprising amount of social

255

theory falls into one or other of these categories, and must
therefore be rejected.[1]

(2) The network/interest theory states that all knowledge is a
constructed simplification. Even the most empirical aspects of
any given network are thus subject to change. To put it in the
language of philosophy, there is no such thing as a neutral
observation language. This has a number of directly-
prescriptive implications. For instance, it means that 'two
language' accounts of science or social science inquiry must
be rejected. It means that 'empiricist' programmes of inquiry
are unlikely to generate any findings of interest. As the
fragments of data so gathered will not, in fact, be theory-free,
but only free of any particular explicit theory, the likelihood
that they will be utilisable in a subsequent, more theory-
directed 'puzzle-solving' inquiry will be slim. It means that the
'ecumenical' approach we mentioned in the last chapter is
most unlikely to bear any fruit.

(3) The network/interest theory of knowledge suggests that
judgements of the *quality* of systems of belief should have no
role with respect to their explanation. It is consistent with the
tenets of impartiality and symmetry and seeks the most
general possible explanation for the origins of belief in
general. It thus explains both those beliefs that are held to be
false and those that are held to be true in terms of the same
kinds of causes. It is accordingly critical of those, whether
philosophers or social scientists, who breach the requirement
of impartiality and advance asymmetrical explanations for
different kinds of knowledge.

(4) The network/interest theory takes a view of the nature of
science, and its conceptual and methodological similarity to
non-science. This implies, prescriptively, that first, the
common assumption that science is epistemologically different from non-science has to be rejected. Marxism, *pace*
Althusser and Winch, is no more 'scientific' or 'non-scientific'
than any other form of social theory. The same is true for
Durkheimian scientism. This leads to a second implication
that there is no virtue in either aping or seeking to avoid 'the
scientific method' in social science, where this method is
understood to be some kind of method, formula or formal
procedure. The Durkheimian desire to collect 'social facts',
the methodological fetishism of much statistical and

mathematical sociology,[2] or the aversion expressed in certain circles of *verstehende* sociology to causal explanation and scientificity, all have, in and of themselves, no merit. They are all based on an erroneous notion of the nature of natural science. The latter, in the network/interest theory understanding, turns out to be a great deal more 'relaxed', if we might put it informally, than the stereotypes to which social scientists have typically reacted. It is unfortunate that these stereotypes are so widespread in social science, particularly at the 'soft' end of the spectrum.

This observation brings us to the question that we want to consider in this final chapter: what should students of the social sciences make of the philosophy of science and social science which generally presents itself as a primarily prescriptive discipline, able to tell the practitioner about the nature of good or bad method?[3] We have touched upon this question at several points, but here we want to approach the problem by highlighting the important differences in approach between this text and other, more standard texts in the philosophy of science and social science. In early drafts this book indeed looked much more conventionally philosophical. That is to say, we tended to take an issue – say the nature of natural science or teleological explanation – consider the major positions adopted by classic writers, offer our critical evaluation of those positions, and end with an outline of our *own* understanding of the issue in question.

In certain places we still adopt this approach. As an overall strategy, however, we abandoned this way of writing very soon and for at least three reasons. First, though perhaps of little importance in itself, we found the task boring. It was not quite clear to us why it was necessary to outline the details of the 'Popper–Kuhn debate' when these were in fact available in the original for anyone who wished to read them. They had, in any case, been the subject of commentary elsewhere. Second, we knew from experience that this kind of approach, though obviously of importance to the rare student who wished to study the development of social thought or philosophy, was very difficult for the majority of students who sought, instead, a simple exposition of 'the truth' rather than a tour of the complicated philosophical scenery. Of course we were not so naive as to believe that there was a single 'truth', but the students seemed to have a point: why this concern with the substantially-rejected views of this or that long dead social philosopher? Third, we found that the standard manner of expressing one's views – as the outcome of a constructed historical dialogue – was an excessively oblique way of expressing what we took to be the case. As we have stressed, our position was grounded not so much in the history of philosophy and social thought, as in largely contemporary empirical claims in cognitive psychology and the history, sociology and philosophy of science. In the face of these considerations we rapidly decided so far as possible to 'de-historicise' our approach, to base it on empirical evidence, and, so far as we were able, to state our views in a simple and unmediated way. Hence the present text, with its generally descriptive bias – albeit a bias that leads, as we have noted, to prescription of its own.

But where does this leave the philosophy of science? And where does it leave the history of the philosophy of science? Answers to both these questions can be unpacked from the proposition that we advanced in the last chapter: that social scientists should allow themselves to be directed by social interests to focus on *particular* problems that may be soluble in terms of *particular* networks. A corollary of this suggestion was that, while they may wish to borrow elements from outside networks, these borrowings should be treated as utilisable resources. They should not, repeat *not*, be used as Trojan horses to introduce the specialist problems preoccupations and pretensions of the disciplines from which they are borrowed.

In the present text we have attempted to follow this dictum. As is obvious, we have borrowed from cognitive psychology. The gist of these borrowings is that perception is best seen as an active process – that something is added by the perceiver to whatever is that he or she obtains from the outside world. Perhaps this not so very startling in the abstract, but it certainly has important consequences for an understanding of the nature of knowledge. What we avoided doing was treating cognitive psychology in its own terms. That discipline has its own problems, its own pretensions, indeed its own divisions. For the cognitive psychologist these are important, as they would be for someone seeking to write a history of cognitive psychology. However, for our purposes they are altogether irrelevant. We do not need become cognitive psychologists. We have no need to take sides their debates. And for our purposes all we need to know is that strong case can be made for the view that perception is active. There is a further point: the pretensions of cognitive psychologists do not extend to telling other social scientists (for instance economists or sociologists) how they should conduct their own inquiries. It does not claim a global right to clarify the procedures or findings of the practitioners of other disciplines.[4] Indeed, the very suggestion sounds strange, but we mention it for reasons that will shortly become clear.

Now consider the case of the philosophy of science (or social science – for present purposes we may treat the two as one). Philosophy of science, like cognitive psychology, is a practice or a set of practices. People there have their problems and preoccupations. There too, they have their debates and controversies. Again, like cognitive psychologists, they have their pretensions. But what are these pretensions like? Listen to Peter Winch:

> . . . the central problem of sociology, that of giving an account of the nature of social phenomena in general, itself belongs to philosophy. In fact, not to put too fine a point on it, this part of sociology is really misbegotten epistemology. I say 'misbegotten' because its problems have been largely misconstrued and therefore mishandled, as a species of scientific problem.[5]

or I. C. Jarvie, a philosopher of science and social science, here writing about the sociology of knowledge:

> The very idea that science or philosophy is *a* symbolic universe, or even *a* way of looking at the world is a gross oversimplification. Philosophy and science can also be seen as the opposite of legitimating symbolic universes. They are rather *methods* of critically challenging and scrutinizing those symbolic universes that are on offer . . . and these methods do not themselves incorporate or favour any particular symbolic universe.[6]

There are differences between Winch and Jarvie, and the precise nature of their respective views should not detain us here. What is of importance is their understanding of the relationship between philosophical and social science inquiry. Winch takes the more radical view. As we have seen, for him sociology and other social sciences are no more than (probably badly done) philosophy. If sociologists wish to practise good sociology they must stop whatever it is they currently do, and take up philosophy instead. Jarvie is somewhat, but only somewhat, more modest. Philosophy (along with science) is an impartial judge of 'symbolic universes'. It weighs, measures, and prescribes. Now notice, despite their differences, what these two views share. They share the assumption that *philosophy is more fundamental than empirical social science, that it is in a position to supervise practice in these disciplines, and that it may properly discriminate between good and bad practice.* Philosophy is accorded a privileged position in each case. Or, to put it more sceptically, it has imperialist pretensions, that were substantially absent in the other case that we mentioned – that of cognitive psychology.

We have discussed the explanatory drawbacks of such normative views at some length in earlier chapters. We have noted that they involve the abandoning of impartial and symmetrical accounts of the causes of knowledge. What we want to underline here is that unless one 'goes native' and becomes a philosopher (which as we have seen, is what Winch proposes) one is under no compulsion to accept this version of the relationship between philosophy and specialist branches of social science. Just because philosophers have evolved a practice that leads them to claim a kind of overlordship over the other disciplines does not mean that those other disciplines should unquestioningly accept that overlordship. Natural scientists, whatever some of them may say about Popper in their spare time, spend precious little of their time thinking about whether or not they are following his methodological dicta when they are working at the laboratory bench or the computer terminal. In the social sciences, however, particularly at the soft end of the spectrum, there are areas where practitioners have lost their nerve and allowed themselves to give up their independence in favour of a philosophical definition of their task. Of course, it is easy to understand why this might occur. In a discipline as fragmented as sociology the pursuit of locally generated puzzle-solving recommended in the last chapter is necessarily in competition with a concern about how one's practice might relate to that of another. Indeed, it is fair to suggest that there can be no rigid distinction between the two concerns. An interest in the inter-relationships between practices is, in some measure unavoidable. Accordingly, the temptation to abandon use of one's own particular practice with its distinctive problems, preoccupations and pretensions in favour of some 'neutral' set of criteria is obvious. The temptation is strengthened by the fact that in many teaching departments the curriculum is based upon a version of the politics of equal time – so many hours on Marxism, so many on functionalism and so on. Nevertheless the temptation must be resisted. An authentic practice does not involve playing second fiddle to philosophy. It does not automatically involve bowing to judgements by those who are not practitioners of the puzzle-solving tradition under question. It involves, rather, the realisation that philosophy is a practice, or set of practices, like any other discipline. And since it is like any other discipline, we may treat it as a resource in our own work. If bits and pieces are useful, they may by all means be borrowed and adapted. But, whatever the philosophers may say, there is no need to take their complaints seriously when these originate from and advance a different set of prescriptive interests. These preoccupations do not form a part of our practice. Philosophers do not use our networks as we do. They are not trying to solve our puzzles and they are not directed by our interests. By all means let them pursue their practice, for who are we to make judgements of a technical nature about issues integral to philosophical practice? By all means, therefore, let them complain when we break their rules. But we should not take those complaints seriously unless they happen to coincide with our own problems and our own concerns. Let us, therefore, pursue our practice and pursue it unashamedly.

To say this is not to advocate sloppy or careless work in social science. It is not to adopt a hedonistic attitude or to imply that 'anything goes'. It is rather to claim that critical standards cannot or should not be imposed from outside. We rather have to evolve them ourselves, as we practise our own puzzle-solving. And, inevitably, those standards will be local, professional conventions for quality control, not global rules.

And so, finally, the deeper rationale for our approach becomes clear. We did not want to write a traditionally philosophical text about science and social science because we did not want to concede that much to philosophy. The understanding of inquiry that we have outlined is empirically based. It rests upon an 'indigenous' social science view of historical, economic, anthropological and sociological ethnography. It rests upon a hypothesis about the way in which people process information, a hypothesis that is economically expressed in a part of the writings of the philosopher Mary Hesse. We have, accordingly, adopted many elements of her network theory. We believe that the view that we have advanced is worth taking seriously. But if it is, indeed, to be taken seriously, it in turn involves local prescription. It assumes that contexted progress can best be achieved when practitioners who have competence in their own practice select resources in an attempt to focus upon and resolve a limited range of puzzles in terms of a local set of rules. In this book we have attempted to take this prescription seriously by writing, so far as is possible, about the way things are to us rather than the way things were, or seem to be, to philosophers with whose conclusions we disagree. We believe that we have thereby drafted a declaration of independence from philosophy – a declaration of independence that takes the form of an empirical understanding of the nature of knowledge. Ironically, of course, we have used the writing of Mary Hesse in the course of doing this. But, as we have tried to argue, there is nothing unacceptable about such borrowing from the standpoint we have adopted – nothing objectionable so long as what is borrowed is treated as a manipulable resource. Social science needs the self-confidence to treat philosophy as a resource rather than as a master.

---

158 The network theory is not only descriptive. It also has prescriptive implications, suggesting, for instance, that agents are active, that 'empiricist' and 'ecumenical' approaches to social science are likely to fail, and that science cannot be distinguished from social science in terms of its methods.

159 The social sciences are not short of prescriptions, many of which come from philosophy. These are often presented in terms of an historical discussion of the development of philosophy.

160 This type of prescription should not normally be taken seriously, because it comes from outside social science practice. There is no reason why social scientists should define their practice in terms congenial to the imperialist claims of another practice, that of philosophy. To do so is an unwarranted failure of nerve.

161 Instead, social scientists should have confidence in their own locally defined practices, and simply treat philosophy as a resource like any other discipline.

Endnotes

CHAPTER 2   CLASSIFICATION

1. H. Helmholtz, quoted by R. L. Gregory, *The Intelligent Eye* (Weidenfeld & Nicolson, London, 1970) p. 30.
2. This is adapted from D. H. Hubel and T. N. Wiesel, 'Receptive fields, binocular interaction and functional architecture in the cat's visual cortex', *Journal of Physiology*, 160 (1962) p. 106.
3. Ibid, p. 30.
4. These figures are adapted from ibid. This and the author's earlier semi-popular book, *Eye and Brain* (Weidenfeld & Nicolson, London, 1973) are a rich source of information and insight for those interested either in the psychology of perception or in using the latter as an analogue for other cognitive activity.
5. Though we are constructing this argument in line with Mary Hesse's network model readers who know the writing of L. Wittgenstein will immediately recognise this as a version of his concept of 'family resemblance'. See L. Wittgenstein, *Philosophical Investigations* (Basil Blackwell, Oxford, 1968) pp. 31–41.

CHAPTER 3   INFERENCE

1. We discuss tacit knowledge and its acquisition in more detail in Chs 9 and 10.
2. We say 'approximate' because it is important to understand that there is not necessarily one-to-one correlation between terms in two different languages.
3. This is a quotation from Barry Barnes, 'Natural rationality: a neglected concept in the social sciences', *Philosophy of the Social Sciences*, 6 (1976) pp. 115–126.

CHAPTER 4   NETWORKS

1. There are at least two reasons for this diversity. First, individuals do not experience the same phenomena upon which to build inductive generalis-ations. And second, the *reasons* for making connections also influence the types of connections made. This is a point that we will develop later, but it will be immediately obvious if exemplified. The network into which an ornithol-ogist links a certain kind of bird will be different from that into which a radio engineer makes connections. Consider the following (real-life) conversation:

Radio engineer:	We can't keep the aerial properly in service because the mast is continually being attacked by woodpeckers.
Ornithologist:	Oh really? What kind of woodpeckers?
Radio engineer:	Darned woodpeckers!

The ornithologist was hoping to discover whether the birds in question were greater spotted, lesser spotted or green woodpeckers. This was of no interest to the radio engineer who (rightly) considered the birds to be an utter nuisance.

2. For the purpose of this example we will endow Xaanthi with altogether human cognitive and perceptual attributes. The lack of realism of this example is thereby revealed, for as recent exo-archaeological excavations have shown, the Martian propensity to classify was structured by the capacity to dig imaginary canals.

3. See Ron Westrum, 'Science and social intelligence about anomalies: the case of meteorites', *Social Studies of Science*, 8 (1978), pp. 461–93.

4. Or again, the whale might simply be ignored, for instance on the grounds that its sighting was unreliable.

5. Readers might like to reflect on the fact that books at the 'British Library' (the British Museum of yore) are classified according to their position on the shelves of that institution.

6. For the ethnography and much discussion see R. Bulmer, 'Why is the cassowary not a bird? A problem of zoological taxonomy among the Karam of the New Guinea Highlands', *Man*, new series, 2, 1, (March 1967) 5–25. A slightly shortened version of this paper is reprinted in Mary Douglas (ed.) *Rules and Meanings* (Penguin, Harmondsworth, 1973).

7. See, for instance, Hilary Putnam, 'The meaning of "Meaning"', pages 215–271 in Hilary Putnam, *Mind, Language and Reality, Philosophical Papers*, Vol. 2 (Cambridge University Press, Cambridge, 1975).

8. Mary Hesse prefers the term 'intensional reference'. See Mary Hesse, *The Structure of Scientific Inference* (Macmillan, London, 1974) pp. 61–6.

CHAPTER 5   LINKS BETWEEN CLASSES: ECONOMY AND COHERENCE

1. See T. S. Kuhn, *The Structure of Scientific Revolutions* (Chicago University Press, Chicago, 1970) p. 78.

2. J. S. Bruner and L. Postman, 'On the perception of incongruity: a paradigm', *Journal of Personality*, 18 (1949) pp. 206–223.

3. Easy, that is, so long as it is assumed that such social terms as class relate to orderings of perceptible phenomena in the same way as the British and the Karam talk of instances of fauna. We will make this assumption here.

4. See David Butler and Donald Stokes, *Political Change in Britain; the Evolution of Electoral Choice*, 2nd edn (Macmillan, London, 1974) pp. 81–8.

5. For a discussion of models and metaphors, see Ch. 11.

6. For a *caveat*, see Endnote 3.

7. R. M. Young, 'Malthus and the Evolutionists: the common context of biological and social theory', *Past and Present*, 43 (1969) 109–45.

8. M. Rudwick, 'Poulett Scrope on the volcanoes of Auvergne: Lyellian time and political economy', *British Journal for the History of Science*, 7 (1974), 203–42.
9. J. Law, 'A Durkheimian analysis of scientific knowledge: J. A. Udden's particle size analysis', *Knowledge and Society*, 5 (1983), in the press.

CHAPTER 6   LINKS BETWEEN CLASSES: STRENGTH

1. We briefly discuss J. S. Mill's induction in Ch. 8.
2. For a recent review of induction and confirmation theory see Mary Hesse, *The Structure of Scientific Inference* (Macmillan, London, 1974) Ch. 4, 'The Logic of Induction as Explication'.
3. See D. C. Bloor, 'Epistemology or psychology?', *Studies in History and Philosophy of Science*, 5 (1975), pp. 382–95.
4. It is important to note that use of the term 'subjective' here should not be taken to mean that beliefs are idiosyncratically personal. We have already seen how social cues direct agents to attend to certain similarities and differences in preference to others.
5. Formally, Bayes's theorem is expressed:

$$p(h/e'\&e) = \frac{p(h/e)\,p(e'/h\&e)}{p(e'/e)}$$

where h = hypothesis, e = prior evidence and e' = new evidence

6. Hesse, *The Structure of Scientific Inference*, p. 105.
7. Bloor, 'Epistemology or psychology?', p. 392.

CHAPTER 7   WORKABILITY AND TRUTH

1. We owe this example to our colleague, Gordon Fyfe.
2. For further, cross-cultural, consideration of this point see Michael Cole and Sylvia Scribner, *Culture and Thought* (Wiley, New York, 1969) pp. 61–98.
3. For the original ethnography, together with extensive analysis, see R. Bulmer, 'Why the Cassowary is not a Bird', in Mary Douglas (ed.), *Rules and Meanings* (Penguin, Harmondsworth, 1973) pp. 167–93.
4. This group of birds is called *ratitae*. Other birds have breastbones in the shape of a keel which permits, among other things, leverage for the developed pectoral muscles necessary for flight.
5. It should be noted that Mary Hesse prefers to make use of the term 'correspondence' in her description of the network theory.

CHAPTER 8   PHILOSOPHIES OF SCIENCE AND THE NETWORK THEORY

1. Though Popper's philosophy of science is spelled out in a number of his texts, its essentials may be found in the early pages of K. R. Popper, *The Logic of Scientific Discovery* (Hutchinson, London, 1959). This is a

translation of Popper's first major work, *Logik der Forschung*, which
appeared in Vienna in 1934.
2. This is because all the terms in a network are ultimately linked together.
3. In actual fact, oxygen theory ultimately carried the day.
4. We put the term 'empiricist' in inverted commas because we are unhappy
(a) about the loose use of this term in contemporary social science, and
(b) about the way in which empiricism is held to be entirely misguided. The
term is used loosely by many critics, particularly Marxists, to mean
theoretical stances with which the critic does not agree. Thus Kuhn's history
of science is sometimes held to be empiricist. Whatever may be held to be
wrong with Kuhn's conception of paradigm-based knowledge, it is most
certainly not empiricist. So far as the purported misguidedness of empiricism is concerned, though we criticise it in this chapter, we also try to show
that in an important respect it is correct. This point has been extensively
argued in Ch. 5 of David Bloor's *Knowledge and Social Imagery*, (see
Bibliography) where he adapts Mill's theory of number by discussing the
role of social factors to produce a conception of mathematics that is entirely
consistent with the Hesse network theory.
5. From John Stuart Mill, *A System of Logic* (Longman, London, 1961) 3, 8.
6. Published in English by the Free Press, New York, 1964.
7. E. Durkheim, *The Rules of Sociological Method* (Free Press, New York,
1964), pp. 43–4.
8. See, for example, Jack D. Douglas, *The Social Meanings of Suicide*
(Princeton University Press, Princeton, New Jersey, 1967) Ch. 12, 'The
nature and use of official statistics on suicide'.
9. See Popper, *The Logic of Scientific Discovery*.
10. For an example of this position – albeit presented in the course of an anti-
Kuhnian polemic – see Imre Lakatos, 'Falsification and the methodology of
scientific research programmes', pp. 91–195 in Imre Lakatos and Alan
Musgrave (eds) *Criticism and the Growth of Knowledge* (Cambridge
University Press, Cambridge, 1970).
11. See David Bloor's argument in Chapter 5 of his *Knowledge and Social
Imagery*, cited in endnote 4.
12. To put it in the more formal language introduced at the end of Ch. 4, the
extension of the term depends upon tacit decisions about its intension.
13. We should briefly indicate one further difficulty with Popper's conception of
falsifiability. This prescriptive criterion of demarcation insists that upon
falsification the scientist must abandon his theory and search for an
alternative and broader conjecture. It enjoins the scientist to abandon ship,
as it were. The network theory tells us that it is not possible to abandon ship,
though it is eminently possible to rebuild the ship on a piecemeal basis
(remember Neurath's raft). Popper's insistence that falsified theory should
be rejected wholesale is thus an impossibility. Lakatos concedes this and
caters for it in his revisionist Popperian position that is developed in the
lengthy paper cited in endnote 10.
14. The positions of both Mill and Popper are more complex than we have
suggested in this discussion. In particular, Mill allocated a greater role to
theory than we have implied, though his name is now inseparably linked
with inductivism.

15. These theories are 'two-language' because, on the one hand, there are terms and axioms which connect those terms and on the other hand there are empirical observations. These two different languages are connected by a dictionary. See, for example, N. R. Campbell, *Foundations of Science* (Dover, New York, 1956) pp. 119 ff.

CHAPTER 9 THE ACQUISITION OF SOCIAL COHERENCE CONDITIONS: PERCEPTION

1. For details see Sonia Cole, *Counterfeit* (John Murray, London, 1955) pp. 40–7.
2. The importance of these observations is this: they suggest that the sense of stability that we have about our customary ways of seeing, our visual data, is not, in and of itself, evidence against the role of socially-constructed coherence conditions. The fact, that is, that we 'see' things without any difficulty under ordinary circumstances does not mean that we would have to see them in that (or any) way without the appropriate cues from proper authority. Whether the books by Carlos Castenada are to be treated as fact or fiction we leave for the reader to decide. Whatever their status, however, they can be read as an example of the reconstruction of perception under the authority of unusual social cues. See Carlos Castenada, *Tables of Power* (Penguin, Harmondsworth, 1976).
3. See S. E. Asch, 'Opinions and social pressure', *Scientific American*, 193 (5), (1955) pp. 31–5.
4. Roger Tory Peterson, *A Field Guide to the Birds Giving Field Marks of all Species found East of the Rockies*, 2nd edn (Houghton Mifflin Co., Boston, 1947) p. 120.
5. Ibid.
6. Roger Tory Peterson, Guy Mountfort and P. A. D. Hollom, *A Field Guide to the Birds of Britain and Europe* (Collins, London, 1974) pp. xix–xx.
7. Thomas S. Kuhn, *The Structure of Scientific Revolutions* (Chicago University Press, Chicago, 1970).
8. Ibid, pp. 189–90.
9. Ibid, p. 190.

CHAPTER 10 THE ACQUISITION OF SOCIAL COHERENCE CONDITIONS: MANIPULATION

1. This point will be intuitively obvious to anyone who has ever watched a baby intent on acquiring control of its hands in order to grasp an object. What the adult, or for that matter the one year old, does effortlessly, is unambiguously hard work for the four-month old. He looks at the object he wishes to grasp, moves his hand to within his field of vision and looks to and fro between his hand and the object. Then, monitoring the former, he attempts to move his hand to grasp the latter – though he also has to learn to co-ordinate grasping with the arrival of his hand at its goal. Many of the advances made by the small child are probably epigenetic in nature, but this does not undermine,

indeed it emphasises, the role of learning. See T. R. G. Bower, *Human Development* (Freeman & Company, San Francisco, 1979).

2. Harry M. Collins, 'The TEA set: tacit knowledge and scientific networks', *Science Studies*, 4 (1974), pp. 165–85.
3. Michael Polanyi, *Personal Knowledge; Towards a Post-Critical Philosophy* (Routledge & Kegan Paul, London, 1972).
4. J. Ravetz, *Scientific Knowledge and Its Social Problems* (Oxford University Press, Oxford, 1971).
5. For an example of this kind of learning in science, consider the case of particle-size analysis in sedimentology – a technique that is reputed to be very easy to learn. See John Law, 'Fragmentation and investment in sedimentology', *Social Studies of Science*, 10 (1980) pp. 1–22.

CHAPTER 11   THE ACQUISITION OF SOCIAL COHERENCE CONDITIONS: METAPHOR AND THEORY

1. Our discussion of John Dalton is drawn from Arnold Thackray, *John Dalton: Critical Assessments of his Life and Science* (Harvard University Press, Cambridge, Mass., 1972).
2. Henry, in this case at least, acted like the perfect Popperian scientist. He set out to refute Dalton's conjecture (which he thought to be wrong) and abandoned his own position in favour of Dalton as a result of the experimental evidence. Such episodes are relatively rare in the history of science.
3. For a discussion of the notion of theory as a coherent story, see Alan Ryan, *The Philosophy of the Social Sciences* (Macmillan, London and Basingstoke, 1970) Ch. 4.
4. Althusser writes 'The greatest disadvantage of this representation of the structure of every society by the spatial metaphor of an edifice, is obviously the fact that it is metaphorical: i.e. it remains *descriptive*'. 'Ideology and ideological state apparatuses' in B. R. Cosin (ed.), *Education, Structure and Society* (Penguin, Harmondsworth, 1972) pp. 242–80, at p. 248.
5. There is an immense literature, both in prose and poetry, which documents this shift. A moving description written by a non-participant is to be found in Vera Mary Brittain, *Testament of Youth: an Autobiographical Study of the Years 1900–1925*, (Macmillan, London and New York, 1933). More succinctly, the change in war poetry reflects the change in perception. Thus, the 'pre-war' poet, Rupert Brooke, wrote of death in noble and patriotic terms – 'dying has made us rarer gifts than gold' (Rupert Brooke, *The Collected Poems of Rupert Brooke, with an Introduction by George Edward Woodberry* (John Lane Co., New York, 1916) p. 109, 'The Dead'). Contrast this with Wilfred Owen's 'Futility':

> Move him into the sun –
> Gently its touch awoke him once,
> At home, whispering of fields unsown.
> Always it woke him, even in France,
> Until this morning and this snow.

If anything might rouse him now
The kind old sun will know.

Think how it wakes the seeds –
Woke once, the clays of a cold star.
Are limbs, so dear-achieved, are sides,
Full-nerved – still warm – too hard to stir?
Was it for this the clay grew tall?
– O what made fatuous sunbeams toil
To break earth's sleep at all?

Wilfred Owen, in Edmund Blunden (ed.) *The Poems of Wilfred Owen* (Chatto & Windus, London, 1955) p. 73.
6. This is known as the 'interaction' view of metaphor. See Mary B. Hesse, 'The explanatory function of metaphor', pp. 157–177 in Mary B. Hesse, *Models and Analogies in Science*, (Sheed & Ward, London, 1973). A similar point, relating specifically to the use of terms, is to be found in Garfinkel's analysis of discourse. See H. Garfinkel, *Studies in Ethnomethodology* (Prentice Hall, New Jersey, 1967) in his discussions of the 'documentary method'.
7. Max Weber, *The Protestant Ethic and the Spirit of Capitalism* (George Allen & Unwin, London, 1930).
8. Weber is probably wrong about the causes of the rise of capitalism and the relationship between ideas and economic activity. See Barry Barnes, *Interests and the Growth of Knowledge* (Routledge & Kegan Paul, London, 1977).
9. For this argument see J. D. Douglas, *The Social Meanings of Suicide* (Princeton University Press, New Jersey, 1967). Emile Durkheim, *Suicide* (Free Press, New York, 1951).
10. For a discussion of the current controversy about the teaching of evolutionary theory in American schools see Dorothy Nelkin, *Science Textbook Controversies and the Politics of Equal Time* (MIT Press, Cambridge, Mass., 1977).
11. We have seen (Ch. 8) one exception to this rule which occurs when alternative theories of knowledge make unrealistic assumptions.

CHAPTER 12 INTERESTS AND KNOWLEDGE

1. For a detailed sociological analysis of the race-intelligence debate see Jonathan Harwood, 'The race intelligence controversy: a sociological approach, (1) Professional factors; (2) External factors', *Social Studies of Science*, 6 (1976) pp. 369–94; 7 (1977) pp. 1–30; 'Heredity versus Environment; an episode in the continuing history of the Welfare State', pp. 231–51 in Barry Barnes and Steven Shapin (eds), *Natural Order; Historical Studies of Scientific Culture*, (Sage, London and Beverly Hills, 1979).
2. For more discussion of such impartial analysis see Ch. 1 of D. C. Bloor, *Knowledge and Social Imagery* (Routledge & Kegan Paul, London, 1976) and the introduction to Part IV of the present text.

3. The noted radical and Marxist, Haldane, was an hereditarian in the generation before the current controversy.
4. Harwood here uses Mannheim's notion of a 'style of thought'. This is briefly discussed in Ch. 20.
5. Naturally, a full empirical description of the debate would involve a much more complex field of interests than that described here. See the Harwood articles cited in note 1.
6. Our description and definition of these two knowledge-generating interests is close to that of Barnes. See Barry Barnes, *Interests and the Growth of Knowledge*, (Routledge & Kegan Paul, London, 1977). However, there is one important difference: Barnes argues that, ideally, it might be possible to envisage knowledge directed solely by an interest in prediction and control, and without legitimating social-control interests. We argue (see Ch. 20 onward) that this is wrong. There are *always* interests in social legitimation present. The important point is whether these are *local* (e.g. professional) or global.

CHAPTER 13   INTERESTS AND THE GROWTH OF KNOWLEDGE

1. This theory of science is to be found in the sociological writing of Merton. See, for instance, 'Science and the social order', in R. K. Merton, *Sociology of Science* (Chicago University Press, Chicago, 1973) pp. 254–66.
2. For details see Irving Langmuir, *Pathological Science*, Report No. 68–C–035 (General Electric Research & Development Center, Schenectady, New York, 1968).
3. For further details see Richard Lewontin and Richard Levins, 'The problem of Lysenkoism', pages 32–64 in Hilary and Steven Rose (eds.) *The Radicalisation of Science: Ideology of/in the Natural Sciences* (Macmillan, London, 1976).
4. This discussion is based on four papers by Steven Shapin and Geoffrey N. Cantor, and closely follows the line argued by Shapin. Readers interested in the example are strongly urged to read these papers as they illustrate with great clarity the differences between a correspondence and network/interest analysis of scientific controversy. G. N. Cantor, 'The Edinburgh phrenology debate, 1803–1838', *Annals of Science*, 32 (1975) pp. 195–218; S. Shapin, 'Phrenological knowledge and the social structure of early nineteenth-century Edinburgh', *Annals of Science*, 32 (1975) pp. 219–43; 'The politics of observation: cerebral anatomy and social interests in the Edinburgh phrenology debates', pp. 139–78 in Roy Wallis (ed), *On the Margins of Science: The Social Construction of Rejected Knowledge*, Sociological Review Monograph, No. 27 (University of Keele, Keele, 1979); '*Homo Phrenologicus*: Anthropological perspectives on an historical problem' pp. 41–71 in Barry Barnes and Steven Shapin (eds), *Natural Order: Historical Studies of Scientific Culture*, (Sage, London and Beverly Hills, 1979).
5. For a development of this position see the paper by Cantor, 'The Edinburgh phrenology debate'.
6. Psychology did not exist as an academic discipline at that time. What might later have been described as speculative psychology was simply part of

philosophy. For purposes of simplicity, however, we use the anachronistic term 'psychology' here.

7. See note 4.
8. To put it crudely, experts are always available for hire if the price is right. (It is, after all, in *their* interests to find a clientele). All contemporary scientific cum political controversies illustrate this. There are experts for and against nuclear power. There are experts for and against the control of atmospheric sulphur dioxide emission by coal-fired power-stations. There are experts for and against the fluoridation of the water supply (though the anti-fluoridation lobby is the less attractive client in this case). There are experts for and against herbicidal spraying. And so on.

CHAPTER 14   NEGOTIATION, PERSUASION AND THE POWER OF KNOWLEDGE

1. Our description of the gravity-wave controversy is drawn from H. M. Collins, 'The seven sexes: a study in the sociology of a phenomenon, or the replication of experiments in physics' *Sociology*, 9 (1975) pp. 205–24. See also H. M. Collins, 'Son of seven sexes: the social destruction of a physical phenomenon', *Social Studies of Science*, 11 (1981) pp. 33–62.
2. In fact the original experimentalist's experiments came to what was, from his point of view, a sad end. A failure to notice the difference in time zones between two linked detectors changed what appeared to be an interesting confirmation of his findings into something that was generally taken to undermine them.
3. Our analysis of the gravity-wave negotiations parts company somewhat from that of Collins here. In his view nothing other than the cultural preferences and social interests of the protagonists has any relevance for the outcome of the negotiations. Our view is that the lumps in nature (here translated into the traces of the instruments) have some relevance for that outcome. This does not, however, mean that they determine it. It is just that all the protagonists presumably accept that the readings of the instruments require explanation. One imagines that the actual explanations of what was going on would vary depending on these readings. The scientists could, of course, in principle ignore the readings, and reclassify them as irrelevant for the debate. In practice, however, given the cultural preferences and social interests of the practitioners, such an outcome is improbable. We are thus in agreement with Collins when he says that culture constitutes data. We part company with him when he says that nature is irrelevant, because once those cultural commitments are entered into, then nature, (as it were) finds its voice and has to be accounted in one way or another if continued workability is to be ensured.
4. Max Weber, *The Protestant Ethic and the Spirit of Capitalism*, (George Allen & Unwin, London, 1930). An analysis of and attack on Weber's idealism is mounted in some detail in Barry Barnes, *Interests and the Growth of Knowledge* (Routledge & Kegan Paul, London, 1977). Following Hugh Trevor Roper, Barnes also attacks Weber's thesis on empirical grounds. See

H. R. Trevor Roper, *Religion, and the Reformation and Social Change* (Macmillan, London, 1967).

5. K. Marx and F. Engels, *The German Ideology*, Part 1 (Lawrence & Wishart, London, 1970).

6. For this criticism worked out in detail see Digby C. Anderson and W. W. Sharrock, 'Biasing the News: technical issues in "Media Studies" ', *Sociology*, 13 (1979) pp. 367–85.

7. See Roland Barthes, *Mythologies* (Paladin, London, 1973).

8. See Gaston Bachelard, *La Formation de l'Esprit Scientifique* (Librairie Philosophique, J. Vrin, Paris, 1980).

9. It was Mannheim who first presented the sociology of knowledge in roughly this way. See our discussion in Ch. 20.

10. See Barry Barnes, 'Natural rationality: a neglected concept in the social sciences', *Philosophy of the Social Sciences*, 6 (1976) pp. 115–26.

11. See Barry Barnes and David Bloor, 'Relativism, rationalism and the sociology of knowledge', pp. 21–47 in Martin Hollis and Steven Lukes (eds), *Rationality and Relativism* (Blackwell, Oxford, 1982).

12. See David Bloor's study of the rationality of the Azande poison oracle for a more extended development of this analysis of logic. David C. Bloor, *Knowledge and Social Imagery* (Routledge & Kegan Paul, London, 1976).

CHAPTER 15   SCIENTIFIC SOCIALISATION AND THE ALIGNMENT OF NETWORKS

1. T. S. Kuhn, *The Structure of Scientific Revolutions*, 2nd edn, (Chicago University Press, Chicago, 1970).

2. Ibid, p. 80.

3. Ibid., p. 189.

4. We consider this eventuality in the second half of Ch. 16.

5. Our example is taken from Lakatos' study which displays the historical debate that took place in the form of a discussion between students and teacher. See I. Lakatos, *Proofs and Refutations* (Cambridge University Press, Cambridge, 1976). For further sociological discussion of this example, see Barry Barnes and John Law, 'Whatever Should be Done with Indexical Expressions?', *Theory and Society*, 3 (1976), pp. 223–37.

6. For instance, if one imagines a cube and then, as it were, flattens it into two dimensions by removing a face, then it looks as we have depicted it in Figure 15.2, and since a face but no vertices or edges have been taken away, it may be described by the formula:

$$V + F - E = 1$$

If Euler's theorem is true, then the latter expression is true for the 'flattened cube'. We can show that this is true for the 'flattened cube' if we triangulate each of the remaining faces. In doing so, we have added five new faces and five new edges and since these additions cancel each other out,

$$V + F - E = 1$$

should still describe the resultant Figure 15.3. Next we remove triangles from

273

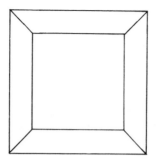

FIGURE 15.2 *Flattened cube*

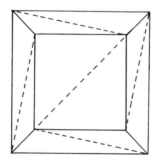

FIGURE 15.3 *Triangulated flattened cube*

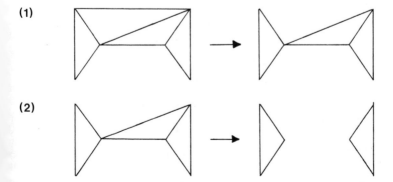

FIGURE 15.4 *Anomalous proof procedure*

the outside inwards. The removal of each triangle must involve removing $1 E + 1 F$ (in which case $V + F - E = 1$) or $2 E + 1 V + 1 F$ (in which case $V + F - E = 1$, still). This process goes on until we are left with one triangle, for which $V + F - E = 1$ can be determined by inspection. All triangles have 3 vertices, 1 face and 3 edges, so $V + F - E = 1$ is true. Hence this expression must be true for the original cube after a face has been taken away (Figure 15.2), so the original cube restored, with its six faces will conform to Euler's theorem of polyhedra $V + F - E = 2$.

7. For instance, the second move in Figure 15.4 above, while removing a single triangle in conformity with the instructions, leads to the loss of $2E$, $1F$, and $0V$.

CHAPTER 16   NORMAL SCIENCE AND THE OPERATION OF INTERESTS

1. Further details and references are to be found in John Law, 'The Development of Specialties in Science: the Case of Protein X-ray Crystallography'. *Science Studies*, 3 (1973), pp. 275–303.
2. T. S. Kuhn, *The Structure of Scientific Revolutions*, 2nd edn (Chicago University Press, Chicago, 1970) p. 24. In this quotation Kuhn uses the term 'paradigm' by which he intends the practically-shared network that comprises theory and exemplary applications. It is also worth noting that the 'relatively inflexible box' of the paradigm is flexible at least to the extent that we have suggested in the preceding paragraphs. Kuhn's extensive use of examples elsewhere in the book – for instance his discussion of dynamics after Newton – makes it clear that this 'flexible' reading is justified.

CHAPTER 17   ANOMALIES AND SCIENTIFIC REVOLUTIONS

1. For further details of this case see Rob Williams and John Law, 'Beyond the Bounds of Credibility', *Fundamenta Scientiae*, 1 (1980), pp. 295–315, and John Law and Rob Williams, 'Putting Facts Together: a Study of Scientific Persuasion', *Social Studies of Science*, 12 (1982) pp. 535–58.
2. We can only guess what might have happened if the results had more consistently pointed to the stimulatory effects of DIVEMAs. Our guess, for what it is worth, is that the scientists would have concluded that such results were genuine and published them. This would have involved generating public anomaly, something contrary to theoretical expectations. Note however, that such theoretical expectations were relatively weak.
3. It is worth mentioning that the biochemists might have undertaken further experiments in order to generate additional data. For reasons that are not important for our present purposes, however, they found the DIVEMA work relatively uninteresting, and were somewhat unwilling to invest more time and effort in what would most probably have turned out to be a wild goose chase.
4. For a further entertaining case, see Ron Westrum, 'Social Intelligence about Anomalies: the Case of UFOs', *Social Studies of Science*, 7 (1977) pp. 271–30.
5. For some further details see Peter Doig, *A Concise History of Astronomy* (Chapman & Hall, London, 1950) pp. 115–16.

6. There is an immense literature on the chemical revolution. Readers might start by looking at J. B. Conant, *The Overthrow of the Phlogiston Theory: the Chemical Revolution of* 1775–1789 (Harvard Case Histories in Experimental Science, Case 2, Cambridge, Mass., 1950).

7. We have seen that any change in a network of terms has implications for the intension and extension of other terms. Accordingly, one cannot claim that there was no change in those observational terms that survived the transformation. Clearly in the new circumstances their significance was somewhat different. Henceforth scientists would use them in subtly different ways. This is, however, theoretically unproblematic for it differs in principle not at all from the situation encountered in relatively minor network changes.

PART IV INTRODUCTION

1. David C. Bloor, *Knowledge and Social Imagery* (Routledge & Kegan Paul, London, 1976) pp. 5, 6.

CHAPTER 18 SOCIAL STRUCTURE OF PRIMITIVE IDEAS: AZANDE POISON ORACLE

1. Lucien Lévy Bruhl, *La Mentalité Primitive* (Alcan, Paris, 1922) p. 506.
2. Ibid, p. 510.
3. Some recent and sophisticated examples of this genre are to be found in R. Horton and R. Finnegan (eds), *Modes of Thought: Essays on Thinking in Western and Non-Western Societies* (Faber & Faber, London, 1973).
4. For a recent example of this see Peter Winch, *The Idea of a Social Science* (Routledge & Kegan Paul, London, 1958). Aspects of Winch's argument are discussed in Ch. 22.
5. E. E. Evans Pritchard, *Witchcraft, Oracles and Magic Among the Azande* (Oxford University Press, London, 1937).
6. See, note 5, p. 348.
7. It is proper to note that this is a conclusion with which the great majority of contemporary commentators are in complete disagreement. See, for instance, the essays on rationality by Steven Lukes in *Essays in Social Theory* (Macmillan, London and Basingstoke, 1977), and most of the papers in M. Hollis and S. Lukes, (eds), *Rationality and Relativism* (Blackwell, Oxford, 1981). Barnes and Bloor, however, develop the view that we argue here, and indeed we draw a part of our argument from them. See Barry Barnes, 'The Comparison of Belief Systems: Anomaly versus Falsehood', in R. Horton and R. Finnegan (eds), mentioned in note 3 and Barry Barnes and David Bloor, 'Relativism, Rationalism and the Sociology of Knowledge'; pp. 21–47 in M. Hollis and S. Lukes (eds), mentioned above. For further discussion of the Azande poison oracle consistent with the position advanced here see David Bloor, *Knowledge and Social Imagery* (Routledge & Kegan Paul, London, 1976) pp. 123–30.
8. Of course, according to network theory all network applications must be seen as extensions to novel instances. There is, however, an obvious and

important pragmatic distinction between extensions recognised as novel and those considered to be routine.

9. Notice that we have avoided saying 'less developed' as this implies that knowledge moves along a scale from less to more developed, from the Azande to us. We may predict that as societies become more complex so knowledge will become more differentiated and esoteric. We may not, however, assume that other esoteric knowledge will look like ours. Remember that any given network is only one possible way of categorising similarity and difference.

10. We include the qualifier 'almost' here for the obvious reasons that a differentiated though perfectly static and homeostatic society is conceivable, though in practice it seems unlikely.

CHAPTER 19   SOCIAL STRUCTURE OF COMMON SENSE

1. The data on children's tests are drawn from H. Mehan and H. Wood, *The Reality of Ethnomethodology* (Wiley & Sons, New York, 1975) pp. 38–43.
2. D. Lawrence Wieder, 'Telling the Code' in Roy Turner (ed), *Ethnomethodology* (Penguin, Harmondsworth, 1974) pp. 144–72.
3. Ibid, p. 160.
4. Ibid.
5. For this position argued elsewhere, see David C. Bloor, 'Epistemology or Psychology?', *Studies in History and Philosophy of Science*, 5 (1975) pp. 352–359.
6. See K. R. Popper, *The Logic of Scientific Discovery* (Hutchinson, London, 1959).
7. We touch upon this writing at the end of Ch. 21.
8. See Gaston Bachelard, *La Formation de l'Esprit Scientifique: Contribution à une Psychanalyse de la Connaissance Objective*, 11th edition, Librairie Philosophique (J. Vrin, Paris, 1980) p. 19.
9. Ibid, p. 55.
10. Ibid, pp. 73ff.
11. Ibid, p. 38.

CHAPTER 20   SOCIAL STRUCTURE OF IDEOLOGY

1. In what follows we do not, of course, offer a full account of the writing of the authors treated.
2. See, for instance, Karl Marx and Friedrich Engels, *The German Ideology* Part 1 (Lawrence & Wishart, London, 1970) p. 37.
3. Ibid, p. 47.
4. Ibid, p. 56.
5. Ibid, pp. 65–6.
6. Ibid, pp. 37 and 40.
7. Karl Marx, *Capital*, Vol. 3 (Lawrence & Wishart, London, 1974) p. 168
8. Karl Marx, *Capital*, Vol. 1 (Lawrence & Wishart, London, 1974) p. 507
9. In some later writers – notably Lukács – Marx's interest-explanation fo

the failure of the bourgeoisie to understand its 'true' position takes an illegitimately idealist form.

10. Karl Mannheim, *Ideology and Utopia* (Routledge & Kegan Paul, London, 1960) pp. 66–7.
11. Ibid, pp. 49–50.
12. Karl Mannheim, 'Conservative Thought' in Karl Mannheim, *Essays on Sociology and Social Psychology* (Routledge & Kegan Paul, London, 1953) pp. 74–164.
13. Karl Mannheim, as note 10, p. 36.
14. Ibid.
15. Ibid, p. 175.
16. Ibid.
17. Ibid, p. 71.
18. Mannheim to some degree excepts certain branches of the natural sciences. It is worthwhile noting that these achieve their exceptional status because they are in some measure detached from the specific social interests of particular scientists and are directed by an interest in contemplation rather than action. See *Ideology and Utopia*, pp. 154–5 and 243.
19. Ibid, p. 31.
20. Ibid, pp. 132 and 144.
21. Jorge Larrain, *The Concept of Ideology* (Hutchinson, London, 1979) p. 118.
22. Barry Barnes, *Interests and the Growth of Knowledge* (Routledge & Kegan Paul, London, 1977) p. 38.
23. We followed a similar though somewhat more guarded line of argument in our discussion of the social contrast between primitive and scientific beliefs in Ch. 18.
24. Barnes, *Interests and the Growth of Knowledge*, pp. 34–5.
25. We discuss the issue of *verstehen* in Ch. 22.
26. Andrew Pickering, 'The Role of Interests in High Energy Physics: the Choice Between Charm and Colour', in Karin D. Knorr, Roger Krohn and Richard Whitley (eds), *The Social Process of Scientific Investigation, Sociology of the Sciences*, vol. 4 (D. Reidel, Dordrecht and Boston, 1980) pp. 107–38.
27. See, in this context, Bruno Latour and Steven Woolgar, *Laboratory Life: the Social Construction of Scientific Facts* (Sage, London and Beverly Hills, 1979) Ch. 5; Trevor Pinch, 'Theoreticians and the Production of Experimental Anomaly: the Case of Solar Neutrinos', in Karin D. Knorr, Roger Krohn and Richard D. Whitley (eds), *Social Process*, pp. 77–106; and Rob Williams and John Law, 'Beyond the Bounds of Credibility', *Fundamenta Scientiae*, 1 (1980) pp. 295–315.
28. Barnes, *Interests and the Growth of Knowledge*, p. 42.
29. Barnes' suggestion that a distinction be made between knowledge that is ideologically determined and that which is not finds an echo in Mary Hesse's finely-tuned concern to find a properly contexted but none the less normative role for the epistemologist. For a discussion of this and related issues to do with social interests see Mary Hesse, 'The Strong Thesis of Sociology of Science', in Mary Hesse, *Revolutions and Reconstructions in the Philosophy of Science* (Harvester, Brighton, 1980) pp. 29–60.
30. We should, perhaps, make it absolutely clear that our position has nothing whatsoever to do with the 'end of ideology' thesis.

CHAPTER 21   THE 'PROBLEM' OF RELATIVISM

1. For a clear exposition of the methodological consequences of a relativist conception of knowledge see David C. Bloor, *Knowledge and Social Imagery* (Routledge & Kegan Paul, London, 1976) Ch. 1.
2. Those who are interested would do well to consult Martin Hollis and Steven Lukes (eds), *Rationality and Relativism* (Blackwell, Oxford, 1982). Only one article in this collection (Barry Barnes and David C. Bloor, 'Relativism, Rationalism and the Sociology of Knowledge', pp. 21–47) is in favour of a form of relativism. The others are opposed to this. See also Mary Hesse, 'The Strong Thesis of Sociology of Science', in Mary Hesse, *Revolutions and Reconstructions in the Philosophy of Science* (Harvester, Brighton, 1980) pp. 29–60.
3. For a sociological version of this view see R. K. Merton, 'The Normative Structure of Science', in R. K. Merton, *The Sociology of Science*, (Chicago University Press, Chicago, 1973) pp. 267–78.
4. This, of course, is what we have tried to do in this text: upon an assumption that people reason in identical ways (i.e. a set of shared psychological coherence conditions) we have tried to show that variation in social coherence conditions is natural.
5. Our own argument, of course, has no finality. Its success rests upon its deployment in a specific set of social and intellectual circumstances. It is thus only contingently workable, despite the fact that we have used such terms as 'accurate' in the course of our discussion and we are, in addition, firmly committed to it ourselves.
6. See Bloor, *Knowledge and Social Imagery*, Ch. 1.
7. K. R. Popper, *The Logic of Scientific Discovery* (Hutchinson, London, 1959).
8. K. R. Popper, *Objective Knowledge* (Oxford University Press, Oxford, 1972).
9. Imre Lakatos, 'Falsification and the Methodology of Scientific Research Programmes' pp. 91–195 in Imre Lakatos and Alan Musgrave (eds), *Criticism and the Growth of Knowledge* (Cambridge University Press, Cambridge, 1970).
10. It should be clear that an *explanation* for the philosophical preference for prescription is no argument against that position. A similar analysis could easily be made of the position we are arguing. Note also that Hesse, *Revolutions and Reconstructions* hopes to find a prescriptive role for epistemology *within* an acceptance of the strong, relativistic, thesis of the sociology of science.

CHAPTER 22   THE PROBLEM OF *VERSTEHEN*

1. Peter Winch, *The Idea of a Social Science* (Routledge & Kegan Paul, London, 1958).
2. Emile Durkheim, *The Rules of Sociological Method* (Free Press, New York, 1964); and in particular, Emile Durkheim, *Suicide* (Free Press, New York, 1951).

3. Max Weber, *Economy and Society*, vol. 1, ed. G. Roth and C. Wittich (ed.) (University of California Press, Berkeley, 1978), Ch. 1, 'Basic Sociological Terms'.
4. We do not, of course, suggest that our account of Winch's position is exhaustive.
5. Winch, *Idea of a Social Science*, p. 23.
6. Empathy requires adequate prior knowledge of the actors' culture.
7. It might be argued that at the extreme the similarities and differences attended to in the case of social institutions are *entirely* dependent upon – indeed are constituted by – social cues, whereas they exist independently of social cues for natural kinds. For a discussion of this possibility see Barry Barnes, 'Social Life as Bootstrapped Induction', mimeo, (Science Studies Unit, University of Edinburgh, 1982).
8. See J. D. Douglas, *The Social Meanings of Suicide* (Princeton University Press, New Jersey, 1967) and J. Maxwell Atkinson, *Discovering Suicide: Studies in the Social Organisation of Sudden Death* (Macmillan, London, 1978).
9. R. Bulmer, 'Why the Cassowary is not a Bird' pp. 167–93 in Mary Douglas (ed.), *Rules and Meanings* (Penguin, Harmondsworth, 1973).
10. D. Lawrence Wieder, 'Telling the Code' pp. 144–72 in Roy Turner (ed.), *Ethnomethodology* (Penguin, Harmondsworth, 1974). This is a particularly interesting study of network acquisition.
11. Winch, *Idea of a Social Science*, p. 89.
12. Winch's position appears to rest upon two unrealistic assumptions: (a) that there is cognitive consensus within cultures, and (b) that the investigator who lives among the natives long enough will partake of that consensus. Proposition (a) is almost always demonstrably wrong and in any case cannot be shown to be correct even where there are no disputes. (If there is any doubt about this, consider the case of Euler's theorem of polyhedra). Proposition (b) is obviously impossible to obtain in the absence of (a) and is in any case more generally governed by the same conditions as (a).
13. The latter typically arise either because the link concerned is of insufficient importance to warrant further investigation, that is to say, it is workable as it stands; or because, despite its importance, it has so far resisted attempts at specification.
14. Steven Shapin, 'Phrenological Knowledge and the Social Structure of Early Nineteenth Century Edinburgh', *Annals of Science*, 32 (1975) pp. 219–43.
15. Our discussion of cause is akin, but not identical, to that of Barnes. Barry Barnes, *Scientific Knowledge and Sociological Theory* (Routledge & Kegan Paul, London, 1974) pp. 71–8.
16. Durkheim, *Rules of Sociological Method*, pp. 89–90.
17. Trevor J. Pinch, 'The Sun Set: the Presentation of Certainty in Scientific Life', *Social Studies of Science*, 11, (1981) pp. 131–58.

CHAPTER 23   SCIENCE AND SOCIAL SCIENCE

1. None of these writers wrote very much about sport *per se*. Marx advocated the development of physical abilities:

Marx was concerned with civil society's need for workers to obtain more
free time – not only for pure leisure but also for recuperating their
strength and applying themselves more vigorously to productive work
after reasonable rest and recreation. (James Riordan, *Sport in Soviet
Society*, Cambridge University Press, Cambridge, 1977)

Weber makes only a passing reference to sport and that in *The Protestant
Ethic and the Spirit of Capitalism*, (George Allen & Unwin, London, 1930).
Here he indicates that sport is acceptable only if it serves rational purposes.
Durkheim, so far as we know, did not comment on sport at all.
2. Paul Hoch, *Rip Off the Big Game* (Doubleday, New York, 1972).
3. Riordan, *Spent in Soviet Society*, p. 399.
4. Jay J. Coakley, *Sport in Society* (C. V. Mosby Company, St. Louis, 1978),
quotes from Rick Barry and Bill Libby, *Confessions of a Basketball Gypsy*
(Prentice Hall, New Jersey, 1972), in which Barry refers to himself and other
professional basketball players as slaves 'Slavery is slavery no matter what
the slave is paid'.
5. Hoch, *Rip Off the Big Game*, p. 10.
6. Writers following the Durkheimian tradition also focus on the alleged
functions of sport. According to Coakley (see note 4) sport fulfils a variety
of functions including pattern maintenance, goal attainment and transmission of values.
7. Interestingly, even the term 'holiday' is derived from holy day.
8. Harry Edwards, *Sociology of Sport* (The Dorsey Press, Homewood, Illinois,
1973) p. 90.
9. Riordan, *Sport in Soviet Society*, p. 90.
10. Ailen Guttman, *From Ritual to Record* (Columbia University Press, New
York, 1978).
11. For some fascinating hints on the processes by which this takes place in
natural science see Andrew Pickering, 'The Role of Interests in High Energy
Physics: the Choice Between Charm and Colour' pp. 107–38 in Karin
Knorr, Roger Krohn and Richard Whitley (eds) *The Social Process of
Scientific Investigation, Sociology of the Sciences Yearbook*, Vol. 4 (D.
Reidel, Boston and Dordrecht, 1980).
12. We would like to thank Michel Callon who first drew our attention to the
'opportunities' for a successful sociology in totalitarian societies. We should
also note that Eastern Europe and the Soviet Union do not closely
approximate to the 'ideal' totalitarian society that we have been discussing.
13. As we have already noted, we deal with the case of philosophy in Ch. 24.
14. Certain social sciences are more prone to ecumenical initiatives than others.
In general the 'harder' the social science, the lower its susceptibility. In
psychology, 'general theory' is wisely eschewed in favour of the development of specialist theory about particular psychological attributes which are
of interest for particular predictive reasons. Even economics, despite the
periodic pretensions of such macrotheorists as neo-Keynesians or monet-
arists, is substantially free from the activities of the ecumenical. Here, as in
psychology, different approaches become fashionable at different times, in
part as a response to changes in the balance of broader social interests. The
disease is most prevalent in sociology where certain practitioners can talk,

without blushing, of a 'general theory' of society. The hopelessness of such an enterprise – indeed its pretentiousness – can easily be seen if one imagines the equivalent in other disciplines: there would be 'general theories' of the mind, the body, or the world. In fact, of course, psychological, physiological, meteorological or geological questions are much more specific and much less synthetic (despite the great success of such theories as plate tectonics) and are in all cases considered in terms of particular interests in simplification, prediction and control.

15. One can readily think of cases – for instance, labelling theory, conversational analysis and the sociology of scientific knowledge – where this has taken place in recent years.

CHAPTER 24   SELF-CONFIDENCE AND REDUNDANCY
OF PHILOSOPHY

1. As an example of the former, consider Max Weber's explanation of the rise of capitalism in *The Protestant Ethic and the Spirit of Capitalism* (George Allen & Unwin, London, 1930). As an example of the latter, many types of structural functionalist theory.

2. On this see John Whittaker, 'Models of Social Space: a Study of a Statistical Coup', *Sociology*, 16 (1982), pp. 43–66.

3. There are naturally exceptions to this rule. See P. K. Feyerabend, *Against Method: Outline of an Anarchistic Theory of Knowledge* (New Left Books, London, 1975).

4. Obviously every rule has its exceptions, but as a generalisation, cognitive psychology does not possess grandiose imperialist pretensions.

5. Peter Winch, *The Idea of a Social Science* (Routledge & Kegan Paul, London, 1958) p. 43.

6. I. C. Jarvie, *Concepts and Society* (Routledge & Kegan Paul, London, 1972) p. 144.

Bibliography

The following is a brief bibliography of works in the area covered by this book that are either important in themselves, important because they represent traditions or styles of work, or useful because they provide a ready point of entry into a particular literature. Much fuller references to specific topics are to be found in the notes to each chapter.

Barry Barnes, *Interests and the Growth of Knowledge* (Routledge & Kegan Paul, London, 1977). Treating knowledge as a resource or a tool, indicates the way in which social interests lie behind and direct it.

Barry Barnes, *T. S. Kuhn and Social Science* (Macmillan, London, 1982). A reassessment of Kuhn's writing from a sociological standpoint which develops a finitist notion of knowledge. Very clearly written.

David C. Bloor, *Knowledge and Social Imagery* (Routledge & Kegan Paul, London, 1976). A bold statement of the claim that all knowledge, whether or not scientific, is susceptible to social influence, and hence open to study by the sociology of knowledge.

T. R. G. Bower, *Human Development* (Freeman & Company, San Francisco, 1979). A fine textbook in developmental psychology with much about infant learning.

Mary Douglas (ed.), *Rules and Meanings, The Anthropology of Everyday Knowledge* (Penguin, Harmondsworth, 1973). A collection of empirical articles on the organisation of everyday knowledge.

Dorothy Emmet and Alasdair MacIntyre (eds), *Sociological Theory and Philosophical Analysis* (Macmillan, London, 1970). A collection of papers by a range of authors on the relationship between scientific and social scientific knowledge.

R. L. Gregory, *The Intelligent Eye* (Weidenfeld & Nicolson, London, 1970). An extremely skilful popular account of mechanisms of perception.

Mary B. Hesse, *Revolutions and Reconstructions in the Philosophy of Science* (Harvester Press, Brighton, 1980). A recent collection of essays from a philosopher sympathetic to the history and sociology of science.

Mary B. Hesse, *The Structure of Scientific Inference* (Macmillan,

London, 1974). A rigorous statement of the network theory of knowledge, with some fairly technical passages.

Martin Hollis and Steven Lukes (eds), *Rationality and Relativism* (Blackwell, Oxford, 1981). A collection of essays that are mostly opposed to relativism, though the piece by Barnes and Bloor is an exception.

Thomas S. Kuhn, *The Essential Tension: Selected Studies in Scientific Tradition and Change* (University of Chicago Press, Chicago, 1977). A collection of essays in which Kuhn tends to draw back from the socially-contexted theory of science that many detect in his *Structure* (see below).

Thomas S. Kuhn, *The Structure of Scientific Revolutions*, 2nd edn (Chicago University Press, Chicago, 1970). The best-known and possibly the most influential 'post-positivist' reassessment of the nature of scientific inquiry and change.

Imre Lakatos, *Proofs and Refutations* (Cambridge University Press, Cambridge, 1976). An attractive constructed dialogue between master and pupils about the adequacy of Euler's theorem of polyhedra.

Imre Lakatos and Alan Musgrave (eds), *Criticism and the Growth of Knowledge* (Cambridge University Press, Cambridge, 1970). A collection of essays which amount to a 'Popper–Kuhn' debate.

Bruno Latour and Steve Woolgar, *Laboratory Life: the Social Construction of Scientific Facts* (Sage, London and Beverly Hills, 1979). The first systematic attempt to describe day-to-day science as it is actually practised in the laboratory.

Michael J. Mulkay, *Science and the Sociology of Knowledge* (George Allen & Unwin, London, 1979). A useful introduction to the analysis of scientific knowledge as a branch of the sociology of knowledge.

Ernest Nagel, *The Structure of Science* (Routledge & Kegan Paul, London, 1961). A standard textbook in the classic philosophy of science.

Ulric Neisser, *Cognition and Reality: Principles and Implications of Cognitive Psychology* (Freeman, San Francisco, 1976). A useful general overview of cognitive psychology.

William Outhwaite, *Understanding Social Life* (George Allen & Unwin, London, 1975). An introduction to the classic debates about *verstehen*.

Michael Polanyi, *Personal Knowledge: Towards a Post-Critical Philosophy* (Routledge & Kegan Paul, London, 1972). A text on the philosophy of science by a working scientist in which the role of the tacit is emphasised.

Karl R. Popper, *The Logic of Scientific Discovery* (Hutchinson, London, 1959). A translation of Popper's pre-war text in which the method of falsificationism is developed.

Alan Ryan, *The Philosophy of the Social Sciences* (Macmillan, London, 1970). A review of the standard issues of the philosophy of science. Useful introduction for those with a specific interest in these.

Arnold Thackray, *John Dalton: Critical Assessments of his Life and Science* (Harvard University Press, Cambridge, Mass., 1972). An example of the fine historiographic work by contemporary historians of science.

Roy Wallis (ed.), *On the Margins of Science: The Social Construction of Rejected Knowledge*, Sociological Review Monograph 27 (University of Keele, Keele, Staffs). A collection of empirical studies of knowledge of questioned status. A good example of recent work in the sociology of science.

Bryan Wilson (ed.), *Rationality* (Blackwell, Oxford, 1971). A series of essays on rationality and problems of translation between and explanations of alien cultures.

Peter Winch, *The Idea of a Social Science* (Routledge, London, 1958). Defines *verstehen* in philosophical terms, and argues that the social sciences are best seen as a branch of epistemology.

John Ziman, *Public Knowledge: An Essay Concerning the Social Dimension of Science* (Cambridge University Press, Cambridge, 1968). Still a good introduction to the sociology of science, written by a distinguished physicist.

Glossary

anomaly Troublesome inconsistency, frequently between the more theoretical and the more empirical sections, within a network. The term 'misfit' is used for an inconsistency that is not held to be troublesome or one that may be easily resolved.

cause A term used in a wide variety of ways in different philosophies of science. In network theory terms, the more interesting and explicit links transferred in the course of metaphorical redescription.

class A term in a network whose meaning (like that of all other classes) is determined by its relationship with other terms in that network (*see* intension) and the objects, events or relationships in the world to which it is applied (*see* extension).

coherence conditions The principles which organise the structure of a network. Some of these are assumed to arise from the way in which human beings perceive and classify information and may thus be called psychological coherence conditions. Others appear to be culturally defined and are described as social coherence conditions. Psychological coherence conditions are presumptively common to all networks, whereas social coherence conditions may differ between cultures.

correspondence theory A theory of knowledge which claims that true knowledge is that which corresponds to that which it describes. This may be contrasted with a pragmatic theory of knowledge which criticises correspondence theory for vagueness.

empiricism The doctrine that knowledge arises from sense experience.

epistemology The theory of knowledge; a branch of philosophy.

extension The objects, events or relationships described or covered by a term. Closely related to intension.

falsificationism Popper's preferred scientific method: that scientists should (i) construct bold but empirically falsifiable theories, (ii) attempt to falsify them and that, having succeeded in this, they should (iii) then proceed to construct a more general but empirically falsifiable theory.

functionalism An explanatory model in social science that stresses that social events and institutions are interconnected and mutually influential. In addition, it often advocates teleological explanation (phenomena are explained in terms of the functions they are supposed to play) and may also imply the use of an organic metaphor for society.

Hesse network or Hesse net *See* network

idealism The doctrine that the explanation of phenomena should be posed in terms of the power of ideas or the ideal: that reality is non-material. This is often set against materialism.

285

ideology A widely and diffusely used term normally used to describe knowledge that is (i) directed by social (e.g. class) interests, (ii) distorts reality by concealing its true (for instance, exploitative) nature, yet (iii) is nevertheless workable in day-to-day practice. The theory of ideology has been particularly developed in Marxist writing. Claim (ii) above is incompatible with the pragmatism of the network theory.

impartiality A part of the strong programme of the sociology of knowledge, the assumption that both true and false knowledge require explanation.

incommensurability The impossibility of translating one system of belief into the language of another; often posed in terms of the non-existence of a neutral observation language.

induction The process of deriving general claims from empirical instances, and hence going beyond those instances.

intension Loosely, the meaning of a term (*but see also* extension). In network theory the properties in terms of which objects, events and relationships grouped together in a class are held to exhibit similarity. Thus the intension of the term 'mammal' includes 'air breathing' but not 'terrestrial habitat'.

interest in natural accounting, prediction and control One of the two basic interests that are assumed to underlie all knowledge. In this case, the aim is to describe, account for and explain events in order to interact more satisfactorily with the natural and social worlds.

interest in social control and legitimation The other basic interest that is assumed to underlie all knowledge. Here the aim is to defend, legitimate or rationalise a general social position advantageous to the group deploying or using the knowledge.

interests Explanatory attributes imputed to individuals or groups in order to understand their actions and knowledge. It is assumed that all knowledge is constructed and deployed (i) with the purpose of interacting more satisfactorily with the natural and social worlds and (ii) with the purpose of ensuring social advantage. In order to explain the generation and use of knowledge it is thus necessary to make a hypothesis about the problems which the knowledge is designed to resolve. The imputed interests are in turn used to explain what count as important problems. Though they relate to both motives and purposes, it is important to note (i) that they are properly used of social groups and not just individuals, and (ii) that they are structural and relational, i.e. a function of the relationship between groups. It should be emphasised that, just as the attribution of knowledge is an hypothesis, so too is the imputation of interests.

Marxism A set of explanatory models (and political commitments) originally associated with the writing of Marx that stresses the importance of (i) the material in general and the economic in particular; (ii) economic class, class antagonism and class contradiction; (iii) qualitative, and sometimes revolutionary, social change; and (iv) the importance of ideology in concealing class contradiction. Marxism is now a wide family of often incompatible doctrines.

materialism The doctrine that the explanation of phenomena (and in particular knowledge) must start with the assumption that there is a material world, that reality is material. This is often set against idealism.

meaning *See* intension, for a network theory interpretation.

metaphor In the network theory of knowledge all classification is seen as metaphorical because it treats objects, events or relationships as if they were the same as other objects despite the fact that there are always dissimilarities. Hence there is no incompatibility between scientific theory and metaphor. Scientific theories are constitutively metaphorical.

network A set of interrelated classes. More generally, a model for talking about knowledge, i.e. about the way in which both individuals and cultures classify and interpret events, objects or relationships in the world. The model does not discriminate strongly, as do some theories of knowledge or description, between theoretical and observational terms. It further assumes all terms (and hence the structure of the network) to be revisable.

network theory A particular theory of knowledge or description. *See* network.

neutral observation language A language of observation that is assumed to be independent of theory and hence relatively stable. Associated with correspondence theory, network theory denies the possibility of a neutral observation language.

normal science Science proceeding under the auspices of, and articulating a paradigm.

ostension The definition of a term by naming while showing or pointing out the phenomenon in question.

paradigm A term from Kuhn's history of science which refers to the complex of theoretical, methodological, practical and metaphysical commitments shared by a group of scientists. In Kuhn's view the role of the practical is of particular importance.

pragmatic theory of knowledge A theory which argues that knowledge, even scientific knowledge, is best seen as a tool for dealing with practical problems. Thus the test of the adequacy of knowledge in this view is its workability in practice and not the degree to which it corresponds to what it describes (*see* correspondence theory). Network theory is a pragmatic theory of knowledge.

pragmatism *See* pragmatic theory of knowledge.

psychological coherence conditions *See* coherence conditions.

reflexivity A part of the strong programme of the sociology of knowledge. The assumption that the sociology of knowledge can explain its own derivation in terms of the same kinds of factors as the derivation of other systems of knowledge.

relativism A doctrine that asserts that there are no absolute standards against which the adequacy of a system of knowledge may be measured. Standards are rather local. The network theory is relativistic.

scientific revolution A term from Kuhn's history of science which refers to the major conceptual changes that occur from time to time in the history of science. These are interpreted as the abandonment of one paradigm by a group of scientists in favour of another.

scientism The inappropriate adoption of a conception of science as a model for explanation in another domain.

social coherence conditions *See* coherence conditions.

symmetry A part of the strong programme of the sociology of knowledge. The assumption that all knowledge, and in particular that which is held to be true and that which is held to be false, may be explained in terms of the same kinds of factors.

teleology Explanation of phenomena not in terms of prior causes but rather in terms of their consequences.

theory A relatively explicit section of a network taking the form of a 'plausible story' that has been metaphorically extended to new phenomena, and which is held to describe, account for or explain these.

verstehen Loosely, the act of understanding the beliefs of another individual or group. It is often defined as the successful acquisition of the language of a group. In network theory, the acquisition and competent use of the network of the culture in question.

weltanschauung World outlook, outlook on life.

workability A term used of networks in the pragmatic network theory of knowledge: a way of talking of the fact that the test for adequacy of a network is not its correspondence to reality but rather how well it serves the purposes of those who deploy it.

Name Index

Subject Index